AF622389

Bridging Souls

A Journey from Mahabharata to Bharata

Arindam Nath

PEACOCK BOOKS

Published by
PEACOCK BOOKS
7/22, Ansari Road, Darya Ganj, New Delhi-110 002
Phones : +91-11-4077 5252, 2327 3880, 2327 5880, 2328 0451
Fax : +91-11-2328 5873
Web : www.atlanticbooks.com
E-mail : orders@atlanticbooks.com

Branch Office
5, Nallathambi Street, Wallajah Road,
Chennai-600 002
Phones : +91-44-6461 1085, 3241 3319
E-mail : chennai@atlanticbooks.com

Peacock Books is an imprint of
Atlantic Publishers and Distributors (P) Ltd.

Copyright © Arindam Nath, 2012, 2013

Cover Design: Shri Dilip Paswan, a Rifleman of TSR

All rights reserved. No part of this publication may be reproduced, stored in a retrieval system, transmitted or utilized in any form or by any means, electronic, mechanical, photocopying, recording or otherwise, without the prior permission of the copyright owner. Application for such permission should be addressed to the publisher.

Printed in India at Nice Printing Press, A-33/3A, Site-IV, Industrial Area, Sahibabad, Ghaziabad, U.P.

Dedicated to

My family members who have helped me to grow as a writer through constructive criticism

Foreword

The book *Bridging Souls—A Journey from Mahabharata to Bharata* makes a fascinating reading. Written lucidly in the form of a diary, it weaves a magical tale that takes the readers' mind back and forth to the glory and grandeur of the epic period of Indian history and present-day realities. The characters in the novel are fictional but the book is grounded on the personal experience and perceptive vision of Arindam Nath, a senior officer of Tripura Police who travelled across the country as a chairman of Tripura Rifles Recruitment Board. The author's knowledge of the epics and his cultivated, discerning and scholarly mind come out through the pages of the book.

The story comes out of the diaries written by one medical practioner, Dr. Ashamanja Bhowmik, who accompanied a recruitment team of Tripura State Rifles, an elite armed police force of Tripura, all over the country. Through the pages of his diary, the author has spun a delightful tale that captivates the mind. The recruitment team traversed different regions of India, where about 5,000 years ago, some of the famous battles and events recounted in Mahabharata had taken place. Acts of heroism as well as frailties of the different 'dramatis personae' of Mahabharata are compellingly and evocatively recounted by one Ambujanaba Sharma, Commandant of the battalion, who headed the team. The pen portrait of the Commandant drawn by the author shows the qualities of his head and heart—a happy blending of scholarship and humanism. He narrated and interpreted in a new light and perspective, and with consummate knowledge to his accompanying colleagues, the characters and events of the Mahabharata. His vivid description of the valour of the heroes as well as the deeds of princes and sages will grip the minds of the readers.

Mahabharata is not merely "a song of victory", it is a *Padma Samhita*, a collection of old legends, and *Itivritta* or traditional account of noble kings, pious sages, of dutiful wives and beautiful maids. It is also *Mokshya Shastra*—pointing ways to salvation.

Mahabharata also lays down rules of conduct for attainment of three great aims animating all human conduct—*Dharma, Artha and Kama.*

Some of the characters in the novel are fascinating. Dr. Bhowmik is an ideal Boswell. He has painstakingly noted down the references, comments and perceptive observations of Sharma after the narration of different episodes of Mahabharata. However, some of the comments of Sharma on the nature of crimes committed by heroes of Mahabharata are somewhat trite and may not stand the glare of scrutiny. Some of the acts of the epic heroes now interpreted as crimes under the Indian Penal Code were not so in the days of yore. They were in accordance with the then prevailing customs.

Against this wider backdrop of acts and transgressions of the heroes of Mahabharata, the author weaves a tender sub-plot of a love affair between the Bengali doctor Bhowmik and the Punjabi girl Dr. Harleen Bedi, a medical officer of CRPF Group Centre, Jalandhar. The pages of the diary unveil the tragic story of the death of Harleen's fiancé, Aman who reportedly committed suicide, but actually was murdered. The untold story could be unearthed by Harleen with the help of the members of the recruitment board. Enchanting romance blossoms between the two doctors, hailing from two different parts of the country. It was indeed *omnia vincit amor.*

The book will enthral the readers and provide them with glimpses of Mahabharata as well as many other events of the past and the present. Issues like Maoism, Gorkhaland agitation, etc. figure in the narrative. Common readers will also gather from the book, some interesting details of the methods of recruitment in the paramilitary forces and the pains taken to select appropriate candidates from different parts of the country. Arindam Nath deserves plaudits for writing an informative and interesting book, revealing his scholarly as well as analytical mind. I am sure that the book will be well received and widely read.

Sankar Sen

I.P.S. (Retd.), Former Director,
National Police Academy

Preface

There is a saying, "In Mahabharata we breathe the united soul of India and individual soul of her people." I was fascinated towards this 'soul' about twenty-five years ago while reading a book *Panchajanya* written by an eminent Bengali writer Gajendra Kumar Mitra. Panchajanya is the conch gifted to Sri Krishna by Agni, a Brahmin for fulfilling his desire to destroy Khandav forest. I was a teacher of Physics in a higher secondary school then. I was a voracious reader of Bengali classics, including the works translated from other literatures.

I was exposed to the world of legal studies in Police Academy which I joined as a commissioned officer after clearing a competitive examination of State Police Service. Before that I had a stint of four years as a teacher. The subject of legal studies enthralled me; my skill in solving Mathematics problems and puzzles helped me a lot in understanding the provisions of law. In particular, I liked Indian Penal Code (IPC) formulated by a British gentleman, Macaulay in 1833 and enacted in 1861. It is amazing that an Act enacted more than one hundred fifty years ago is still serving our purpose in the 21st century, with very few amendments. Many a time, I used to toy with IPC sections, like, while travelling by a vehicle, it would invariably come to my mind what IPC offences can be constituted with the registration number of a vehicle.

My fascination towards the epic Mahabharata, and IPC enriched my imagination to a great extent. I started thinking what would have been the fate of the mighty Pandavas and the Kauravas in a democratic set up. I wrote a short-story in Bengali, narrating my encounter with Eklavya in a dream. I heard the story of Eklavya whose right hand thumb was cut off as a reward for his percept master Dronacharya. In the story, I announced imprisonment for three years for Drona for his alleged abetment. The story earned good acclamations, especially from my friend Manas Paul, a senior journalist and writer of

The Eyewitness, the most trusted book on the ethnic conflicts in Tripura. He insisted upon me to write a book by portraying other such events in the epic which might attract penal provisions of law. He urged me to write it in English in order to attract attention of a wide cross-section of people, as the work would be extraordinary.

After receiving such inspiration from my friend, I tried my best in the next few years to put up some draft. But every time it failed to satisfy me as it appeared to be a narration without any life or humour. My poor knowledge of literary English also proved a stumbling block for me. In 2008, I got a chance to visit states like Delhi, Haryana, Himachal Pradesh, Punjab, Uttarakhand, Uttar Pradesh, Jharkhand, Bihar, Orissa, Andhra Pradesh, Tamilnadu and West Bengal, in the course of recruitment in Tripura State Rifles (TSR), against the outside state quota. I was the Chairman of Recruitment Board, and our team could touch almost all the historic places where events of Mahabharata had taken place more than five thousands years ago. It was a maiden experience for me to travel by road more than ten thousands kilometres.

As an ardent reader of prolific writer Satyajit Ray and his immortal creation, 'Professor Trilokeshwar Shanku', I decided to weave my fiction, *Bridging Souls: A Journey from Mahabharata to Bharata*, in the form of a diary. Anyone acquainted with Ray's work will appreciate the simplicity of his writing style. I tried to emulate his style of writing to overcome my shortcomings of literary English.

I have narrated the journey in the novel similar to the itinerary of TSR Recruitment Rally. While acknowledging the hospitality of CRPF, BSF, ITBP, State Police Forces and other organizations, I would like to state with confidence that the characters portrayed in my fiction which have acquaintance with these august houses will not injure their reputation. These characters in the novel are fictitious and any resemblance with any individual's personal life or organization will be a mere coincidence.

The book will appeal to a wide cross-section of people, who will not only find it interesting but also informative.

Arindam Nath

Acknowledgements

I express my sincere thanks to Shri Sankar Sen, I.P.S. (Retd.), Senior Fellow and Former Director, National Police Academy, Hyderabad and also the Former Director-General, National Human Rights Commission for taking pains to write a beautiful 'Foreword' for my book and thereby bringing a new dimension for my work. I also express my heartfelt gratitude to the beautiful couple, Mrs. & Mr. K.S. Ali, I.P.S., Addl. Director CBI, New Delhi for their excellent cooperation and guidance. In particular, I like to appreciate the painstaking task taken by Mrs. Ali, in correcting the manuscript in its initial stage.

I take this opportunity to convey my regards to Shri B.L. Vora, I.P.S. (Retd.), Shri G.M. Srivastava, I.P.S. (Retd.) and Shri Pranay Sahay, I.P.S., all former DGPs Tripura, Shri Sekhar Dutta, Senior Journalist of *The Telegraph*, Shri Amitabh Kar, I.P.S. (Retd.), DG Fire Services Tripura and my senior officers, teachers for their blessings and suggestions which helped in qualitative improvement of my writings. I also like to convey my sincere thanks to my colleagues, friends, my family members and well-wishers for their valuable suggestions which helped me a lot. I am indebted to my friends Shri S. Talapatra and Shri Manas Paul for their constant inspiration which eventually made me to make the daring venture to write a book in English. A word of praise for Shri Monoj Kumar Sole, Naib Subedar (Clerk), TSR and Shri Sukanta Banik, LDC of Police Headquarters, Tripura, Agartala for taking pains to decipher my handwritings, beyond their office hours to type it into soft copy in computer. Last but not the least, I cherish my association with my team for Recruitment Rally for TSR which paved the way for this book.

Any word of praise will be insufficient for my friends in Delhi like Srimati Sharmila Chandra, Shri Tinku Roy, Shri Pradeep Kapil, Shri Subash Saluja and the editorial team of Atlantic Publishers & Distributors (P) Ltd., without whose support perhaps this book would not have seen the light of day.

Arindam Nath

I

It reminds me of one of the worst April summers, I've ever seen. I was posted as Medical Officer at the 5th Battalion of Tripura State Rifles (TSR) then. A drought-like situation was prevailing even in Tripura, where it rains more than 200 days a year. Sitting at Battalion Headquarters, Daluma, Amarpur, we would discuss the vagaries of nature and how long the hot spell would continue. Added to the misery was the ever-increasing number of causalities of our jawans from malaria Plasmodium Falciparum and water-borne diseases as a corollary. Our deployment was in Kalajhari and in Baramura-Deotamura hill-ranges of the state. It spreads over three subdivisions—Amarpur, Gandacherra and Sabroom. I felt disheartened to receive an order at that juncture from my Directorate on 17th April 2008 asking me to move as Medical Officer with a Recruitment Board constituted for the recruitment of TSR personnel against the vacancies of outside state quota.

I have to bear the scorching summer while moving with the Recruitment Board across the country by road to places like Delhi, then Punjab in the north-west, Dehradun in the north, followed by Maoist-infested Jharkhand, Bihar and Orissa in the east, and then to Vizag and Nellore in the south, and finally back to the north-east corridor to Siliguri of West Bengal. The itinerary circulated by the Recruitment Board, spanning over a period of more than 45 days seemed highly impractical. The task appeared Herculean to me when I received information about the possible size of candidates' gathering, their relatives and innumerable touts. I left no stone unturned to avoid this job. But, the seniors in my department insisted that I move with the team. Even I realized that it would be a unique experience to travel more than 10,000 k.m.

on Indian roads in hot summer. The police personnel of the Board also encouraged me and assured me of all their assistance.

I tried to ascertain the reason behind their interest in attending this uphill task, but remained clueless. My Directorate also didn't pay any heed to my prayer for exemption from this assignment. I was left with no option other than to prepare for the journey. Fortunately for me, the Chairman of the Recruitment Board, Shri Ambujanabha Sharma was known to me, as he hailed from my native subdivision. We imbibed our primary education at the same school, though he was pretty senior to me. He was in the arts stream, while I opted for science and was successful in becoming a medical graduate. Mr Sharma completed his post graduation in History, and after a brief stint in a college as a part-time lecturer, he joined police service as Deputy Superintendent. Presently, he was serving as Commandant of a TSR Battalion, after putting in more than 15 years in police profession.

The Board had two more members in the persons of Sri Kaushik Roy, an Additional Superintendent of Police and Sri Ajit Debbarma, an Assistant Commandant of TSR. Both of them were new for me, like the rest of the 16-strong staff ranging from the rank of Inspectors of Police to drivers, constables and Enrolled Followers down below to support us.

Mr Sharma took a meeting in his office at Agartala on the 23rd April 2008 morning with all the Board members and support-staff, which I also attended. We had a long discussion to chalk out the paraphernalia required for the recruitment rally. It came out as a long list of more than 150 articles ranging from all-pins to wooden structures for chin-up exercises, measuring devices for physical measurements, hoardings on plastic flex containing information and instructions for the candidates, cooking utensils, etc. Really speaking, it took the shape of an expedition, and I felt encouraged. I didn't book my tickets till that period. Mr Sharma was approaching the local police administration at the venues for recruitment to ensure services of local medical officers.

The main body of the Recruitment Board would move in three vehicles, one Maruti Gypsy, one Bolero Jeep and one Swaraj Mazda mini-bus under the command of Ajit Debbarma, carrying all materials directly to the CRPF Group Centre at Jalandhar, Punjab on 24th April 2008 by road. The driver of the jeep, Joginder, with one constable, Narayan would pick up Mr Sharma and another senior member, Kaushik Roy on 30th April 2008 from Delhi Airport, as they will travel by air on that day itself. From 30th April 2008 onwards, the whole team would move by road till the end of the recruitment rally at Siliguri on 13th June 2008.

Finally, I surge up my hesitations and resolve to move with the chairman by air. Fortunately for me, flight tickets for Agartala-New Delhi route in Indigo airlines were still available for the day, which I booked gleefully. The ardour and fervour were also beginning to grip me. I recollected the famous lines of Johann Wolfgang von Goethe:

> Rest not! Life is sweeping by; go and dare before you die.
> Something mighty and sublime, leave behind to conquer time.

I decided to pen down the happenings in the course of the tour in my diary.

❖❖❖

II

Now it's seven in the night of 1st May 2008. We're comfortably placed at Officers' Mess, CRPF Group Centre, Jalandhar. It's a nice accommodation. There are 16 AC rooms on two floors. Mr Sharma has got his room on the ground floor, a better-equipped room, while rooms of Kaushik and mine are on the first floor, side by side.

Last night after arrival, I took a bath and enjoyed sound sleep. When I got up today, it was already seven, but the sun looked very young. It evoked the advice given by Kaushik the previous day regarding time zone. The room attendant was perhaps waiting outside. No sooner did I open the door than he entered my room with tea and biscuits. He's Shyamal Biswas, a CRPF constable and is a native of Cooch Bihar District of West Bengal. Shyamal had been entrusted for looking after all three of us by the Mess Commander, Mr Bhatia, a Deputy Commandant of CRPF.

As I was gathering information from Shyamal, Kaushik entered my room.

- Good morning doctor.
- Very good morning. You're looking very fresh!
- I've just taken a bath. It's so refreshing! You also take a bath. Till then, I can watch news on TV.

I obeyed the suggestion and within 15 minutes we came out of my room to meet Mr Sharma who was expecting us. He instructed Ajit Debbarma about the arrangements for the next day and asked him to visit the ground of district police, Jalandhar with his team and wait for our arrival around noon.

We came across Mr Bhatia at the breakfast table. Mr Sharma appreciated him for maintaining the mess so well. After breakfast we'd a walk around the CRPF Group Centre. The campus was huge, spreading over more than 100 acres of land by the side of National Highway (NH)-1, about 12 kilometres from Jalandhar towards Amritsar. The venue for the recruitment rally was chosen by officials at Police Headquarters, Agartala. But, after seeing the beautiful grounds and other infrastructure at the Group Centre, Mr. Sharma suggested before us, "Don't you think we should hold the recruitment rally here itself?"

Kaushik opined, "Sir, we should call the candidates to this place after initial enrollment. Otherwise, it'll create confusion, since in the advertisement; the name of this location wasn't mentioned."

The Chairman agreed to Kaushik's proposition and with this plan in mind, we went to meet with Mr Sultan Ahmed, Deputy IG, CRPF Commanding Officer of this Group Centre. Mr Ahmed had earlier served in Tripura as Commandant of a CRPF Battalion, and he was acquainted with Mr Sharma. We received warm greetings from him and assurances of all sorts of assistance. Mr Sharma approached him for the permission for using the ground at the group centre from 3rd May 2008. He also requested for the service of hospital staff of CRPF group centre, as there might be casualties during physical tests in this hot weather. Mr Ahmed immediately rang up Dr Jagjeet Chauhan, CMO of the CRPF Hospital in the group centre and narrated our programme to him. The latter in turn assured all possible help. Mr Ahmed then called Mr Bhatia and instructed him to make necessary arrangements from the next day onwards. He requested us to meet Dr Chauhan in his hospital, located at walking distance from his office.

So we walked off to meet Dr Chauhan. He was waiting for us with one of his colleagues Dr (Miss) Harleen Bedi. Dr Chauhan was in his early forties. He had obtained his MBBS degree from Christian Medical College, Ludhiana and PG in orthopaedics from AIIMS. He is a native of Bhatinda, Punjab.

Dr (Miss) Harleen Bedi had joined CRPF about a year back as Asstt Commandant. She is a tall, slim, fair-complexioned and charming lady. She hails from Malwa region of the state of Punjab, and graduated in medical science from Government Medical College, Amritsar.

It was around 11 in the morning. Temperature outside was rather high, probably hovering around 43°C. Hardly any patient took notice of us in this 50-bedded hospital. It is basically meant for CRPF personnel and their family members from five CRPF battalions under this sector who are staying at quarters here. Two more doctors are posted in this hospital; one is presently on leave while the other has gone for visiting the units.

Mr Sharma apprised Dr Chauhan that we were expecting a huge gathering, as it was the recruitment venue for candidates from five states, namely Punjab, Haryana, Rajasthan, Himachal Pradesh and Jammu and Kashmir. He requested Dr Chauhan to depute a medical officer for our assistance. The CMO immediately detailed Dr Bedi for our help from 3rd May 2008.

Here, an interesting thing happened, which I should mention. When we were about to leave the hospital, Mr. Sharma asked Dr (Miss) Harleen Bedi, "What's the meaning of your name 'Harleen'?"

She replied, "It means one who's absorbed in the Lord's love."

I asked Mr Sharma, "Sir, by the way, what's the meaning of your name?"

He appreciated my query, "Good question, Doctor! You should always ask a person the meaning of his name. Only then you can recollect his name even years after. Literary meaning of 'Ambujanabha' is one who's having lotus flower in his umbilical region (navel) and it indicates Lord Vishnu."

"Like your name is 'Ashamanja' meaning 'un-similar', but I'm sure your parents have named you after the name of eldest son of King Sagar of Mahabharata era, whose name was also 'Ashamanja'."

I felt encouraged to disclose, "In our school days, we were fond of translating Bengali names and in the process we find some interesting meanings. Some of these, I still remember. It goes like: 'Surya Mondal...Solar System', 'Jagat Roy... Universal Opinion', 'Sushil Nath...Faithful Husband', 'Durjoy Pahari...Unconquerable Mountaineer', 'Becharam Kar...Sales Tax', 'Nirmal Pathak...Pure Reader', 'Hiranmoy Pal...Group of Deers', 'Mahabir Singha...Mighty Lion', 'Manab Biswas... Humam Faith', 'Sajal Ganguly...Flooded River', 'Sagar Majhi ...Sea Sailor', 'Akash Samanta...Air Force', 'Antara Roy... Interim Order', 'Chanchal Sarkar...Unsteady Government', 'Santana Dey...Console', and so on."

"Excellent!" said Mr Sharma, "Doctor, it's really very fascinating."

I told Miss Bedi that Mr Sharma had an in-depth knowledge of history and mythology. Yesterday, Kaushik and I were treated to some fabulous stories related to Panipat and Kurukshetra battles while coming to Jalandhar from New Delhi by road.

Dr Chauhan and Miss Bedi were enjoying our company. Dr Chauhan surmised, "I've always noticed Bengali people to have keen interest in literature and travelling. I've a Bengali friend, Dr Jayanta Mallik from Kolkata from my PG days in AIIMS. He's a voracious reader and travelling is his pastime."

Mr Sharma asked Dr Bedi, "What's your husband doing?"

At this she became a little aloof and with a weak smile, she disclosed, "I'm a maiden."

Dr Chauhan changed the topic by saying, "Mr Sharma, I believe you've not visited Jalandhar city ever."

Mr Sharma thanked Dr Chauhan for the reminder, "We have an engagement with the District Superintendent of Police, Jalandhar."

We left the hospital for District SP's office, Jalandhar. Driver Joginder was rested for the day, instead one Rafique was driving the vehicle. He had come to Jalandhar with the advance party the previous day, and seemed to have gathered very good knowledge about Jalandhar within a single day. Except the highways, all other infrastructures in the city have come up in an unplanned way. There is hardly any space in the city for expansion and it causes regular traffic congestions. All this while, Kaushik had been keeping mum at the CRPF hospital. Suddenly he burst out, "Dr. Bedi perhaps has suffered some tragedy in her life!"

"It's quite possible", Mr Sharma supported Kaushik, "The way Dr Chauhan changed the topic about her marital status suggests this."

"It was apparent from her body language as well", Kaushik tried to lend weight to his conjecture.

It had caught my notice as well, but I preferred to remain silent. Today being May Day, the offices were closed. The District SP wasn't available in his office. He was out with some law and order commitment. One Mr Paramjit Bist, Addl. SP (Headquarters) Jalandhar was waiting for us. Mr Bist also raised the same question, which we had faced the previous day at Kurukshetra, "Why are you recruiting police personnel from outside the state? Don't you've any unemployment problem in Tripura?"

After a round of refreshing tea in big decorative cups, Mr Sharma enlightened Mr Bist about the recruitment rules of Tripura State Rifles (TSR). Mr Bist was a national-level long distance sprinter and he'd been to Agartala, Tripura. He shared his experience of running up to Bishalgarh from Agartala as part of a practice session, in one early winter morning during the Athletic Meet. He was particularly amused by the small size of goats in Tripura. Mr Bist took us to nearby District Police Ground in his AC car. Ajit Debbarma with his team was already there to receive us. The ground was small, compared to the ground at CRPF Group Centre. It was very dusty and close to the quarters, and porous from all sides. But one advantage of this ground was the easy availability of security forces for law and order duties, apart from the presence of a residential Medical Unit of District Police in close vicinity.

Mr Sharma didn't reveal his plan of shifting the venue to Mr Bist. It was 2 in the afternoon; Mr Bist took us to a nearby Gurudwara, where some religious festival was in progress as part of Baishakhi. We were served with sweet dishes and milk cake. We returned to the campus by 3 p.m. I took a light lunch and didn't venture out of my room except for taking dinner at 9.30 p.m. Mr Sharma gave me some more respite by allowing me to appear at the ground by 8 a.m. For others, including Mr Sharma, the reporting time was 6 a.m.

III

We had a hectic schedule yesterday, the last day of April. Our Indigo flight from Agartala via Kolkata landed at Indira Gandhi Airport, New Delhi sharp at 1.30 p.m. We were three of us, Chairman Mr Ambujanabha Sharma, Co-chairman Mr Kaushik Roy and I, Dr Asamanja Bhaumik. The flight took off at about 9.30 in the morning. We travelled continuously to Delhi, except for a brief halt at Dum Dum Airport for about an hour. Coming out of the domestic terminal, we had the first taste of the severity of the heat outside. The temperature was around 43°C and the sun seemed to be right above our head.

Kaushik advised, "Dr Bhaumik, you turn your watch two hours behind to be able to do justice to the task here."

I thanked Kaushik for his practical sense, and jokingly replied, "Yeah! I realize, we're presently in the north-west part of our country. There should be a separate time zone for the north-east." Kaushik was more or less of my age, but was endowed with a great deal of common sense.

In the parking we found our jeep. Driver Joginder and constable Narayan greeted us. They had reached Delhi yesterday and after spending the night in the house of Joginder at adjoining Gurgaon, were waiting for us from mid-noon. Joginder was driving the vehicle almost continuously for the last seven days which was evident from his appearance. But the distress and fatigue was more noticeable in Narayan as his complexion had become darker compared to that of Joginder. The obvious reason behind this was that the latter being a native of this area, was accustomed to such weather. For us, it was difficult to even stand outside. We were in a dilemma about whether to go to Tripura Bhawan, New Delhi for a change or to proceed directly to Jalandhar. We held a long discussion sitting inside the jeep. Joginder was in favour of driving straight to Jalandhar and to take rest for a day. Considering the approximate distance between Delhi and Jalandhar, which was 380 k.m., we decided to complete the journey without wasting time at Tripura Bhawan.

Mr Sharma asked Joginder to stop at a suitable roadside restaurant for our lunch on the way. We covered our faces, especially ears with towels and kept the doors and windows of the car closed for possible prevention from the hot 'loo' winds blowing outside. The humidity level was very low and as a result there wasn't much sweating. The road was very wide with double lanes. We began to enjoy the journey, listening to old Hindi duet songs of Lata and Kishore Kumar on the CD player.

After leaving Delhi, we first crossed a small township, Naraina followed by Azadpur. Mr Sharma told us that he was in Azadpur before undergoing training at National Security Guard (NSG), Gurgaon, Haryana in the early-1990s. After Azadpur, the next big town was Panipat as indicated by a milestone. It was four in the afternoon and we were feeling hungry, and so we entered a roadside AC restaurant to feel cooler. We spent quite some time in the restaurant and contacted our advance party led by Ajit Debbarma. They'd already reached their destination and were settled comfortably at CRPF Group Centre, Jalandhar, Punjab.

As we came out of the restaurant to resume our journey, towards the next milestone which was Panipat, Mr Sharma opened the floodgates for some untold stories of history, which sounded highly eloquent in his voice with the backdrop of classical Hindi music by Manna Dey: "During the period of the Mahabharata, the name of Panipat was 'Pandupath'. It was one amongst the five villages namely Indraprastha, Panduprastha, Soneprastha, Tilprastha and Bagprastha demanded by the Pandavas from Kauravas for their livelihood and stay. Indraprastha is the present day New Delhi, Panduprasth as I've already mentioned is present Panipat, Soneprastha is present Sonepat, Tilprastha is present Tilpath and Bagprastha is present day Bagpat, located in Uttar Pradesh. Except for Indraprastha and Bagprastha, the rest three are probably located in the state of Haryana and dominated by people from the Jat communities. In fact, Bagpat has now become synonymous with our late Prime Minister

Choudhury Charan Singh, for he was elected from the Bagpat constituency to the Parliament six to seven times."

Here, Kaushik interrupted, "His son Sri Ajit Singh is presently the MP and the legacy of this family over this constituency may continue for many more decades."

We tittered at the consciousness of Kaushik, as Mr Sharma continued with his story, "Panipat is about 90 k.m. from Delhi while Kurukshetra is at about 160 k.m. north of the national capital. The battle of Kurukshetra in the Mahabharata spreads over a radius of 80 miles or approximately 120 k.m. centring Kurukshetra. In a sense, Panipat was very much within the battle zone of Kurukshetra."

Kaushik quizzed, "In that case, history should be re-written again, for we all know about the three battles of Panipat. The battle between the Pandavas and Kauravas should be the first battle of Panipat and the subsequent battles of Panipat from 16th century onwards should be re-scheduled."

Mr Sharma thanked him for his wit and for evoking interesting comparison of these battles, "It may just be a coincidence that in all these four battles, the sides having more fire-power and manpower were the losers. Perhaps, the battle of Leningrad in Russia during Second World War has the only resemblance."

Seeing our bewilderment, he explained, "Let us take the case of Kurukshetra battle; the Kauravas carried 23 tons of eatables as against 2 slabs of PEK with accessories carried by the Pandavas."

Both Kaushik and I exclaimed, "what?"

We did it simultaneously and so loudly that the startled driver stopped the vehicle.

Mr Sharma giggled and affectionately asked the driver to carry on as nothing had happened. He then turned towards us and explained, "You can take it as a formula to recollect the names of the kings and the states who had taken side with the Kauravas and the Pandavas in Kurukshetra war. As many as 23 kings joined the side of Kauravas, as against six in favour of the Pandavas."

Kaushik said, "But, what's the similarity between eatables and explosives?"

With a smile on his face, Mr Sharma replied, "It is just an empirical formula, prepared with the first alphabets of the states that joined the respective sides in the battle. English is a funny language and perhaps you can prepare an even better formula than me."

"Is it like BODMAS, the formula in Mathematics meaning 'Bracket, Of, Division, Multiplication, Addition and Subtraction, the order in which a problem of simplification should be carried out?", I suggested.

"Exactly!" he said.

We laughed heartily, thoroughly enjoying the company of this gentleman, as he continued narrating, "The Kauravas carried five tons each of apples and bananas, six tons of kulfi, three tons of mangoes, one ton each of guavas, honey, potatoes and tomatoes."

We were rendered speechless even as we tried to follow his train of thought, "By five tons of apples, I mean to say the five ancient states, namely Ambasta, Avanti, Anga, Ahichetra and Ashmak."

Ambasta was the present day Ludhiana in Punjab and its king was Shratayu. Avanti was the present day Ujjain in Madhya Pradesh. As regards Anga, there were actually two states with name Anga and both of them fought in Kurukshetra battle in favour of Kauravas. One of course was the present day Kabul in Afghanistan and it was under the influence of Gandhara. Duryodhana declared Karna as the king of Anga when Bhima objected to the latter for challenging Arjuna, during the Royal Tournament of public exhibition of skill and prowess by the princes of Hastinapura on completion of their arms training. Karna was the son of Kunti, born through Sun god before her marriage with Pandu, the king of Hastinapura. The newborn baby was wrapped in silk and placed in a wooden box by his mother Kunti, and was swayed away by the waters of Yamuna River. He was picked up by a childless couple, Adhiratha and his wife Radha. They adopted him. Karna was called Adhiratha Sutaputra, and also Radheya, by his adopted mother's name. Duryodhana was Karna's bosom friend.

The other Anga was located in Champa, the present day Bhagalpur in Bihar; Dand Dhar was its ruler. The surname sounded very Bengali. In fact, Bhagalpur produced many eminent Bengali writers; Sarat Chandra Chatterjee and Banaful were prominent amongst them.

Ahichetra was close to present day Ramnagar, District Barreilly in Uttar Pradesh and Dronacharya was its ruler. Last in the apple series was the state of Ashmak, located on the northern bank of river Godavari, the Ganges of Deccan."

Kaushik interrupted, "In that case, in your apple series the number of pro-Kaurava states was six, since there were two Angas."

"Yes, you're right and there are many other small states and kings as well, who participated in the Kurukshetra battle or as you termed, the original battle of Panipat", Mr Sharma responded.

"Let us listen to the list of banana states from Sir," I suggested.

He started again, "Here, my concept is different from banana republic which is a term that refers to a politically unstable country dependent upon limited agriculture (e.g. bananas), and ruled by a small, self-elected, wealthy and corrupt politico-economic. The original concept of *banana republic* had a direct reference to a 'servile dictatorship' that abetted the exploitation of large-scale plantation agriculture, especially banana cultivation. The term 'banana republic' was first used by the American writer O. Henry in *Cabbages and Kings*, a book of short stories derived from his stay in Honduras, where he was hiding from U.S. law for bank embezzlement in U.S.

Prominent amongst my banana states are Balhik, Bidharbha, Bideha, Batsya and Bhoja. Balhik was actually located in Punjab, in present day Pakistan and its capital was Harappa. Somdutta was its ruler. Bidharbha was located on the bank of river Tapti, the present day Bhusawal, Maharashtra. Its ruler was Bhima and his daughter Rukmani was married to Sri Krishna.

There's a school of thought about participation of this state in favour of the Kauravas. The king of Bidharbha, Rukmi, came with a huge army to participate in the battle in favour of the Pandavas. But, Arjuna refused to take his help as he was very proud of his bravery. He then went to Duryodhana. He also refused his help saying that he wasn't in such dire need as to accept the assistance of a king rejected by the Pandavas. Thus, neither party accepted him. But, his moral support was with the Kauravas.

Bideha was in north Bihar and its capital was Mithila, the present day Muzaffarpur on the bank of river Gandak. Batsya was the present day Allahabad in Uttar Pradesh and Bhoj was in present day Gujarat."

By that time we reached the outskirts of Panipat, a small town. The fields on either side of the road were even and extended up to the horizon, making it a suitable stage for a huge battle. We didn't stop at Panipat and moved ahead. Kaushik reminded Mr Sharma about his unfinished task of describing the states related to kulfi, guava, mangoes, etc.

He resumed, "Kaushik, tonight we shall of course take kulfi or ice-cream, but I'm afraid, none of the six kulfis namely Kekoy, Kamboj, Kaushal, Khudrak, Kalinga and Kukkur are in existence today with their original names.

Kekoy was in Punjab, comprising districts Shahpur, Jhelum and Gujarat, and its capital was Girivraja in Gujarat. It was basically the fertile land on the banks of rivers Jhelum and Chenab. Famous king Sibi was the ruler during Kurukshetra battle.

Kamboj was located north of Madra and Kekoy and Gandhar corresponded to the present day Jammu and Kashmir. The rulers of this state were descendents of Druhya, of Chandra dynasty.

Kaushal was near Ayodhya and its ruler was Brihddal. Actually Kusha, the son of Lord Rama, was the founder of this state. The state Khudrak was adjoining Kaushal and as the name suggested, it was a small state ruled by descendents of Surya dynasty.

Kalinga was present day Orissa and it had the same name during the period of Ashoka as well. The state had two parts during Mahabharata period, one ruled by Bhanuman and the other by Srutayu. Both the kings participated with their troops for the Kauravas.

Last amongst the kulfis was state Kukkur, the present day Sourashtra. Kukkur was a tribe that is believed to be the forefather of Jats. The name 'Jat' came from the 'Jata' of Lord Shiva."

"In that event, the Jats have the same origin as that of river Ganges," Kaushik suggested.

"Obviously, you're referring to the story, 'In search of Bhagirathi's origin', written by Acharya Jagadish Chandra Bose," Mr Sharma reacted.

"Yeah!" said Kaushik. "This Bengali prose was in our higher secondary curriculum."

"I've also read this" Mr Sharma confirmed, as he went ahead with his description: "These are mythological stories; we should go by their spirit rather than by their words. It's the season of mangoes, but except for east Magadh, present day south Bihar, none of the other two states from mango series, viz., Madra and Mahishmati is famous for mangoes. Madra was in north Punjab, and Sakala was its capital. This is present day Sialkot in Pakistan, and their rulers were again descendents of Yayati of Surya dynasty. The land was encircled by rivers Chandrabhaga and Irabati.

Mahishmati was in Madhya Pradesh, located at about 40 k.m. from Indore, on the banks of river Narmada. Its capital was Mahishmati and king was Neel."

Kaushik chipped in, "I've been to that place in June 1992 during the Kumbha Mela. It's a pilgrimage centre for the Hindus. An old temple of Shiva on the banks of river Narmada is the centre of attraction."

I couldn't resist the temptation to showcase my wisdom, which I sometimes feared, was rather pseudo in nature. So, I suggested, "Perhaps it's the same temple which Tagore and Jibanananda Das have dreamt separately in their poems 'Swapna' and 'Banalata Sen' respectively."

Mr Sharma, maintaining a smile on his face remarked, "These areas were once culturally very rich. Remember adjoining Ujjain was the birth place of great poet Kalidas."

Kaushik requested Mr Sharma, "Sir, you continue with your story, we can discuss this some other day."

"I've almost completed the description of allies of Kauravas in Mahabharata battle, only the guava, honey, potatoes and tomatoes are left. Can you guess what these states are?" Mr Sharma queried.

I couldn't name a single state. Kaushik correctly identified two states, Gandhar and Hastinapura.

Mr Sharma affirmed, "The remaining two are Pragjyotishpur and Trigarta. Pragjyotishpur is our neighbouring state Assam. Its capital was at Tezpur and Bhagadutta was its ruler. Sri Krishna killed one of his predecessors Mura and earned the epic name 'Murari'. Sri Krishna also killed his yet another predecessor Narakasura and freed a large number of abducted women kept by Narakasura. It is doubtful that Bhagadutta fought in favour of Kauravas.

Trigartha is Jalandhar where we're going tonight. Apart from Jalandhar, the state Trigartha included part of Kangra and Himachal Pradesh. The capital was Prasthala, present day 'Kapurthala', once ravaged by Khalisthan insurgency. Its ruler was Susharma.

Gandhar is present day Rawalpindi in Pakistan. Subala was the ruler of Gandhar. His son was Shakuni and daughter was Gandhari. The latter, in fact, was the mother of the hundred Kaurav brothers and their sister Dushala.

Last, but not the least, in the list of allies of Kauravas was Hastinapura. It was the Kuru state named after its capital Hastinapura and basically consisted of Delhi, Meerut and its adjoining areas.

Kauravas were supported by eleven akshauhini sansaptak soldiers, whose motto was to fight unto death."

"This motto is universally adopted by almost all security forces", Kaushik emphasized.

'Yeah! You're right Kaushik', Mr Sharma said. "But it is easier said than done. As compared to the Kauravas, the composition of the allies of Pandavas was compact and they had clear domain over those states. They were from areas centring Indraprastha.

As I've mentioned there were two slabs of PK explosives, meaning the four states of Panchal, Paschim Magadha, Kashi and Karush, and accessories in the form of one detonator Dhristaketu, and one match switch Morya."

"So it was the first nuclear blast!" I passed a casual remark, causing an outburst of laughter.

"Definitely, explosives were used in the battle", Mr Sharma reacted to my suggestion, "but I mean to say that the allies on the side of Pandavas were explosively charged to take revenge. Take the example of Panchal, its king was Yojnasena Drupada, the father of Draupadi and Dhrishtadyumna; he was the father-in-law of all the Pandav brothers. Originally, Panchal consisted of districts Budayun, Barreilly, Sahajahanpur, Farrukhabad and Etah in Uttar Pradesh. It was located on either side of river Ganges. Drupada was compelled to donate the northern portion of his state, consisting of districts Budayun and Barreilly to Dronacharya. In fact, Arjuna captured it from Drupada before his marriage to Draupadi and offered this portion, named Ahichhatra to Dronacharya as a gift to his guru. Drupada was the natural enemy of Hastinapura and in particular of Dronacharya. His son Dhrishtadyumna was the chief of the army for the Pandavas during the Kurukshetra war.

Paschim Magadha was the present day Rajgir in Bihar. Jarasandha was the ruler of this state. He was a natural enemy of Sri Krishna since he had killed his son-in-law, Kansa. Before the Rajsuya Yagya of Yudhishthira, Jarasandha was killed by Bhima in a feint duel. His son, Sahadeva was crowned as the king of Magadha with the condition of enduring as an ally for the Pandavas.

The capital of Kashi was Varanasi. Abhibhu was the king of Kashi. He had two daughters, Bhanumati and Balandhara. The elder daughter, Bhanumati got married to Duryodhana while younger daughter, Balandhara got married to Bhima. Abhibhu fought in favour of the Pandavas.

Karusha was the adjoining state of Kashi, located on its southern side, Rewa region of Madhya Pradesh. Dantavakra was the king of Karusha and he was great friend of Shishupala and an adversary of Sri Krishna. Sri Krishna killed Dantavakra and forced the state to support the Pandavas.

Dhristaketu was the present day Bundelkhand region located in between Godavari and Narmada rivers. Its capital was Suktimati, and is currently known as Sagar. This state was also named as Chedi. Damaghosa and then his son Shishupala were the sovereigns of Chedi state. Sri Krishna killed Shishupala since the latter was his strong critic.

The last major state was Matsya. It comprised of Jaipur, Alwar and Bharatpur regions of Rajasthan. Its capital was Viratnagar, present day Jaipur. King Virata was the descendant of Vasu and his daughter Uttara got married to Abhimanyu, the son of Arjuna. The Pandavas also took shelter in this state incognito during the 13th year of their exile. The Pandavas had also the support of their mentor Sri Krishna; some powerful Gods from the Himalayas and seven akshauhini soldiers."

After an interlude Mr Sharma resumed, "We all know how the Pandavas achieved victory. One may say everything is fair in love and war, but as far as perfidy is concerned, the score would be 3-1 adversely against the Pandavas."

Kaushik and I looked bemused, so he elucidated, "The death of Abhimanyu goes against the Kauravas on the count of sham, as against the deaths of Bhishma, Drona and Karna inflicted by the Pandavas, not to speak of deaths of Jayadratha and Duryodhana."

Kaushik signified the killings of Jarasandha and Shishupala as fraud and violation of human rights as well. It was about

6.30 in the evening when we arrived at Kurukshetra. We respectfully touched the ground of this holy place. Kaushik had been given the responsibility of our food during travel by the chairman. We reminded him about our promise to eat ice-cream tonight. Fortunately for us, we found a bakery where ice-cream was available. We ate ice-creams while Joginder and Narayan took lassi. We were in Haryana and driver Joginder was a native of the state. He disclosed our identity to the shopkeeper in his mother-tongue. Soon, there was a small gathering. They all wanted to know the reasons for recruitment from outside the state in TSR and whether there was no unemployment in the state of Tripura. With great difficulty Mr Sharma clarified their doubts. It appeared to me that he performed better in describing the battle lines of Kurukshetra war to us, a short while ago. The bottom line was that the shopkeeper gave us almost fifty per cent discount.

❖❖❖

IV

We left Kurukshetra after about half an hour and decided to have our dinner at Ambala as we had to travel another 250 k.m. to reach Jalandhar. Karnal was the next major town, located within the district of Kurukshetra.

This time Mr Sharma proposed, "We can start with the first Panipat Battle!"

Kaushik reacted sharply, "It should be the second battle of Panipat, if we treat the battle of Kurukshetra in Mahabharata, as the first."

Mr Sharma agreed smilingly, "OK, Kaushik, I shall go by the dates of the battle to avoid confusion."

Kaushik replied, "No Sir, it'll create further confusion, instead you go by the conventional way."

The latter began his story with a warm smile, "The first battle of Panipat took place in the month of April, under a similarly scorching sun, precisely on the 21st April 1526. It was Wednesday, like today."

Both Kaushik and I were at a loss, and as a concession to our amazement, he explained, "There are certain formulae with which you can ascertain any day of the Gregorian calendar. I know a formula personally. Some formulae you'll find in the books of Shakuntala Devi. You can check by asking me a date."

Kaushik said, "OK, Sir, 21st April 1998?"

After thinking for a while he answered, "It was a Tuesday."

"Yes, it indeed was a Tuesday. I joined Police service on this date", Kaushik expressed his admiration of Mr Sharma.

We didn't notice when we crossed Karnal as were enjoying the story, "The dateline of first battle of Panipat was drawn in 1523, when a Mongol prince, Zahir-ud-Din Muhammad, known as Babur promised to help Daulat Khan Lodhi, the Governor of Lahore in his fight against the Sultan of Delhi, Ibrahim Lodhi. Babur made many invasions into Punjab and occupied Punjab in 1525 AD. He along with his 12,000 strong dedicated soldiers, crossed the Indus in the month of December 1525. After crossing Sutlej at Ropar, they reached Panipat without any resistance on 1st April 1526. The entire area was barren wasteland, dry and naked with only a few thorny bushes.

The Afghan Sultan of Delhi, Ibrahim Lodhi advanced from Delhi with an army of 100,000 and 1,000 elephants to meet the invader. Babur had strong artillery which he pressed into service.

The battle started early in the morning. At about 400 yards from each other, Babur's cannons opened fire. Noise and smoke from the artillery terrified the Afghans and the attack lost momentum. Though Ibrahim Lodhi had elephants and a huge army, he didn't know how to control them. The elephants were scared by the gun shots and the noise. As a result, the elephants went out of control and trampled Lodhi's own army. He lost a large number of soldiers in the process.

Here the Afghans encountered for the first time, the real weapons of Mongols—the 'Turko-Mongol Bow'. With such a bow, a Mongol warrior could shoot three times more rapidly than a musket from a distance of 200 yards and with more accuracy."

"It seems that there was no planning on the part of Afghans against the ambush carried out by Babur", Kaushik tried to analyse.

Mr Sharma agreed with Kaushik, "Exactly, Ibrahim Lodhi was overconfident as he had a huge army when compared to Babur's troops and his army was accustomed to the climate of the area. Only about 6,000 troops led by Ibrahim Lodhi took part in the actual battle. Most of his army stretching behind up to a mile never saw action. Battle ended in three hours with the death of Ibrahim Lodhi, who was at the forefront. His head was cut off and taken to Babur.

Ibrahim Lodhi was buried at Panipat. When Afghans fled, they left 20,000 soldiers either dead or wounded. Fatalities to Babur's army were heavy in terms of percentage. About 4,000 of his troops were killed or wounded. Had Sultan Ibrahim survived another hour of fighting, he would have won, since Babur had no reserves, and his troops were rapidly tiring under the Indian mid-day sun. Babur entered Agra two weeks later where he was presented with the famous 'Kohinoor' diamond. Babur celebrated his victory in a lavish manner and occupied Delhi and Agra."

In the meantime, we had crossed Pipli, a small town and were close to Shahabad. Mr Sharma went ahead with his story, "The Second Battle of Panipat was fought between the forces of Samrat Hemchand Vikramaditya, popularly called Hemu and the army of Mughal emperor Akbar, on 5th November 1556. It was a Monday."

Saying this, he cast a glance at Kaushik, who reciprocated with a smile, "On January 24, 1556, Mughal Ruler Humayun died and was succeeded by his son, Akbar. He was only thirteen years old when he was enthroned as the king, on February 14, 1556 in a garden at Kalanaur in Punjab."

"What's the significance of 14th February, Doctor?" suddenly he asked me.

I was able to respond as the answer was known to me, "It's Valentine's Day."

"Yes, you're right. I decided to ask you this question as you are a bachelor", he then added, "Do you have any lover?"

I nodded negatively, to which he put a further question, "What's your present age?"

"I'm twenty seven", I replied.

Summoning up all his wisdom, he remarked, "Without a lover's acquaintance one cannot enjoy the nature. Only the artificial delicacies will catch your eyes. Hope that you'll get someone during this tour."

I felt shy and didn't say anything.

Kaushik changed the topic, "14th February is also the birthday of Smt Sushma Swaraj, former Union Cabinet Minister. She was probably born and brought up in Ambala Cantonment in Haryana."

Mr Sharma upheld Kaushik, "You're right and thanks for reminding me the birthday of Smt Swaraj. In fact, the celebration of her birthday and protest against the celebration of Valentine's Day by her party activists are witnessed together. She's an excellent lady and I believe she was judged the Best Speaker of Haryana State Assembly for three consecutive years, before earning the status of a national leader."

It was 8.30 in the evening as we passed Shahabad and headed towards Ambala. Mr Sharma asked, "Where were we?"

"We were left with 14th February 1556, the Valentine's Day and accession of Akbar as the king of Mughal Empire", I reminded.

"Yes doctor, you could be a good writer like Dr Watson of Conan Doyle if you follow the stories so minutely", he reckoned.

I thanked him for the compliment, "Sir, I've decided to write down the happenings of this tour in my Diary."

Accepting my tributes he began, "At the time of accession to the throne by Akbar, the Mughal rule was confined to Kabul, Kandhar, parts of Delhi and Punjab. He was then campaigning in Kabul with his guardian, Bairam Khan.

Hemu was the Prime Minister and Military Chief of Adil Shah Suri. He was trying to expel the Mughals from Delhi. At the time of Humayun's death, Hemu had quelled a rebellion in Bengal. He then started a major campaign, winning battle after battle throughout northern India. When he attacked Agra, the commander of the Mughal forces in Agra ran away. A large area of Ettawah, Kalpi and Agra states came under Hemu's control.

He then moved towards Delhi and stationed his forces outside the city at Tughlaqabad. In October 1556, his army faced first Mughal resistance. After a fierce fight, Akbar's forces led by Tardi Beg ran away, allowing Hemu to capture Delhi without much difficulty. Around 3,000 soldiers were killed. Hemu was coroneted at Purana Quila.

The subsequent development was the brain-game of Bairam Khan, the guardian of the teenaged emperor Akbar. Reminding them about Hemu's valour, many Mughal generals advised Akbar and Bairam Khan to retreat to Kabul. But Bairam decided in favour of war. Akbar's army marched towards Delhi. On November 5, both armies met at the battle field of Panipat. Hemu's army had initial success and it seemed that they would defeat Akbar's forces. However, Hemu was accidentally struck by an arrow in the eye by an archer. The loss of Hemu caused panic among the troops, which turned the tide of the battle. Shah Quili Khan captured Hemu and took him directly to Akbar and Bairam Khan. He was killed in front of Akbar. This battle resulted in re-establishment of Mughal Empire in India."

It was 9.15 in the evening when we entered a roadside restaurant at Ambala for dinner that consisted of wheat chapattis and vegetables. We resumed our journey within half an hour. Driver Joginder had been driving the car non-stop for the last one week, and so, to keep him awake we decided that it was best for Mr Sharma to continue narrating his story. He started from where he had left, "The duration of the third Battle of Panipat was by far the longest. In terms of number of casualties also, it was the highest. Let me explain the background of this battle. The Mughal Empire had been on the decline since the death of the last Mughal Emperor Aurangzeb in 1707. The decline was accelerated by the invasion of India by Nadir Shah in 1739. Continued rebellions by the Marathas in the south, and the de-facto separation of a number of states including Hyderabad and Bengal weakened the empire further. Within a few years of Aurangzeb's death, the Marathas had reversed all his territorial gains in the Deccan. They conquered almost all Mughal territory in central and north India. In 1761, they wanted to expand further in the north and the north-west, where their path crossed that of Ahmad Shah Abdali—the ruler of Afghanistan. He had been making raids into Punjab for the last several years.

The battle preparedness was very strong in the Maratha side. It included empires like Sadashivrao Bhau, Ibrahim Khan Gardi, Janokji Shinde, Malharrao Holkar, Sardar Purandare, Sardar Vinchuruar, with 40,000 cavalry, 200 pieces of modern long-range French made artillery, 15,000 infantry, 15,000 Pindaris and 300,000 non-combatants comprising pilgrims and camp followers.

On the contrary, Afghan Emperor Ahmed Shah Durani was supported by Nazib-ud-Daula and Shuja-ud-Daula with 42,000 cavalry, about 130 pieces of cannon, 38,000 infantry in addition to 10,000 reserves, 4,000 personal guards and 5,000 Qizilbashas as well as a large number of irregulars."

Kaushik interrupted, "Except for three lakh irregulars including pilgrims in Maratha side, both the sides were evenly matched."

"You're right and these three lakh irregulars became a burden when Afghans seized the supply line for more than two months. The 70 odd additional cannons had become futile", he stressed.

"On the final day of the battle, on 14th January 1761 at Panipat, the two groups came in such close proximity that the shots of long-range cannons of Marathas became useless."

"Then it was close-combat battle", suggested Kaushik.

Approving Kaushik's remark, he went on to elaborate, "The two armies fought at Karnal and Kunjpura in early October, 1760 in which Afghans suffered heavy losses. Ahmad Shah was encamped on the left bank of Yamuna River, which was swollen by rains and hence, powerless to aid his forces. The massacre of the Kunjpura garrison within the sights of Durani camp incensed him to such an extent that he ordered crossing the river at all costs. Ahmed Shah and his allies crossed the river Yamuna at Bagpat unopposed between 23rd and 25th October 1760. Next day, they encountered Marathas at Sambalka located between Sonipat and Panipat. In the skirmishes, Govind Pant Bundela with 10,000 light cavalry was counter-ambushed by an Afgan force near Meerut. This was followed by another loss of 2,000 Maratha soldiers who were delivering salaries to the soldiers from Delhi. The Jat leaders, except Ala Singh of Patiala, didn't support the Marathas.

Maratha soldiers and their horses were virtually starving, as the impasse continued despite several attempts by the Marathas to break the shackles. As a result, when close-combat-battle began on 14th January 1761, the Marathas could hardly put up any resistance.

The casualties on either side were enormous. The Marathas lost about 35,000 men on the battle field and 10,000 in the massacres that followed the next day, as against the loss of 30,000 to 40,000 men by the Afghans and 500 to 600 deaths in counter-attacks the next day. The numbers of persons injured were countless. The victorious army led by Durrani oversaw the cremation of the bodies of Viswas Rao and the Bhau. Many Maratha generals were executed by the victorious army. The overriding legacy of the battle was the halting of Marathas' advances in the north."

It was 11.30 in the night as we were crossing Ludhiana.

"Interestingly", Mr Sharma added, "The Marathas captured some Afghan soldiers during the siege of Kunjpura. Amidst the general melee, the slaves revolted. This brought confusion and great dismay among the loyal Maratha soldiers, who thought that the enemy had attacked from their rear. Noticing his forward lines dwindling, Sadashivrao Bhau came down from his elephant and led the battle at the head of the troops. Some Maratha soldiers, seeing that their general had disappeared from his elephant, panicked and began to flee. Viswasrao had already fallen to a shot in the head. Bhau and his loyal bodyguards fought to the end. Bhau's wife Parvatibai, escaped to Pune with her bodyguards."

Kaushik was silent all along, suddenly he charged up, "Sir, I'm sure your Ahmad Shah Durrani had genes from some characters of Mahabharata. The possibility of existence of Karna's genes in the blood of Abdali can't be ruled out."

"Comparisons between Shakuni and Durani can be made, as Gandhara was Shakuni's kingdom", said Mr Sharma, "but why have you brought lion-hearted Karna into this comparison?"

"It's due to the Bhishma connection. Moreover, 'Anga', the realm of Karna was part of Gandhara", replied Kaushik.

We looked towards Kaushik, confused.

He explained, "The third battle of Panipat took place on 14th January 1761, the uttarayan day. It commemorates the death of Bhishma. Karna was deprived by Bhishma to fight in the Mahabharata battle alongside him. Probably, he proved his mettle by winning a battle single handed through his progeny, Ahmad Shah Abdali,"

"Bravo, my boy!" Mr Sharma encouraged Kaushik. "But you've changed the religion of Karna."

"Karna was harassed badly in Mahabharata for no fault on his part", Kaushik responded. "So it was quite natural that he was vulnerable for conversion."

"Hope, this is the ultimate battle of Panipat or greater Kurukshetra", I said, as we entered Jalandhar city after crossing Phagwara at midnight. My wish received thumping support from Kaushik Roy and Mr Ambhujhanabha Sharma.

❖❖❖

V

One new officer, Mr Anup Kumar, Deputy Commandant of BSF has joined our team today, the third day of our tour. He'll work as a representative from Central Para Military Force (CPMF) in the recruitment board. He has been accommodated in the same mess.

We had some bad experiences during the day. There was a huge gathering of about five to six thousands people in the ground, at District Police Lines, Jalandhar, right from morning. They came from various parts of Punjab, Haryana, Rajasthan, Jammu & Kashmir, Himachal Pradesh and Maharashtra. Truly speaking, it was difficult to accommodate them in the small ground and to carry out their physical, written and oral tests. Police personnel with red caps, armed with lathis tried to maintain state-wise queues. Most of the candidates had brought application forms in a format circulated in the newspapers. But, some local agencies brought out printed application forms mentioning age relaxation of 3 years for OBC contenders. This wasn't there in our advertisement and caused serious difficulties for us. We had a tough time trying to convince the youths who were holding such application forms that they were being eliminated for being over-age. The candidates from Haryana were the most unruly, followed by the aspirants from Rajasthan. There was no problem from the rest.

They were sent to my counter for medical tests after their height and chest measurements were taken. We continued with the enrolment and tests despite the scorching sun, and in between took our lunch. By six in the afternoon, we reviewed the situation. The crowd was unending and even the disqualified candidates preferred to stay in the queue with fresh application forms. We changed the process, and decided to issue signed tokens to the candidates in the queues. They were instructed to report to the same venue next morning by 6 a.m. Our hectic schedule continued till 8.30 in the evening.

After dinner, we sat down in the lobby. It was very pleasant outside. Anup Kumar was also giving us company. Mr Sharma told us about the arrival of the Aryans in our country and the evolution of Hinduism. At one point of time, he commented, "The Pandavas are basically imperialists."

Kaushik reacted sharply, "Is there really any legitimate ground for saying this, sir?"

He was waiting for just this question and delighted at having an attentive listener like Kaushik, he said, "Yeah! The Pandavas may be termed as imperialists if you believe in Aryan Invasion Theory (AIT)."

"Sir is there any other theory for explaining our Vedic culture?" this time, it was Anup Kumar.

He elaborated, "One school of thought has recently come up and it may have caught your notice. According to this, there was no Aryan invasion during the Indus Valley Civilization. The pioneers of the ancient Vedic culture were indigenous people of mother India. It is said that renowned Indologist from Germany, Max Muller introduced AIT in 1853 but in the latter part of his life in 1888; he himself refuted his theory. Unfortunately, I am not a believer of this new theory and cannot elucidate much on it."

"I've also not heard this", Kaushik opined by reciting a few lines from Tagore's poem 'Bharat Tirtha', which supported AIT.

"I don't know about Dr Bhaumik, but it's clear that the majority of us are in favour of AIT", said Anup Kumar. "Sir, you should throw light on the issue of imperialism."

"Don't drag me in this? I prefer to play the role of an umpire", I proposed.

Mr Sharma approved of the idea, "OK, Doctor, in that case you should keep a close watch on my arguments."

I gladly accepted the proposal, allowing him to begin his speech, "Imperialism is social Darwinism, or the belief that all human groups compete for survival and that the stronger groups will replace the weaker groups. It occurs when a strong nation takes over a weaker nation or region and dominates its economic, political or cultural life.

Aryans were from the southern side of Ural Hill Range in Russia and were nomads, basically warriors. Their land was plain and full of dry grass, with plenty of wild horses. They harnessed the horses to earn a means for moving from one place to another at a fast pace."

Here, Kaushik interrupted, "Sir, are the Aryans a race?"

"I'm coming to this", Mr Sharma didn't want to break the flow, "the term 'Aryans' is not a 'race', rather it's a 'dialect'. The people, who used this 'dialect' for conversation, were called 'Aryans'. With the help of fast-moving horses, they came to India from an extremely cold place to the temperate zone.

When the Aryans came to India, the Indus Valley Civilization was at its peak. The exact time of the Aryans' invasion couldn't be ascertained. But it would be around six to seven thousand years ago. According to famous astrologer Makarachhakar, the Kurukshetra battle took place 3179 years prior to the commencement of Shaka era, which would mean that the battle took place exactly 5140 years from 2008."

He took a pause, to see if there were any queries and then continued, "Rig Veda depicted the arrival of Aryans through their conflict with indigenous people. The Indus Valley Civilization was at its peak at that time. It was an agro-based civilization. It had facilities like settled agriculture, irrigation schemes, granaries for storage, and boats for sailing in Indus river. The township was also developed with facilities like drinking water, sanitation, bathrooms, etc. They invented tools like dao, axe, fishing hooks and weaving kits. Alphabets for expressing their feelings and for communications were also developed. They worshipped many gods and goddesses, Lord Shiva being the most prominent among them. But, they didn't have warriors to protect their country.

Compared to indigenous people, the Aryans were nomads. They were fond of animal milk and meat. So they didn't like the lifestyle of civilized indigenous people. They felt envious and termed the natives as 'Asuras', 'Non-Aryans', dacoits, slaves, etc., with hatred. They began to vandalize the areas of the civilization and specially exploited native women. Their population was dominated by males. So for biological need, they started mixing with indigenous females. This they termed as marriage between gods and Asuras. Consequently, in accordance with the rule of heredity, we noticed pure Aryans, indigenous people and hybrids between the two groups."

Here, after a long pause, he said, "Dr Bhaumik may explain it in a better way."

I insisted that he should continue. He started again, "But there was serious conflict between two antagonistic cultures. This is evident from the hymns of Rig Veda, the first of the four. It goes like: 'Give us wealth of enemy, property, cows and their girls', 'Give us all their belongings', 'O, Lord Indra, never give them horses', 'Let them not dare to stand before our chariots', 'O, Indra, give us their wives, their meals', 'Please give us power to fight against them and beat them' and so on.

One glaring example of these conflicts is the epic Ramayana. The battle was fought in Ramayana between Aryans and Non-Aryans. Between incarnations of Vishnu, namely Rama, and Rakshasas led by Ravana. Rama got the support of a section of indigenous people termed as monkeys. The root cause of the battle was domination over a woman, and might also be agricultural land symbolized by 'Sita'.

Aryans were accustomed to only one type of marriage. To their advantage, they found that eight different types of marriages prevailed amongst the indigenous people. So they accepted this and in this way, assimilation of culture of Indus Valley Civilization with that of the Aryans took place, resulting in Hinduism."

Mr Sharma took some time as he drank water, "Hinduism is nothing but a way of life with maximum power resting with Brahmins and Kshatriyas. People who didn't demonstrate faith in the Vedas or who didn't accept the supremacy of Brahmins were looked down upon and termed as Daitya, Danav, Asura, Rakshas, Bhoot, Pishach, monkey, cow, snake, etc., irrespective of whether they were Aryans or indigenous people. Charbak was a great sage. He came from a poor Brahmin family. He was an atheist. Brahmins killed him for calling them cunning frauds. Interestingly, people like Rama, Krishna and Krishna Daipayan Vyasa were dark in complexion. This is an indigenous characteristic, yet they were Aryans. Probably, they had hybrid genes."

He turned towards me, and asked, "What's the score, Doctor?"

"There's no hope for indigenous people, except for some individual performances", I replied.

"You've not yet caught up with the game", he reacted, "anyway it'll be clear tomorrow. Let us call it a day. It is already eleven."

So, the stumps were drawn.

❖ ❖ ❖

VI

At the ground, everything was in order on 3rd May 2008, Saturday. We could call off the day's proceedings by six in the evening with instructions to the candidates aspiring to become riflemen to report at CRPF Group Centre, Jalandhar the next morning. The others would attend a rally at Police Ground, Jalandhar. Accordingly, our duties were re-assigned. Mr Sharma had a talk with Dr Chauhan over telephone, requesting the latter to send Dr Bedi to the CRPF ground from next morning onwards.

Today, we came to the lobby a bit early. Anup Kumar requested Mr Sharma to unravel his story.

He began from where he had left last night, "Dr Bhaumik couldn't draw the score-line yesterday. To make it easy, 'The Pandavas were imperialists' may be treated as a motion for debate. We may further draw some similarity between the two antagonists of Mahabharata battle with the Warsaw and NATO countries. Obviously, I'm talking about the cold war days between USSR and USA of last century."

Kaushik responded, "Both USA and USSR had imperialistic characteristics."

"Yes, you're right, but we can always compare the degree," Mr Sharma commented. "Forget evil portrayals of Duryodhana, he was a sensible man and was loved by people. You'll find temples in his name, even these days. Similarly, Karna is also worshiped.

My question is why great men like Bhishma, Drona, Karna, Bhagdutta and many others supported the Kauravas. How come the number of states participating in favour of Kauravas out numbered those in favour of Pandavas?

As I had stated the other day, the ratio of 23:6 states, was adversely in favour of the Pandavas. As many as 59 tribes were on the side of Kauravas as against 38 in favour of Pandavas. The propaganda indulges in by Vidura and his associates that the Pandavas were following the path of Dharma obviously didn't endure. In a democratic set up, the Kauravas could have easily won the mandate to rule."

"The question of people's mandate is certainly a strong point in favour of the motion", I suggested.

"OK scorer", Mr Sharma acclaimed my judgement. "The Warsaw group is no longer in existence; we can compare it with Kauravas, the losers in the Kurukshetra battle. The role of Shakuni had to be comparable with the chief of intelligence wing of USSR, namely KGB. The Pandavas, in that case would be the NATO Group, with Vidura taking the role of chief of US intelligence agency, namely CIA."

"Who can be compared with Mikhail Sergeyevich Gorbachev?" Kaushik put up the question in a flash.

We all giggled. Mr Sharma accepted the query, "It's a good question, Kaushik. I think the answer will be none other than Bhishma."

"Sir, this is not acceptable", all three of us objected strongly.

"I say this with a particular purpose", he disclosed. "This will be clear from the example of Varanabata. Popular belief is that Duryodhana, Karna, Shakuni and Dushasana had carried out a criminal conspiracy to kill the Pandavas out of jealousy owing to the popularity of the Pandavas. If we analyse; an interesting feature will emerge, even if we accept that a conspiracy was hatched by Duryodhana and his associates.

Under our Indian Penal Code (IPC), the preparation for dacoity is regarded as an offence under section 400 IPC. No other preparation of crime is an offence. Vidura came to know about the conspiracy and accordingly, intimated Yudhishthira. As Kshatriyas, they could have fought it out or taken some alternative steps at Varanavata, other than digging a tunnel with the help of a miner. The Pandavas weren't chained at Varanavata, and could have taken any number of alternative steps to defeat the conspiracy. Instead, they invited a Nishad family of similar composition, mother and five sons, made them eat lavishly and got them intoxicated. Finally, Bhima set fire upon the wax palace. All the six members of Nishad family and Purochana, the main accomplice of Duryodhana, died.

Is it not peculiar that the murderer is killed by would-be victims?

Is it not possible that Purochana was killed just to distort the evidence?

Had this incident occurred today, television serials would have been made on it. It would have invited a serious case under section 436/302/201/34 IPC for arson, murder and elopement of evidence. The Pandavas would face death sentences for this gruesome act.

Here, the surprising fact is the silence on the part of Bhishma. He was informed by Vidura about the actual incident in Varanavata, and was categorically told that the Pandavas were alive. Yet, he allowed Dhritarashtra and other Kauravas to carry out the last rites of Pandavas, on receipt of information about the gutting of the wax palace and the recovery of seven charred dead bodies, alleged to be the dead bodies of Kunti, her fives sons and Purochana.

A man like Bhishma should always have been sceptical about the identity of Pandavas, but he behaved peculiarly in the epic. I place Bhishma in the place of Gorbachev for his openness and accepting Pandavas as offspring of Pandu. The only difference is that after all his experiments with 'Glasnost' and 'Perestroika', Gorbachev has taken shelter in USA."

"I didn't know that", Anup Kumar demonstrated his surprise; "it is really unbelievable that Bhishma didn't have the courage to declare the truth."

"Yes, my dear", Mr Sharma stressed. "This is the state of affairs. Does it mean something else? I would not be surprised if it was found that Bhishma was dictated to by some external forces, to show favour towards the Pandavas."

"But for that reason, we can't put Bhishma in the place of Mikhail Sergeyevich Gorbachev", Kaushik stressed. "Bhishma should be treated as the father of the nation, and in respect of USSR, he should be none other than Vladimir Lenin."

"Who will be Joseph Stalin then?" I asked.

"Doctor, we can't yet solve the problem of Gorbachev, and you've brought another", Mr Sharma remarked with a smile.

"I think there can't be any doubt vis-à-vis the identity of Joseph Stalin, he should be Dronacharya", Kaushik suggested.

We all agreed with this postulate. Finally, after a detailed and thread-bare discussion, we accepted that Gorbachev should be compared with none other than Shakuni. The names of Duryodhana and Karna also came in for consideration, but ultimately their names were dropped.

"Sir, you were mentioning about a suspicion regarding the identity of the Pandavas", as usual, Anup Kumar didn't want to miss any point, "Will you please elucidate?"

"Certainly!" replied Mr Sharma, "consider the first arrival of the Pandavas in Hastinapura. Pandu died on the 14th birthday of Arjuna. It was spring time, and so decomposition of the body would be faster, compared to winter. Dead bodies of Pandu and Madri were brought to Hastinapura in a procession, led by Kunti with the Pandavas and Brahmins from the woods seventeen days after the death. Condition of the dead bodies is quite imaginable unless there was mummification or preservation by using chemicals like formalin.

No reference of use of preservatives is available in the Mahabharata. So, it can be presumed that the dead bodies were in putrefied condition and that these were beyond recognition.

Bhishma welcomed the Brahmins and sages who had accompanied Kunti and the Pandavas. Dhritarashtra asked Vidura to make all arrangements for cremation of Pandu and Madri. Kunti initiated the cremation of Madri. Kunti, Bhishma and Dhritarashtra together carried out the last rites of Pandu. The Pandavas were accommodated in the Hastinapura as princes. For the next thirteen years, the Pandavas learnt lessons in weaponry from Dronacharya alongwith the Kauravas. Think about the circumstances. After 16 to 17 years, suddenly if some one appears and puts a claim on the monarchy, that too without proper identity, will any one accept this? Moreover, the five Pandavas were fathered by Devas, not by Pandu!"

"You are really making a strong case", I couldn't resist from commenting.

"Actually, we've never considered it from that angle", Kaushik emphasized.

Mr Sharma explained his case further, "Dhritarashtra has been depicted as a villain, despite all his broadness. He gave his younger brother Pandu the chance to rule over Hastinapura first, on the ground that he was blind. Was he incapable as a king? Then, how was he able to rule the country for more than 50 years, once Pandu retired to the woods? Was there even an iota of greed in his action?

It was Vidura and his associate Brahmins who orchestrated all this propaganda to create an evil atmosphere, and to believe that Dhritarashtra was prejudiced towards his sons."

There was pin-drop silence this time, as he unfurled his story, "After their marriage with Draupadi, the Pandavas were provided with five villages; Panduprashta, Banprastha, Indraprastha, Soneprastha and Tilprastha. They weren't happy with this. They set the entire Khandavprastha on fire to build their capital. In the process, they killed thousands of tribes living in that forest, not to speak of casualties to animals, and damage to the flora and fauna.

This is again a serious offence punishable under section 435/302/429 of the IPC. Also, section of 436 IPC would have been attracted for mischief by fire or explosive substance to destroy houses, etc., which prescribes stringent punishment, from that of section 435 IPC for causing damage to agricultural produce. For causing the death of hundreds of people, they would face capital punishment in the form of death sentence. Section 429 of the IPC prescribes five years' imprisonment for mischief by killing or maiming animals. In addition, it would have attracted violation of Wild Life Protection Act and an officer of the rank of Deputy Inspector General of Police or above would have to be entrusted for investigations."

"It sounds like modern day Singur", Kaushik surmised like an expert.

"Not exactly, there were no such atrocities in Singur", Mr Sharma reacted. "However, 'imperialism' is a term associated with industrialization. For industrialization, it is necessary to identify lands in the vicinity of townships with easy availability of raw materials and connectivity. Khandavprastha forest was located on the bank of river Yamuna. Since boats were in use those days, it could be concluded that waterways were a means of transport. In this sense, the two cases are alike."

It was 10.15 p.m., so we decided to bring our chatting to an end and proceeded for dinner.

❖❖❖

VII

Everything went as per schedule on the fifth day of our ongoing tour. The recruitment rally is basically a method of elimination. Amongst all outdoor tests, the most difficult is chin-up in-beam. One candidate has to perform 10 chin-ups as per the timings given by our instructors. Usually, three persons perform this exercise at a time. As in-charge for this test, Kaushik soon became a terror for the candidates. Physical measurement of height and chest alongwith the checking of certificates were carried out at two counters; one headed by Mr Sharma and the other headed by Anup Kumar.

As for me, my counter was located near the counter of Mr Sharma. After completion of physical measurements and verification of documents, candidates report to me for a medical test. I am required to check deformities like flat footedness, varicose veins, knock knees, eye-sight problems, colour blindness, any deformities in limbs, etc. Riflemen S.K. Madhaban and Bimal Kumar Negi are my helping hands. They're basically nursing assistants of TSR.

Dr (Miss) Harleen Bedi joined our team at around 10.30 a.m. By four in the afternoon, we completed the medical tests of all the candidates. Mr Sharma left the ground at around 5 p.m. for the other venue after instructing Kaushik to set questions for the written test. I also accompanied him in his vehicle. At District Police Ground, Jalandhar, our staff had carried out an excellent job by reducing the number of candidates to only seventy-seven. I examined eleven doubtful cases. These are mainly cases of obesity, so I requested Mr Sharma for introducing of Body Mass Index (BMI) as a criteria for selection of candidates. He gladly accepted my proposal. The simplest way of finding the perfect weight in MKS system is by multiplying the square of height in meters with 23. I instructed my staff accordingly.

While returning, Mr Sharma enquired, "Dr Bhaumik, what about Dr Bedi? Did she narrate her story to you?"

"No, today we hardly had any time to chit-chat. She's very sincere in her work and performs her job without any fuss", I replied.

- She has a tragedy in her life. I've learnt this from Dr Chauhan.
- Tragedy! Regarding what?
- She was deeply in love with a Captain of Black Panther Rifles, who committed suicide in the Officers' Mess of Black Panther Rifles at Bharatpur in May, 2006. The boy was from Ambala. Since then, Miss Bedi has become introverted.
- It is really very sad.
- Try to be friendly with her; I've faith upon you since you have ample patience.

I kept mum, as I became thoughtful.

- Tomorrow you've very little work to do in the afternoon. Take my vehicle and enjoy a toss around Jalandhar with Dr Bedi.
- Sir, you're unnecessarily taking pains for me. Infatuation, love, marriage, etc., are all matters of coincidence.
- Don't be a fatalist, my boy. She's such a beautiful girl and it is her age for enjoying life. I feel pity for the girl. I'm sorry if I have hurt you.
- No Sir, I don't mean that.

He remained silent for almost ten minutes, till our return to the mess. We went to our respective rooms with a promise to meet over dinner. Inside the room, I switched on the TV and tried to watch an IPL match between Rajasthan Royals and Chennai Super Kings. But, I couldn't focus on TV.

I went to Kaushik's room. Anup Kumar was also there, watching the cricket match. At around nine, we jointly went to Mr Sharma's room, and with him we came to the lobby. Our purpose was to hear the remaining part of his story. Somehow, we feel that TV programmes have attained saturation and have come monotonous. We took tea, and asked the mess boy to serve dinner a little later.

As usual, Anup Kumar reminded Mr Sharma that he had left us at Khandavprastha the previous day. He thanked Anup Kumar for recollecting the last reference, and resumed his narrative, "Greatness of sage Vyasa is that despite his tacit weakness towards the Pandavas, he narrated the incidents on their merit. We can make inferences from his descriptions."

"It is something like the decisions taken by appellate courts, on the basis of depositions made in the trial courts" Kaushik made a passing remark.

"Well said!" he appreciated the comment and unfurled his story. "According to the Mahabharata, Arjuna got married to Draupadi at the age of 29 and the next 5 years they spent celebrating their marriage and enjoying times with their relatives at Hastinapura. Shifting of the kingdom and consequent construction activities took 23 years under the monarchy of Yudhishthira. The Pandavas were living happily, and their children were taking lessons in arms and warfare. The subjects were equally happy and had cordial relations with the rulers.

The day Krishna and Arjuna came across Agni, a Brahmin, to take decision to set entire Khandavprastha on fire is really interesting. On that evening, Krishna and Arjuna went to Khandavprastha with their wives. Their wives were taking drinks with the native women who were also beautiful. The ladies were dancing with joy on getting the acquaintance of the queens. Krishna and Arjuna were at a little distance, with river Yamuna flowing behind them. Just at that joyful moment, Agni, a Brahmin appeared there. He disclosed his plan to convert Khandavprastha into a modern township. He told Krishna and Arjuna that he had tried seven times in the past to evict these people, and set fire to Khandavprastha. But, every time Lord Indra prevented his efforts for his friend Thakshak Nag, an inhabitant of the forest.

The role of Agni is comparable with the modern day real estate promoters. Krishna and Arjuna agreed to Agni's proposal to wipe out the entire habitation of Khandavprastha for creating Indraprastha township. In exchange, Krishna got the Sudarshana Chakra (Discus), Kaumodini mace, and his famous Panchajanya conch from Agni. Arjuna received the Gandiv bow, chariots and two consignments of un-diminishable arrows. In the fifteen days' long fire, Krishna and Arjuna killed the entire population living in Khandavprastha, including animals and vegetation ruthlessly.

Indra tried his sincerest best to preserve the forest and succeeded in saving only six creatures, Ashwasen, the son of Takshak; an Asura named Maya and four birds."

"Indra is like modern day social activist and ecologist", I suggested.

"You're right, doctor" Mr Sharma expressed solidarity with me. "We should give a big hand to Indra for his excellent gesture. Maya, the great architect of Asuras, was then compelled to build a vast and marvellous palace in fourteen months' period. Yudhishthira ruled for 27 years during this tenure. As the years rolled by, the Pandavas grew more and more powerful and a greater number of kings accepted Yudhishthira as their real lord and sovereign. The Pandavas led a peaceful and contented life. Yudhishthira devoted himself to the welfare of his subjects.

One day, Narada, the sage of gods visited Yudhishthira and advised him to perform the Rajasuya sacrifice. Narada was a peculiar character and his basic duty was enticement, having access to all sects, Deva, Nara and Asuras. But he was basically, prejudiced towards the gods and men of upper castes. On being enticed by Narada, Yudhisthira consulted his brothers, and of course Krishna about this great sacrifice. Krishna opined in favour of the ceremonial sacrifice, but told him about the powerful king Jarasandha, who still continued to defy the authority of Yudhishthira. The very idea of the Rajasuya sacrifice was an imperialistic attitude, which perhaps helped alienating many states from the Pandavas, and they fought in favour of the Kauravas.

Jarasandha, Shishupala, Bhagadutta and a few other kings like them were basically enemies of Yadavas. Shri Krishna availed the opportunity of the Rajasuya sacrifice of Yudhishthira to settle his personal scores. Thus after reigning for 27 years, when Pandavas went to exile with their wife Draupadi, following loss suffered by Yudhishthira in a game of dice, the divisions amongst the states in favour and against the Pandavas became distinct. Battle lines were already drawn. It is not wholly true that Pandavas made use of the sentiments and zeal arising out of the humiliation suffered by Draupadi in Hastinapura assembly only.

Such anguish generally doesn't continue for a long period, and is quite unlikely to percolate to others not directly connected with the events, to fight, treating the same as a common cause. Moreover, the manner and the act of Yudhishthira to get involved in gambling wasn't worthy of a king of Yudhishthira's stature. It would have invited a criminal case under the Gambling Act, had it happened today.

Even after 27 years of reign for the first tenure, the Pandavas, led by Yudhishthira, did not remain satisfied with their five villages. So they adopted the policy of 'might is right', which was nothing but neo-Darwinism or imperialism. So they killed Hidimba, Bakasura and many other strong personalities who were active amongst the indigenous people. They adopted the principle that 'king has no rule', and resorted to insolent activities like polyandry and polygamy. Polyandry wasn't certainly the order of the day. In the entire Mahabharata, only two female characters, namely Kunti and Draupadi were involved in polyandry. We may leave out widows of Vichitravirya who bore children through Niyoga, which may amount to adultery."

"Sir, after listening to your story, I don't find any difference between Pandavas and the present day Western society", Anup Kumar surmised.

"In a sense you're right", he supported the point raised by Anup Kumar partially, "they maintained polygenic relations to create progeny, but always under some pretext. Thus, all the Pandav brothers had three to four wives. I shall elaborate some other day but this wasn't the case with the Kauravas."

"We never analysed this from this angle", Kaushik reacted this time, "this is really surprising. Both Kauravas and Pandavas were brought up in identical environments, yet compared to the Kauravas; the Pandavas led more vile and lascivious lives."

"Very correct, Kaushik", endorsing the views of Kaushik, he concluded, "it is almost half past ten, before I finish, let me tell you, imperialism, as defined by the Dictionary of Human Geography is the creation and maintenance of an unequal economic, cultural and territorial relationship, usually between states and often in the form of an empire, based on domination and subordination.

A controversial aspect of imperialism is the imperial power's defence and justification of such actions. Most controversial of all is the justification of imperialism done on scientific grounds. Like it may be said, 'It is desirable that the earth should be peopled, governed and developed, as far as possible, by races which can do this work best, i.e., by the races of highest 'social efficiency'. Like in the case of Mahabharata, it's termed as a victory of 'Dharma' over 'Adharma'.

Arjuna even used 'chemical weapons' once in battle against all approved norms. This is again a lengthy story. I shall relate it some other day."

He took a pause, and asked, "Doctor, what's the score?"

"That the Pandavas are imperialist", I replied, "is proved beyond any shadow of doubt. But, sir, like Emily Dickinson says,

> Yesterday is History, 'Tis so faı away
> yesterday is Poetry, 'Tis Philosophy."

VIII

Today is 5th May 2008, Monday. We have completed the physical tests and the written tests. The questions are of objective type on current affairs, sports, literature and local customs, culture and the like. After the written examination, 309 candidates for riflemen and 66 candidates for enrolled followers remain in the fray for oral test. Dr Bedi and I have evaluated some answer scripts. By eleven in the morning, we were practically free. Our company, especially given the affectionate attitude of Chairman Mr Sharma, made her feel comfortable.

The tent for the medical unit was pitched under a peepul tree. It was breezy, and despite the blistering sun outside, it wasn't so unpleasant. While Mr Sharma, Kaushik and Anup Kumar were busy with the viva voce of the candidates, I spent the day chatting with Harleen. In between, we were served with soft drinks and refreshments by our TSR attendants. In the process, I could gather some knowledge about the socio-cultural heritage of Punjab. Our discussions became lively as we spent time together and got to know each other better. We discussed various issues from general nature to her personal likings, dislikings, her upbringing, etc.

She's from Malwa region of the state of Punjab, the centrally-located district of the state, namely Ludhiana. It is separated from Jalandhar by the river Sutlej. The same river has also formed the boundary of the district with Hosiarpur. It has common boundaries with Rupnagar, Moga, Sangrur and Patiala. She has an elder brother and a younger sister and both are married. Her father is no more. Her brother looks after their family business of hosiery. Ludhiana is known as "Manchester of India".

She has studied in Khalsa College of Girls in Ghumar Mandi, Ludhiana before taking admission in Government Medical College, Amritsar in 2002. It meant that she was three years younger to me. She was in love with one Amandeep Sandhu, a boy from Khalsa College for Boys, Ludhiana from her school days. Later, the boy joined Black Panther Rifles as a commissioned officer. He committed suicide by firing bullets from his service pistol under suspicious circumstances on 2nd May 2006 at Officers' Mess of Black Panther Rifles, Bharatpur Rajasthan. Amandeep was from Ambala Cantonment, Haryana and was the only son of his parents. Aman's parents felt that their son committed suicide because she didn't agree to marry their son before completion of her studies. Officials of Black Panther Rifles, who were close to Amandeep, also made similar observations. Harleen couldn't accept this slur, but could do nothing to quell the slander.

After completion of her internship from Dayanand Medical College (DMC), Ludhiana in 2006, she spent a few months in her house. She joined CRPF in September 2007, on the advice of Dr Jagjeet Chauhan, their family friend.

Punjab was split between two nations, Pakistan and India at the time of our Independence in 1947. In 1966, Haryana and Himachal Pradesh were carved out of Punjab.

Punjab means the land of five rivers. Gurmukhi is the state language of Punjab-India and the language of Sikhs. Their surnames are categorized into three clans or professions or castes. Jat or Zat or Jutt are land owners/farmers and it is not a surname. Aroras are merchants/businessmen and it is a fairly common surname. Khatiris/Khatters are warriors and can also be merchants. Sandhu is a Sikh surname which goes back to the tribal name Sandhu or Sindhu. Bedi is common with Hindus (Khatris) and is a Sikh name. It is derived from Sanskrit word 'Veda', one who knows the Vedas. Guru Nanak, the founder of Sikh religion was from the Bedi clan. It is said that the founder of the clan studied the Vedas in Banaras.

Origins of Bhangra are imbedded in the farming community of Punjab. It is an expression of joy associated with the harvest festival of Baishakhi (April 13). It is a male dance. Baishakhi marks the new year in Punjab. It also commemorates the foundation day of Khalsa brotherhood of the Sikhs by Guru Govind Singh. Apart from Bhangra, Lohri is a major festival for Punjabis. Gidda dance is also very popular. Lohri marks the end of winter and is celebrated on 13th January. It's an auspicious occasion for the Jat-Sikh community.

Harleen stays alone in the campus with a female attendant. Her favourite colour is pink. But, these days, she prefers light yellow and white attires. Her hobbies include reading books, besides playing guitar. She is the only graduate from her family.

Our lunch was arranged in the stadium with our staff. Harleen also shared lunch with us. This helped in saving considerable time for us. Here, I should mention that the food served during lunch was cooked by the shortlisted candidates for enrolled followers (cooks) as a part of practical test. The food that they prepared was appreciated by Miss Bedi as well.

Realizing her depth of her love for Amandeep Sandhu, I casually stated, "I believe the tragedy has made you more matured to withstand the realities in life."

My words made her lose her composure and she was on the verge of tears, as she said, "But, why didn't he give me a hint? Aman behaved absolutely perfectly till his death. There was no misunderstanding between us."

I couldn't find words to console her. 'One should embrace death as his lord...' I took recourse in my poet Tagore, "Probably Captain Amandeep had gathered this courage from his association with you to avail his journey to the land of peace."

"Why did he not even hint even once that he might take such a desperate step?" up came her question.

I had no answer and felt distraught, like the fate of the peepal tree under which we were sitting, "The tree gazes in love at the beautiful shadow, which is its own and yet which it never can grasp."

Her eyes became moist, but she quickly regained her composure. It was five in the afternoon. Some Sikh gentlemen with turban offered us soft drinks and sweets. They were from a Gurudwara located on the other side of the ground behind the gallery, which had escaped my notice till then. It was time for her to go. I wanted to see the Gurudwara, and so I proposed, "Let us walk up to the Gurudwara."

The people who were engaged in kar-seva, in the form of providing soft drinks and sweets to our people and the candidates, greeted us, "Sat Shree Akal Ji!"

I responded, "Sat Shree Akal!"

We sat for some time on the floor of the Gurudwara before "the Granth Sahib", as Sabad kirtan was being played on the microphone. As we came out of the Gurudwara, Harleen appeared extremely thoughtful. I didn't dare to disturb her.

Before departing for the day, I requested her, "May I expect your company to Jalandhar tomorrow morning? I want to purchase some books."

She nodded affirmatively. I wished her good night, though there was still day light.

I came to the place where Mr Sharma was doing the interviews. Mr Sharma greeted me, "Please come doctor, I hope all is well on your front."

As I sat down on a vacant chair, he announced a temporary break and offered me tea.

- Sir, how long will it take to complete the interview? I'm missing your stories badly.
- Look doctor, it is as good as seeing patients in your chamber. Anyway it is expected to be completed by tomorrow afternoon. But why do you ask this question?
- I want to discuss something about Harleen.
- You're always welcome, doctor. I shall be in the ground up to 8 p.m. You better come to my room at nine; from there we shall go for dinner. Is it alright?
- It's perfectly OK. We may invite Dr Harleen Bedi for a dinner one day.
- That is an excellent idea. I'm thinking of a trip to the Golden Temple, Amritsar and Wagha Border, day after tomorrow with our boys. Why don't you invite her to accompany us?

- OK Sir, I'll request her. Tomorrow we're planning to visit some book stalls at Jalandhar.
- Go ahead my boy; Joginder will be at your service with his vehicle.

After tea, I returned to my room for the day while Mr Sharma and others continued with their task. It was 6.30 in the evening. I took a shower and watched an IPL match between Bangalore Royal Challengers and Kings XI Punjab before leaving for Mr Sharma's room.

He was alone in his room. I narrated to him the account of the suicidal death of captain Amandeep with his service pistol at Officers' Mess of Black Panther Rifles at Bharatpur on 2nd May 2006, as disclosed to me by Harleen. Since the death of Amandeep, his parents have been very harsh to her. They insisted that she marry Amandeep when he went home to spend his holidays during Baishaki in April 2006. But she didn't agree to the proposal as she was preparing for her final MBBS. Aman's parents treat her like a flirt and a loose woman and hold the view that their son was suffering from mental depression caused by her refusal to marry him, resulting in his untimely death. They're not ready to accept the fact that Harleen and Aman were true lovers.

Mr Sharma became silent for quite some time. Then he suggested, "Tomorrow I shall remain busy. Can you bring her day after tomorrow; say at around 8 in the morning? I want to ask her a few questions. I think there's some injustice meted out to her."

I gladly accepted the proposal, feeling happy that I could do at least something for her. We went for dinner at around quarter to ten. Kaushik and Anup Kumar were waiting for us in the lobby. We skipped our after dinner gossip.

IX

I didn't visit the ground today in the morning. Instead I rang up Harleen on her cell phone at around 9.30 after breakfast. She was ready for our trip to Jalandhar. I picked up her from her quarters in the Bolero Jeep. She was wearing a pink salwar and kameez with matching dupatta around her neck. She looked beautiful as usual. We were sitting side by side in the middle seat. I felt amused that she had taken my advice positively.

She asked me, "What type of books are you looking for?"

- Fiction, thriller, anything, actually I've not carried any book with me. It is disgusting to watch TV all the time.
- In that case, we may stop at Jalandhar bus stop; there will be plenty of book stalls around that place.

We left our vehicle at Jalandhar motor-stand. The temperature had come down considerably following a light drizzle last night. After visiting four or five stalls for more than an hour, I purchased the following books, mainly from the stall of National Book Trust Limited (NBTL).

The Wall and Other Stories of NBTL;

Bridging Connections, a Collection of Sri Lankan Short Stories;

Code Name God: The Spiritual Odyssey of a Man of Science by Dr Mani Bhaumik;

Kagaz Te Kanvas by Amrita Pritam;

The Phantom Rickshaw and Other Eerie Tales by Rudyard Kipling.

I gifted Harleen Maitreyi Devi's *It Doesn't* Die (*Na Hanyate*).

- You'll find answers to many of the questions which might have confronted you last night.

- I've to struggle hard, for I've forgotten how to read books these days. You're so caring.
- Thank you for the compliment. If you wish, you can share your feelings with me after reading this book.

We moved around the city for some time and took some refreshments in a restaurant. I purchased one blood pressure measuring instrument before returning to the campus around 1 p.m. Chairman Mr Sharma and others were giving finishing touches to the recruitment rally. Only 25 to 30 candidates were in the queue for taking eligibility certificates.

Mr Sharma greeted us, "Welcome doctors. Please take your seats. I hope you had a nice time. Let me have a look to what you've purchased."

We handed over the books to him. Dr Bedi told him, "It is of course a gift form Dr Bhaumik."

He perused the books for a while and said, "Dr Bhaumik, you've a nice choice. I've read the books by the two ladies, Maitreyi Devi and Amrita Pritam, marvellous works."

Kaushik, who was sitting next to him, stressed, "I've read the Bengali version of 'It Doesn't Die'. It's the real life story of Maitreyi Devi. Her philosophy is inspiring."

"There's good news, doctors. Since it'll take quite some time to complete the clerical works, we've decided to arrange tonight's dinner on this ground itself, around a camp-fire", Mr Sharma conveyed.

"It'll be a maiden experience for me. I've only heard about camp-fires", I replied.

He then turned towards Harleen smilingly, "May I invite your gracious presence at our dinner tonight?"

She laughed to declare, "How can I ever say no?"

"Then I've another request", he continued, "tomorrow, we're going to visit the Golden Temple, Amritsar and Wagah Border in the afternoon. Why don't you accompany us?"

"In that case, I've to take permission from Dr Chauhan", she replied.

"You're still on duty with the Recruitment Team and we're leaving day after tomorrow only", Mr Sharma joked.

"No problem Sir, Dr Chauhan will give me permission", Harleen assured him. "Its been a long time since I visited Amritsar."

"Every thing is settled doctors, we may take a break now", he passed instructions to Ajit Debbarma for arranging a grand dinner tonight.

❖❖❖

X

After lunch, I took a nice nap in the officers' Mess. When I came out to the ground with Kaushik and Anup Kumar on foot, it was 5.30 in the afternoon. Three or four candidates were still in queue before our officials. Harleen came next. She was wearing a magenta coloured salwar-kameez with a dupatta. Here, I noticed that unlike Bengali girls, Punjabi girls put their dupatta around their necks with both the free ends slinging on the back. She was looking marvellous. Mr Sharma came sharp at 6 p.m. and asked Ajit Debbarma to arrange tea.

Anup Kumar apprised Mr Sharma with the latest development, "Sir, I've spoken with my batch mate Akhilesh Kumar of BSF posted at Wagah Border over telephone today. He has promised all support for our visit tomorrow."

"Excellent! When shall we leave tomorrow?" he wanted to know.

"We can go to Wagah Border first to witness the 'lowering of the flags' ceremony followed by a visit to Harmandir Sahib. It'll take one and a half hours to reach Wagah. We can start by three in the afternoon", Anup Kumar proposed.

He accepted, "So, the programme is fixed. We shall move in a mini-bus from here. Drivers of the light vehicles will also accompany us, leaving their vehicles in the campus."

We expressed our assent to the suggestion.

After this initial discussion, Anup Kumar put up a query, "Sir, Kaushik has told me the story of the battle of Mahabharata narrated by you the other day while coming to Jalandhar. Since I'm from Bhagalpur, from my childhood I know that the kingdom of Anga was ruled by Karna and it consisted of Bhagalpur and Munger."

"I've got your point, you want to say that Karna hailed from your region", he reacted, "actually we get reference of two Angas in our history. The one you're referring to is located in eastern India and generally pronounced together with Banga and Kalinga and the other was in present day Kabul in Afghanistan. I feel both are true."

Kaushik and Anup Kumar together uttered with surprise, "How?"

"In that case I've to relate the story of Karna's birth", said Mr Sharma.

Meanwhile tea and snacks were served. He put forth a question, "Who was the mother of Karna?"

"Kunti" Anup Kumar replied almost instantly.

He appreciated the reply, "You're absolutely right. Her original name was Pritha and she was of celestial origin, her mother was a nymph. Her father Sura was a holy Brahmin and her brother Vasudeva, was the father of Krishna. Pritha was noted for her beauty and virtues. Sura's cousin Kunti Bhoja was childless. So Sura gave his daughter Pritha to Kunti Bhoja in adoption. From that time onwards, she was known by the name of Kunti after her adoptive father."

"I didn't know that!" Harleen expressed surprise.

"Yes, my dear", he assured her, "the next story is more interesting. When Kunti was a little girl, the sage Durvasa stayed for sometime as a guest in her father's house. She served the sage for a year with care, patience and devotion. The latter was so pleased with her that he gave her a divine mantra. Durvasa told her that if she called upon any God repeating that mantra, he'd manifest himself to her and bless her with a son equal to him in glory.

Out of impatient curiosity, Kunti tested the efficacy of the mantra, then and there, by invoking the Sun God whom she saw shining in heaven. At once the sky grew dark with clouds. Under cloud-cover, the Sun God approached the beautiful princess Kunti. Hypnotized, Kunti asked him who he was. Sun God disclosed his identity and told her that he had been drawn to her by the spell of the son-giving mantra. Horror-stricken, Kunti requested him that she didn't desire motherhood as an unwedded girl. She prayed to him to go back and forgive her. The Sun God assured her that no blame would be attached to her after bearing his son and she would regain her virginity."

Here, he gave a pause and then turning towards Harleen and me, enquired, "Two doctors are here, tell me if your medical science allows this hypothesis of regained virginity."

Harleen remained silent, but I gave a routine reply, "I've not come across any such instance in my study. I suppose that this is against the principle of nature. May be, medical science was much more developed those days."

Accepting my version, he said, "Yes, it's difficult to judge if the virginity of the teenaged girl Kunti was restored or not. But the first part of his assurance that no blame would be attached to her wasn't fulfilled. We all know that Kunti conceived by the grace of the Sun and divine birth of Karna took place without the nine months' weary course of gestation. Sun God could have taken the custody of the new-born baby. But instead, he preferred to escape, leaving Kunti traumatized. She wondered what she could do with the child. To hide her fault, she placed the child in a sealed box and set it afloat in river Aswa."

He took a break and then looking towards Kaushik said, "The other day you were commenting about human rights violation in Kurukshetra Battle. In fact you were right to point out that track record was 4:1 against the Pandavas. Now, tell me if this incident of gestation and desertion of the child takes place in the modern era, what shall be the consequences?"

Kaushik was not ready for the question, yet he replied smartly, "It would have invited a case of rape against Sun God under section 376 of IPC and under section 317 of IPC against Pritha alias Kunti for exposure and desertion of a child under twelve years of age."

Mr Sharma applauded Kaushik, "Bravo my boy! You may have the liberty to fix Sun God as an abettor for the charge of desertion of the child. Perhaps, an investigation would have revealed the real identity of Sun God as none other than sage Durvasa."

We were enjoying the lively discussion. In between, occasional snacks and soft drinks were served by TSR attendants, Mr Sharma went ahead with his story, "This maiden experience of motherhood by Kunti perhaps initiated the Mahabharata war. The basket carrying newly born Karna drifted down the river Aswa, until it reached the Yamuna and from there, into the Ganga."

After a pause, he turned towards Anup Kumar, "Finally it reached your place which was called Anga at that time. Radha, a native of Anga and a peerless beauty was childless. Her husband Adhiratha was a charioteer. By sheer chance, Radha went to the river bank and beheld the basket drifting on the waves. She was surprised and delighted to see within it a gorgeously beautiful child. Thus Karna, the son of Sun God, came to be brought up as charioteer's child. Karna became a powerful young man and a mighty archer."

"I have also heard this story several times in my childhood from my grandmother", Anup Kumar confirmed.

Mr Sharma unveiled his story further, "But here I differ, the kingdom Anga ruled by Karna was different from the Anga in your state on two counts. There's reference of at least 361 tribes in the Mahabharata. Out of them, 38 tribes fought in favour of Pandavas in the Kurukshetra Battle, while 59 were in favour of Kauravas. The rest were non-warrior tribes and their participation couldn't be confirmed. Almost all these tribes had

Jat Gotra. The tribes in the eastern part of India had proficiency in fields of wrestling, boxing, mace, etc. Karna was basically an archer, which suggested that he was trained in north-western areas."

Here, Anup Kumar interrupted, "Sir, tribal people of Bihar, especially the Santhals of Chota-Nagpur, now in Jharkhand, are very good in archery."

Mr Sharma accepted the argument, "Good point, Mr Kumar, sometimes I really feel surprised about the means of connectivity of ancient people. Probably, they had some form of aircrafts other than the conventional means of conveyance like chariots, boats, horses, elephants, etc. Otherwise it would have been difficult for people like Karna to take lessons from Parasuram, who was from Malabar region, in the extreme south."

"So it wouldn't be wise to judge Karna as a native from the north-western part of India", Anup Kumar reacted.

"I think I shall clear your doubts", he continued, "the introduction of Karna in the Mahabharata was through the test and exhibition of proficiency in the use of arms by the Kauravas and the Pandavas in the presence of the royal family and the common masses. Arjuna displayed superhuman skills with his weapons. The vast crowd was lost in wonder and admiration. Duryodhana felt humiliated and was envious of the Pandavas. Just at that moment, Karna entered into the arena and told Arjuna in a thundering voice that he would show greater skill than what Arjuna had displayed. Bhima objected to the challenge of Karna, saying that he wasn't a Kshatriya. Duryodhana crowned Karna as the king of Anga instantly and gave him Kshatriya status."

He took a pause and resumed, "I agree with the views of historians who felt that Anga was part of Gandhara, the present day Kabul. Remember, the mentor of Duryodhana was his maternal uncle Shakuni. The latter was the king of Gandhara. Duryodhana wasn't a king at that time. Unless he holds authority over the land, he couldn't crown anybody else as king of a state. That authority was probably given by Shakuni to Duryodhana. Karna became a bosom friend of

Duryodhana. It was on the strength of Karna that Duryodhana challenged the mighty Pandavas."

"Karna remains a tragic hero in the Mahabharata", suggested Harleen.

"Yes, my dear lady", he welcomed her views, "there's an interesting story involving Karna in the version of Mahabharata of tribal Bheels of Rajasthan. It is a bit lengthy. You'll find its online version."

"No matter Sir, you please tell us", I requested.

Our boys were also enjoying the evening. They organized a music-jalsha on the ground, a little away from us. One of our cooks, Arjun Paul was a very good singer, especially of Punjabi songs. Ever since we landed at Jalandhar, his talent was being revealed to the local Punjabi people. He was regularly performing at Jalandhar, especially at Police Lines. Mr Sharma gave him a free hand for identifying good singers from the aspiring candidates. Some of these new talents were also trying to enthral our staff with orchestra, in the form of beating of utensils and clapping of hands. It made a good symphony and we were also enjoying the music from a distance.

The weather was excellent and dust-free despite the hot summer, due to the drizzle last evening. Mr Sharma began his story, "Draupadi was sleeping one afternoon in Hastinapura. Her maids were gently combing her hair as she snoozed. As they did so, a single hair form her golden curls broke off and came loose. The maids were terrified. Out of fear, they decided to hang the hair from the window, hoping that wind would carry it away.

The wind saw the strand of hair and decided to play a prank. Storm after storm rushed towards Hastinapura. The single hair hanging from the royal window was lifted up, carried far and dropped. But it was so heavy that the earth couldn't bear it and split open. The hair floated down right into Patala where the king of serpents and the king of the nether world, Vasuki Naga had been asleep for twelve years. His queens were fanning him. The strand of hair fell on his chest. Unable to bear its weight, Vasuki started having chest discomfort and he woke up with a shock. He picked up the hair and studied it. Finally, he came to the conclusion that it was a woman's hair.

He sprang up and went to the seventh chamber in the basement. The chief queen Padma Nagin realized that he was going to the earth in search of the woman. She tried to desist him, warning him against entangling with a woman who didn't belong to their clan. But she couldn't stop him. Vasuki took sixteen sringars and mounted his horse. He eventually reached a lake on the outskirts of Hastinapura.

After taking a little rest, he mounted his horse again, whipped it and the horse started fleeing towards Hastinapura. The bird of good omen called and the king's heart filled with joy. In the royal gardens of Hastinapura, he tied his horse under a champak tree and gave it fresh grass. Then, whip in his hand; he started merrily walking towards the palace. Draupadi was then sitting on a swing.

The rays of the sun fell on her hair through the window. The light was reflected on Draupadi's golden hair and it blinded Vasuki for a moment. He felt enthused and his feet quickened. Draupadi saw him and thought that a guest had lost his way and coming towards the queen's apartments instead of going to the royal assembly. She sent her maids to show him the way. He pushed them away roughly and proceeded towards Draupadi undaunted. Seeing him approaching, Draupadi got up to go to the inner chambers. But, before she could do so, Vasuki swung the whip and lashed at Draupadi's thin waist. Draupadi fell down, her scarf moved off and Vasuki realized that she was the woman he had been looking for.

Draupadi shouted at him and asked him to go away if he wanted to remain alive, for the Pandavas would kill him if they came to know of his insolence. Ignoring her words, Vasuki picked her up and carried her to her bed. Draupadi yelled from the bed, but her protests had no effect on him. Instead, he ordered her to warm water for his bath. After the water was heated, she bathed him. He then asked her to prepare a thirty-two course of meal for him.

She did so and then served the meal in gold plates and while he remained reclining on the bed, she fed him, placing the food with her hands into his mouth. As she fed him, she wondered who that obstinate man was. When the meal was over, she again told him to hurry up and go away. He told her that he had come for spending the night there.

In the meantime, the Pandavas' assembly was over and the sounds of the people dispersing could be heard. Vasuki told Draupadi not to worry, let her husband come. So powerful were the steps of Arjuna as he approached that the very roof top of the palace quaked. As Arjuna entered the chamber, Vasuki jumped up from the bed and gathered Arjuna in a mighty stranglehold in his arms. The fight that ensued was terrible and it took the two of them down to the Patal, back to the earth, then to the skies. Eventually, Vasuki defeated Arjuna and sitting on his chest, tied up his hands and legs with a hair pulled out from his moustache. He then hoisted him up on to a peg on the wall.

Draupadi then got her bed ready for them. Fragrant flowers were spread on it, musk and flowers' essences were sprinkled. Seated on the bed, the Pandavas queen and the king of Patala played a game of dice. Arjuna, hanging from the peg, was a mute witness to the game. After the game of dice, the two of them moved on to another game. Draupadi and Vasuki had sex sometimes tenderly and sometimes vigorously, right before the eyes of Arjuna. In the morning Vasuki left, promising to come back again in the evening. Before leaving, he picked up his shining sword and cut off the whisker with which he had bound Arjuna's hands and feet. Arjuna fell to the ground with a thud.

Draupadi came running to Arjuna, raised him up, consoled him and leading him to the bed, laid him down on it. She heated water to bathe him. She also massaged him. She cooked another thirty-two course meal and fed him. Arjuna told Draupadi that his bones had broken and she should find out a way to kill Vasuki for it would otherwise become a daily affair. Back in Patala, Vasuki found no more pleasure in the company of his wives or the food that they served him. He passed the day impatiently waiting for the evening.

In the evening back at Hastinapura, he found Draupadi restlessly waiting for him. Arjuna was again tied up and hung from the peg and became a helpless witness to their games. Before that, however, Draupadi through a clever pretext learned from Vasuki that he wasn't in the least afraid of Pandavas and the only one he feared was Karna, who belonged to the Kauravas.

The next morning after Vasuki had left; Draupadi again raised Arjuna like the previous day. She revealed the secret of killing Vasuki to Arjuna through Karna. Arjuna was reluctant to take help from Karna as that would be humiliating to him. Draupadi convinced him that there was no other way. Agreeing, he went and sat under a tree waiting for Karna who would pass that way on his way to Kauravas.

As Karna saw him and greeted him, Arjuna acknowledged the greeting with his foot, raising it to receive it. Karna became furious at this insult. He asked him the reason for the insult so early in the morning. Arjuna asked who Karna's father was and added that being father-less, Karna had spoiled his days by showing his face.

In rage, Karna went to his mother Radha and demanded to know who his father was. Initially she maintained that she and Mali were his parents. But when he threatened her, she admitted they were his foster parents and they had brought him up after finding him in a rubbish heap. She advised Karna to go to Kunti. He went straight to Kunti and asked her how many children she gave birth to. When Kunti said five, he threatened her too and then she admitted that she actually gave birth to six children, and she buried him under a rubbish heap. Under pressure, she admitted that he was the son of Surya, the sun god. When he asked for proof, she gave him an agan-pichhaura and a ball of wax and asked him to go to Bengal and meet the rising Sun there.

Karna proceeded towards Bengal. Having reached there, as the Sun rose up in the east, Karna covered it up with the agan-pichhaura. Surya tried to free himself from the agan-pichhaura but failed. He asked Karna who he was and why he had stopped his rays. Karna told him that his son had come to meet him. Surya asked him to free him, but Karna wanted Surya to promise him that he would meet him face to face. Surya promised but on the condition that Karna passed a test to prove that he was really his son. The freed Surya attacked Karna with a thousand blazing rays. The rays passed through him without harming him. Karna had won the test; Surya acknowledged him and the father and the son met affectionately. Karna asked Surya to give him his weapon so that he could teach the Pandavas a lesson and punish Arjuna for insult.

Surya advised him to be patient and gave him an agankatari, a fire dagger, asking him to keep it in a wax scabbard given to him by his mother, and never to take it out except in dire necessity. The dagger was stated to be a dangerous weapon by Surya. If it was taken out without real need, the earth would split and the nine hundred thousands stars would burn down to ashes, and so would the gods in heaven, the gods in the nether worlds, the forest with their trees and bushes, and even the winds alongwith all the water on the earth.

As a happy Karna returned towards Hastinapura with lively steps, Draupadi saw him from a distance. She hurried to him, stopped him on the way and told him why Arjuna had insulted him. She told him about Vasuki's atrocities and the terrible misery he had unleashed upon her and Arjuna. They were dying due to Vasuki's atrocities. So she requested Karna to save them. Karna accepted the request of Draupadi and promised her to do what she desired. She told him that Vasuki would be coming soon as the Sun reached west.

That evening Vasuki came as usual. After tying up his horse under the champak tree, he proceeded to Draupadi's palace, swinging his whip merrily. He tied up Arjuna as usual and hanged him up from the peg from where he watched with unblinking eyes as the king of Patala took his pleasure by enjoying Draupadi all night. As he left the next morning, Draupadi told him she loved him and that there was no hero on earth like him and added that she couldn't live a moment without him.

So, Draupadi requested that Vasuki should give her the promise of early arrival next evening. Vasuki assured Draupadi that he would arrive early the next day. His heart was filled with the loving words of Draupadi. Strolling through the Pandavas' garden the next morning, Karna came across Vasuki's horse. He took out Surya's fire dagger from its wax scabbard and placed it before the horse. Every limb of the horse was burnt. As Vasuki approached, Karna placed the agankatari before him and Vasuki fell down on the ground. Karna burnt up eight of the nine hoods of Vasuki. As his body caught fire, Vasuki joined his hands in supplication and begged for his life, promising Karna never to come that way again. Karna was moved by the begging and let off the now single-hooded Vasuki."

Every one was listening to the stunning story mesmerized and no one interrupted Mr Sharma. Even our staff assembled near our tent, leaving their jalsa, to listen to the story. We were speechless. Mr Sharma was the first person to break the silence, "What are the differences you've noticed between the conventional Mahabharata and tribal Bheels' Mahabharata?"

"Apart from the inclusion of Vasuki, the king of serpents and the role played by Karna in taming him in Bheels' Mahabharata, is there any other difference?" Kaushik suggested.

"There may be two or three differences from the conventional Mahabharata", this time it was Harleen, "which I don't know whether they can be counted. Like here, Kunti is treated as mother of all the five Pandavas, and there's no reference to Madri. Again, Karna's foster father is described as Mali in place of the charioteer in the conventional Mahabharata. Draupadi is famous for her long black hair, but here she has golden hair."

"Excellent!" Mr Sharma was enthused with the answer, "You've a keen sense of observation, young lady!"

"But, it is a rare story and such humiliation of Draupadi is beyond imagination", Kaushik emphasized.

"Why? What about the pulling of clothes of Draupadi by wicked Dushasana inside the Hastinapura assembly? Wasn't it an atrocious offence?" Harleen queried.

"That was certainly an atrocious and humiliating offence upon Panchali, my dear sweet lady", replied Mr Sharma, "but law is blind in such respects. It constitutes a mere case of outrage of modesty under section 354 of IPC, which is cognizable and bailable. Law implementing agencies like the police shall have no option other than to release Dushasana and his associates on bail."

"Is it so?" Harleen expressed her surprise.

"Yes, my girl, but don't be upset as these are hypothetical issues and there's a huge generation gap" replied Mr Sharma.

"But it is said in the Mahabharata that we breathe the united soul of India and individual soul of her people," Harleen stressed. "Then why this discrimination? An act for which a battle was fought would invite a mere simple punishment!"

I felt proud of this young lady for her strong opinions. It was 8.45 p.m. Ajit Debbarma approached Mr Sharma for permission if soup could be served. The latter nodded his head and then turning towards Harleen said, "I appreciate your courage and probably this is the secret behind births of innumerable fighters in our country, from this land of five rivers. This is the reason for our arrival here all the way from Tripura to recruit boys in our elite TSR.

But at the same time, I must tell you that the Indian Penal Code was formulated by one British gentleman, Macaulay in 1833, and on the recommendation of the Law Commission of India constituted in 1834, this Penal Code was adopted in 1860. There's hardly been any amendment of sections of this Act, even after independence. Now, social organizations and conscious people like you have pointed out the need for amendment of some sections related to offences like outrage of modesty, rash driving, causing death by negligence for which the punishment prescribed is very low.

Provision for punishment was deliberately kept at so unreasonably low for these offences. One reason may be that Britishers and influential people used to be offenders in such cases. Like the British imperialists, you can also perceive the Pandavas engaged in thwarting laws at their will. So you'll find them involved in social crimes like polygamy, polyandry and even illegal murders."

"It would have been my proud privilege to listen to these invigorating tales from you Sir, but alas I don't have the opportunity!" Harleen expressed her regret.

Accepting the compliment, he said, "The most atrocious offence upon Draupadi, as per prevalent IPC was committed by Jayadratha while the Pandavas were in exile. He kidnapped her from their hut at Kamyakya forest taking advantage of the absence of her husbands, despite resistance from their priest Dhaumya. Bhima and Arjuna rescued her and detained Jayadratha. They brought him to Yudhisthira in their hermitage. Before that, Bhima being annoyed, shaved Jayadratha's head in five places and made him swear to declare himself the slave of the Pandavas in public. Dharmaraja did his 'forgiving and exhortation of virtue' routine.

The act of abduction by Jayadratha and his associates attract stringent section of law, 366 IPC which is cognizable, non-bailable and punishable by ten years' imprisonment and fine. On another occasion, Draupadi was kidnapped by Jatasura while the Pandavas were living in the jungle. Panchali was rescued and Jatasura was killed. The action was justified as per provision of right of private defence under section 100 of IPC."

"But you've not narrated the incident of attempted molestation of Draupadi by Keechaka, the commander-in-chief of Matsya country, when the Pandavas were living incognito in the house of king Virata", Anup Kumar threw the question towards Mr Sharma.

"This is again a simple case under section 354 IPC, cognizable and bailable", he replied, "but I wonder if the act of killing Keechaka by Bhima can be justified as a general exception under IPC. The act of Bhima is not commensurate with the gravity of offence committed by Keechaka. Here, Bhima has got ample time for taking recourse to law. Well, these are all the possibilities in this case, morally, and as a human, I support the action of Bhima."

We had enjoyed soup in the meantime. The taste was excellent. Mr Sharma praised the same in his inimitable style, "It seems that the soul of Draupadi as Sairandhri has cooked the food."

Accepting applauds, he added, "I shall commit injustice if I don't say a few words about a brave Bhil boy, Eklavya. The fame of Drona as a preceptor was spread far and wide. Many rajas and warriors took their sons to Hastinapura for tuition. All were welcomed except one and he was the son of the Raja of Bhils. This young man pleaded that he be trained as an archer, but without avail. Drona said that he was a Bhil and a cattle lifter. It would be a sin to impart knowledge of weapons to him.

When he heard these words, the Raja's son was stricken with grief and he turned homewards. But he resolved to become an accomplished warrior. So, he fashioned a clay image of Drona and worshipped it, and wielded the bow before it, until his fame as an archer became widespread.

One day, Drona went forth with the princes to hunt in the Bhil kingdom. Their dog ran through the woods and it beheld the dark son of the Raja of Bhils and barked at him. The young man shot seven arrows into the dog's mouth to make it stop barking. Moaning and bleeding, the animal thus returned to the princes. Wondering greatly, the princes searched for the skilled archer who had done this and found him busy with his bow.

They asked: 'Who are you?'

The Bhil answered: 'I'm a pupil of Drona.'

When Drona came to the place, the young man kissed his feet.

The wise preceptor said: 'If you're my pupil, I must receive my reward.'

The young man replied: 'Command me, and I'll give you whatsoever you desire.'

Drona said deceitfully: 'I should like to have the thumb of your right hand.'

The faithful prince of Bhils didn't hesitate to obey his preceptor; with a cheerful face he severed his thumb from his right hand and gave it to Drona.

After his wound had healed, the young man began to draw his bow with his middle fingers, but found that he had lost his amazing skill, whereby Arjuna was made happy. He was Eklavya, son of Hiranyadhanu."

After a pause, Mr Sharma concluded, "Had this happened today, Drona would have to face serious consequences and may be booked under provisions of ST/SC Atrocities Prevention Act and for abetment of offence under section 326 IPC, for he forced a minor boy to severe his thumb. As regards allegation of being a cattle lifter against Eklavya, cattle lifting was a noble profession those days. Drona himself with Bhishma, Karna, Duryodhana and others had received a serious thrashing at the hand of Arjuna, when they attempted to rob away cattle from the Virat kingdom."

"Perhaps it was for this sin that Drona was deceived even by Yudhisthira during the Kurukshetra battle", suggested Harleen.

"This may well be a good clue for investigation", Mr Sharma appreciated Harleen's remark. "I am sure that the tribal boys from Rajasthan whom we've short listed will pull the triggers of their rifles with their middle fingers, as this custom prevailed even afterwards amongst the tribals."

Fluttering of wings of a nocturnal bird in the peepul tree clapped in appreciation of Mr Sharma's narratives, which reminded of Emily Dickinson lines:

Yesterday is mystery
Where it is today
While we shrewdly speculate
Flutter both away

❖❖❖

XI

I got up quite early, by 5.30 in the morning and completed some paper work before leaving for the Harleen's quarters. She was ready in her apartment, and came out the moment I arrived. She was wearing a white salwar kameez and dupatta today. Mr Sharma was waiting for us, as we entered his room sharp at eight. He ordered tea and snacks.

After we took our seats, he said to her, "Dr Bhaumik has told me about the tragic death of Captain Amandeep, day before yesterday. It's just for academic interest; I want to ask you a few questions. Will you mind, my dear sweet lady?"

She remained silent with her head bowed but she nodded in affirmation.

He began, "I know you're in a state of trauma, ever since the death of Captain Sandhu in May 2006. Even allegation of abetment to suicide has been brought against you by his parents. But, joy and woe are woven fine in our life, be steady in replying to the questions. I believe you've not committed any sin."

His vocal consolation helped her to regain her composure. She wiped her wet eyes with her handkerchief and looked at Mr Sharma.

"Right", said Mr Sharma, "you can share with us your journey with Aman. How did you come close to each other?"

Harleen replied, initially with a quivering tone and then steadily, "Ours was a family of five, my parents, my elder brother Gagandeep and my younger sister Harjot. I was born in September 1984. My brother is three years older than me and my sister is one year younger to me. I'm from Ludhiana which is a centrally-located district of Punjab. We own a hosiery shop. After demise of my father in a road accident in June 2004, my brother has been looking after our business."

Here, she took a break as an attendant brought tea and snacks. She helped in serving the tea. After his departure, she continued, "I completed my secondary education from Khalsa College of Girls in Ghumar Mandi, Ludhiana. Aman was four years senior to me. He was from Ambala Cantonment area and his father was in the Forces. He studied from Khalsa College of Boys, Ludhiana and received his degree in electrical engineering from Guru Nanak Dev Engineering College, Ludhiana.

We first met during a quiz competition in Ludhiana. He was an amiable boy, very sober and disciplined, and quite different from other boys of his age. He was the only son of his parents. His parents accepted our relationship and so did my family. I took admission in Government Medical College, Amritsar in 2002, while Aman was doing MBA from Punjab College of Technical Education, Baddowal after completion of his engineering degree. But before completion of MBA, he joined Black Panther Rifles as a commissioned officer, and got his posting in the 15th Battalion, Black Panther Rifles. Their headquarters was at Jamshedpur, Jharkhand. 15th Battalion, Black Panther Rifles used to be one of the elite forces of the British and their battalion had earned two Victoria Crosses. This 15th Battalion, Black Panther Rifles continued its devoted service even after independence and earned many laurels for the country. The performance of their unit during Kargil war was also exemplary. Aman was very happy with his posting, especially with his colleagues and jawans.

In the meantime, I suffered a setback on 24th June 2004. My father died in a road accident, while returning to Ludhiana from Phagwara, after completing a business transaction.

After his basic training in Pune, Aman was posted with his unit at Rajouri, Kashmir. During Baishakhi on 13th April 2006, he was with his parents. I also went to their house. He was expecting his next posting at the headquarters at Jamshedpur, Jharkhand after a ten-day regiment level mock field exercise, christened 'Operation Bikram', scheduled from 18th April 2006 at Indo-Pak border near Bikaner, Rajasthan. After 'Operation Bikram', their units were assembling at Bharatpur, Rajasthan. In the meantime, there were two fire incidents in ammunitions depot of Black Panther Rifles in quick succession, one at Mirdhwal in Rajasthan's Ganganagar district on 24th April 2006 and the other on 26th April 2006 at Pathankot, Punjab.

In these two incidents, huge number of small arms, ammunitions and artillery stocks were destroyed, besides death of three defence personnel. In terms of money value, the loss was more than ₹ 40 billion, as Aman told me on 1st May 2006 in his last telephonic talk with me. He told me that a high-level court of inquiry was ordered from Black Panther Rifles, headquarters to ascertain why such accidental fires had become a routine phenomenon in the forces. There had been a similar fire in Bharatpur, the year before as well. All those who had participated in 'Operation Bikram' were asked to stay back at their respective locations in Rajasthan and Punjab till completion of the enquiry. Aman's unit was inducted in the mock operation through Bharatpur. So, they stayed at Bharatpur, Rajasthan.

I was in my medical college at Amritsar, as I was preparing for my final MBBS. I promised his parents that I would marry him but only after my final MBBS in November 2006, but they were insisting for a 'Sagai' ceremony during Baishakhi. Actually, I didn't want to lose focus from my studies."

Here, again Harleen took a break as tears had welled up in her eyes. She took a glass of water and started narrating her story again, "Sorry, I couldn't control my feelings. I got the information from my brother on 2nd May 2006 in the night at around eleven thirty. The incident took place at around nine in the evening at officers' mess of Black Panther Rifles, Bharatpur. Aman's parents got the information first; my brother got it from a relative of Aman.

I still remember the day vividly. It was a Tuesday and I was preparing for a class test for the next day. I was expecting a call from Aman. He used to call me around 9.30 to 9.45 p.m. That day, I didn't receive any call from him. When I tried after ten, his phone was switched off. Finally, my brother gave me the news. He tried to get confirmation from Aman's parents. But they misbehaved with him.

Even then, I attended Aman's funeral with my sister-in-law. His parents treated us as aliens. According to them, the incident wouldn't have happened, had I agreed for 'Sagai' during Baishakhi. We spent the night with one of our relatives at Ambala. I had to spend the next ten to fifteen days in my house, to recover from the initial shock. Thanks to the support from my family, especially from my sister-in-law Khushpreet Kaur, I could complete my MBBS."

Then, after a pause, she declared, "It is probably just a coincidence. Exactly after two years after the date I last heard from Aman, I've come across you on 1st May 2008. Dr Chauhan is caring, but this is the first time that I have met someone as affectionate and caring as Aman, outside of my family."

Mr Sharma took his time to speak, "As a police officer, we deal with many such cases and have the practical knowledge about the anguish of the victims, either directly or indirectly. Our experience makes us practically a psychologist, though we may not have the requisite qualifications. When a girl of your age suddenly becomes introverted, it would mean that some serious injustice had been done against her. Someone who is actually guilty in such a case wouldn't be so depressed."

Harleen kept mum, with her face towards her toes. He put a further query, "Tell me what was the weapon used by Aman and how many rounds were fired?"

Harleen thought for a while and then replied, "It was certainly a pistol. Probably the old newspaper containing the news of Aman's death is still lying with me. Two bullets were fired. There were two entry wounds at the temple region. I noticed this at the time of laying a wreath on Aman's body.

These wounds were covered with cotton. The upper portion of his head was smashed by the exit wounds."

Her eyes became wet, as she narrated the wounds on the body of her departed lover. But, Mr Sharma seemed elated, "Doctor, you should treat us to a party, as we can do away with the slur upon our dear lady. It's an out-and-out a murder case."

Harleen and I became speechless. He ordered second round of tea with some sweets over the intercom.

He explained, "It's a simple case of medical jurisprudence. Since pistol is a semi-automatic weapon, after the first shot is fired on the temple region, there's no scope for a person committing suicide to pull the trigger again. In fact, there is every chance of instantaneous rigor mortis. This should have come into the mind of doctors who had performed the post-mortem. They should have suspected why two rounds were fired. Alternatively, they might have been purchased by the persons who committed this murder.

From the intensity of fire, I doubt if at all a pistol was used. Bullets might have been fired from firearms like AK 47 or SLR which have higher muzzle velocities.

Obvious conclusion is that Captain Amandeep Sandhu was murdered on the night of 2nd May 2006 at Officers' Mess of Black Panther Rifles, Bharatpur, by a person or a group of persons for reason not known to us."

"I've also done many post-mortem examinations of gun shot cases, but never taken this into consideration", I confessed.

"Suicidal deaths with gun shot injuries always require extra care and it should be corroborated with circumstantial evidence", Mr Sharma opined.

"Here there's hardly any circumstantial evidence that Aman was under mental depression", I suggested.

"Probably, Aman's father accepted the version of suicide given by force officials", Mr Sharma presumed. "He might have risen from the lower ranks."

Harleen immediately confirmed this, "Aman's father had joined as junior commissioned officer, and ultimately retired as captain a few years back."

"In the forces, junior and subordinate ranks always remain subdued", he tried to emphasize with all his experience. "In a regimented organization like Black Panther Rifles, senior officers are treated like God. These old people are victims of generation gap and can't cope up with the opportunistic, corrupt and showy officers of present days."

This time I put the question, "Sir, what should be our course of action now?"

He became thoughtful for a while and said, "It's just a ray of hope which may help Dr Bedi to get rid of the slur brought upon her. It needs to be consolidated. Fortunately, Right to Information Act 2005 would be a great tool for us. She should write for a copy of the First Information Report filed with regards to the incident of Aman's death, police investigation report, post-mortem examination report, seizure list of articles seized from the place of occurrence, video-photographs, or if not available, normal photographs of the place of occurrence, statements of witnesses examined and any expert opinion on the fire arms and fired bullets. Even the newspaper-cuttings will be of immense importance. Side by side with these prayers under the RTI Act, she may also apply for certified copies from the court by depositing the requisite fees. To do all this, she will have to visit Bharatpur."

"It is essentially a private investigation", I said.

"Yes, you're absolutely right", he replied, "but we shouldn't waste time. I think I can help her by preparing a draft RTI prayer."

Meanwhile, attendant Shyamal Biswas served a second round of tea with sweets. Mr Sharma called his clerk Akhilesh Kumar and dictated the text of the application. Harleen and I remained silent. Akhilesh started preparing the draft on his laptop, sitting in Mr Sharma's bedroom. Mr Sharma turned towards us and said, "I believe, Aman had his personal laptop."

Harleen replied affirmatively, "Probably it is lying in his house at Ambala. During the rituals, I saw all his belongings including the laptop inside a room in their house. I don't think uncle and aunty would allow anybody to touch these articles."

Mr Sharma said, "This laptop may be a store-house of information for us. You should try to secure this at any cost."

In the meantime, Akhilesh completed his task, Mr Sharma gave a print out to Harleen, after some corrections. He then personally deleted the file from the computer and said to Harleen, "I'm sure, once you send these prayers after filling up dates, names, address, etc., with fees, a lot of developments will take place."

It was 12 noon, when I escorted Harleen up to her apartment. I asked her to get ready for our trip to Amritsar on time.

❖❖❖

XII

In the afternoon, we started for Wagah via Amritsar sharp at 3 p.m. It was a 32-seater Swaraj Mazda bus. Harleen and I took seats just behind Mr Sharma. He occupied a seat close to the front door on the left side. Anup Kumar and Kaushik sat in line with him on the right side of the aisle. One seat was lying vacant by his side. We moved along the Grand Trunk Road.

Anup Kumar broke the silence first, "Sir, is there any reference of Wagah in the Mahabharata?"

We laughed, but he replied with authority, "Of course there's reference of Atari in Mahabharata. Your vision should be clear, only then can you realize or observe something. It is mentioned as Atreya, north-western primitive tribe located in Atari between Lahore and Amritsar. They were later included in the Brahmin gotras of Atri and Bhardvaja. Thus,

Mahabharata tribe Atreya may be identified with Jat Gotra-Atri. "

I was overwhelmed by the company of this person, as he narrated, "But I've not found reference of Amritsar in the Mahabharata. The reason may be that Amritsar was set up in the 16th century. It is named after a tank excavated by Guru Ram Das, the forth Guru of Sikhism. Harmandir Sahib, meaning the abode of God was constructed in the middle of this tank and it became the supreme centre of Sikhism. Its sanctum came to house the Adi Granth comprising compositions of Sikh Gurus and other saints, e.g. Baba Farid, Kabir, etc. Maharaja Ranjit Singh arranged gold plating of this temple in the early-19th century. Since then, it is known as the Golden Temple.

This temple was damaged many a times, the last being during Operation Blue Star in June 1984, led by General Kuldip Singh Brar. Terrorist leader Jarnail Singh Bhindrawale and his followers had taken refuge in Harmandir Sahib and were indulging in terrorist activities. They were killed along with many soldiers. The official tally was 80-odd soldiers and about 490 civilians killed.

Many Sikhs regarded the attack as a desecration of their holiest shrine. Their alienation caused assassination of Indira Gandhi by two of her bodyguards, both Sikhs, the following October. Sonia Gandhi in 1998 officially apologized for the assault on holy Harmandir Sahib, and acknowledged it as a great mistake. A new Sri Akal Takhat Sahib was completed in 1999 through Kar Seva.

There are four entrances to the temple, signifying the importance of acceptance and openness, and anyone who wants to enter Harmandir Sahib may do so, irrespective of religion, colour, creed or sex. The only restrictions are that the person mustn't drink alcohol, eat meat or smoke cigarettes or imbibe other drugs while in the Shrine and must cover his head as a gesture of reverence."

We got a fair idea about Harmandir Sahib from Mr Sharma. Harleen told me a beautiful story written by Punjabi writer Rajendra Singh Bedi involving Wagah

Border, in her sweet voice. It was a story about a Hindustani girl Lajbanti alias Lajo. She was very beautiful, with a thin waist. Once she came across one Sundarlal, a potbellied man during the marriage of her sister. They fell in love. Soon, they got married and started their life as husband and wife. Lajo was faithful to her husband, despite habitual roughness and occasional physical torture unleashed upon her by the latter. During the partition of the country, many women, including Lajo were abducted by Pakistanis from the Indian side. There were similar kidnappings of Pakistani women by Indian miscreants. Sundarlal was looking after the rehabilitation of such kidnapped victims on the Indian side. It was during this period that Sundarlal realized the importance of Lajo in his life.

He was frantically searching for Lajo. One evening, some people were reciting the Ramayana over a microphone. When the portion about the exile of Sita was about to be recited, Sundarlal forcibly snatched the microphone. He declared that he didn't agree with Rama for accepting criticism over the sanctity of his wife for her captivity in Lanka. Obviously, he was moved by his feelings generated by Lajo's absence from his life. After this incident, Sundarlal became a hero, particularly before women folk of the small town.

After a few days, he received information about exchange of sixteen abducted women on either side, between India and Pakistan at Wagah border. More importantly, in the group of abducted victims to be handed over by Pakistanis, Lajo was there. Sundarlal immediately rushed to Wagah border. In fact, he could see his Lajo standing with other fifteen kidnapped females, on the other side of the border. The authorities on both the sides were arguing over the old age and obesity of the women victims. Pakistani authorities objected to this, showing Lajo who was still maintaining a thin waist and looking very young. The exchange of rescued women was delayed for a day, over this issue.

> Finally, Sundarlal got back his Lajo and started living with her again. He became polite with her. Gradually he came to know that she was in the house of a Sheikh who also loved her very much and never tortured her. Life went on, but the couple felt that they were missing some of their earlier affections.

We reached Wagah border at around 4.45 p.m. The BSF personnel greeted us, giving us VIP status. We were provided with seats just behind a retired chief of the armed forces who also visited Wagah by coincidence. Harleen told me that the ceremony was being performed as a co-ordinated daily ritual for the last 56 years, barring war-days.

Wagah is the only by-road border crossing between India and Pakistan and lies on Grand Trunk Road between the cities of Amritsar, India and Lahore, Pakistan. Wagah village itself is located on the controversial Radcliffe Line. The village was unified before partition in 1947. Today, the eastern half of the village remains in India whilst the other half is in Pakistan.

About 3,000 spectators took their seats behind the border post on the Indian side. Around 1,000 Pakistanis took their seats on the other side of the Baab-e-Azadi (Gate of Freedom). The Indians shouted, "Jai Hind" (Long live India) and it was reciprocated with shouts of "Pakistan Zindabad" (Long live Pakistan). The Indians played war music; the Pakistanis played religious music. The Indian spectators danced on the street and clapped. The Pakistanis remained seated and only one septuagenarian gentleman named Mehradin, dressed in national colour green, sporting a white beard, waved a large Pakistani flag.

Pakistani Rangers in charcoal salwar-kameez, without weapons, started the ceremony. It was repeated identically on the Indian side starting with the Guard of Honour by a ceremonial guard. Pounding the ground with long strides, a Ranger goose-stepped hurriedly towards the gate for a gruff exchange of mimicked threats with his Indian colleague. A second joined them, then a third in a bizarre battle punctured by glowering glares and warrior moustaches. The gates opened. Two officers approached each other and after briefly coming face-to-face, shook hands.

Soldiers on either side then started lowering the national flags fixed high on poles planted at the foot of the gates. Only the clacking of boots and the snorts of the soldiers could be heard, as silence fell. The flags were carried away warily by the goose-stepping soldiers. The two officers then shook hands on the white border for a final time with calm. The gates were shut and on both sides, a trumpet announced the end of the display.

The heights of the Pakistani soldiers are attractive and certainly they're chosen from all over the country. On the contrary, the Indian soldiers are of ordinary heights and even the shades of their uniform are not perfectly matching. These shortcomings are however compensated by the vibrant crowds on the Indian side, who enjoyed greatly in the backdrop of patriotic songs.

We left Atari at around 6.30 p.m. for Harmandir Sahib. Harleen guided our group inside the temple. We carried out a bit of Kar Seva by washing plates and partook of the food from the 'langar' with pleasure. Then we entered the Golden Temple and spent some time listening to religious songs. She showed us the three holy trees (Bers) each signifying a historical event or a Sikh saint. We enjoyed long photo sessions, covering our head with traditional yellow head scarves.

When we were visiting the Jallianwala Bagh, at a walking distance from Harmandir Sahib at around 8.30 p.m., Harleen gifted me a kripan, a bangle and a wall-chart containing replica of Golden Temple with some verses in Gurmukhi as mementoes. I became mum for few moments, standing in front of the garden which had witnessed brutal slaying of 379 people and injury of another 1,200 on the 13th April 1919 at the hands of General Reginald Dyer and his men. I came to my senses when Kaushik made a comment, "The place is so uncared for! It is unbelievable! This single incident shook each and every Indian and caused Tagore to give up his Knighthood."

On way back to the campus, we took dinner at a roadside restaurant. I thanked Harleen for the gifts and requested her to provide tips in future to ensure proper use of these priceless articles. She smiled for a moment and slept without hesitation keeping her head on my shoulder. Beauty of this tall slim girl in cherry coloured salwar-kameez with a black mole on her right cheek enchanted me. She was such an easy-going and free-from-fuss girl that I started feeling affection for her. I tried to find similarities between her and a blooming May flower I saw on the road. I felt happy that by giving her company in the last few days, I could bring some crimson to her soul, which was evident from the change of her attire.

❖❖❖

XIII

Temperature was still hovering around 40°C at Jalandhar. So we decided last night to leave early on 8th May 2008, Thursday for Dehradun, our next venue for the recruitment rally. We had covered more than 400 k.m. in a day. Accordingly, Mr Sharma announced the time of leaving as 5 a.m. while alighting from the bus last night. Our boys had loaded our luggage and articles last night itself. But still, we couldn't start before six in the morning.

Harleen came sharp at 5 a.m. to bid us adieu. Just before the start of our journey, Mr Sharma took her aside and told her something which she listened to attentively. Kaushik and Anup Kumar raised eyebrows to know from me what they could possibly be talking about. But I preferred not to make any guess and told them that I was clueless.

This time the jeep is a little crowded as Anup Kumar has joined us. Constable Narayan was accommodated in the rear seat, while Mr Sharma, Kaushik and I sat in the middle seat. Our three vehicles moved in a convoy up to Ludhiana. From

Ludhiana, the mini-bus and the Maruti Gypsy moved ahead at around 9 a.m., giving us scope for shopping and breakfast.

Here, Kaushik took the lead role. He had been to Ludhiana before which he didn't disclose earlier. Except me, all the other three purchased two or three leather jackets each. We purchased some clothing as well during our brief stop at Ludhiana for about two hours. Kaushik made a joke by suggesting that we should visit Harleen's house for lunch. Obviously, it is an effort to tease me.

As if on my behalf, Mr Sharma replied, "Harleen is a nice girl and I hope she'll give us the chance to visit her in the future."

While coming from Jalandhar, Joginder was playing an album of Sufi Songs on the car's CD player. He had purchased this album from Jalandhar and its flavour was different. We were all enjoying the same and there was no customary discussion. Now, at the time of departure from Ludhiana, the driver again loaded the song. Mr Sharma objected, "Don't play this album. Play some old Hindi melodies."

We were quite surprised and Kaushik asked, "What's the reason for your dislike of this album, Sir?"

He replied, "Sufi songs are good to listen, but there's a saying that they make people mad!"

I didn't find any logic in this, except for the fact that it was sung by a Pakistani singer. We preferred to remain silent on this issue and started listening to "Bindiya chamke gi...." One advantage of this type of Hindi songs is that we're accustomed to their rhythm and lyrics and even while discussing some other issue, we can concentrate on listening to the song.

Just as we crossed Rajapura and were approaching Ambala, Mr Sharma put a question, "By the way, whom will you term as a terrorist in the epic Mahabharata?"

Kaushik smartly replied, "It'll be none other than Parasuram."

"Excellent! I also hold the same view", he said.

Kaushik confessed, "Parasuram is always an interesting character; everyone will like his stories."

He was probably waiting for this request, so he began, "There was a king named Gaadhi. He had a daughter named Satyavati. A sage named Richik wanted to marry Satyavati. But, the king didn't find Richik to be the proper husband for Satyavati. He didn't want to say no directly and as a clever move, he put a difficult condition for Richik to bring one thousand horses, each shining as moon, and each having one black ear. Gaadhi felt that Richik wouldn't be able to fulfil the condition. After all he was a poor man, and would not be in a position to bring so many horses.

But sage Richik gave one thousand horses to Gaadhi after managing the same from Varuna, the rain god. Gaadhi solemnized the marriage of his daughter Satyavati to Richik.

Once, it so happened that Richik's wife Satyavati and her mother, both were carrying. They requested sage Richik to prepare some auspicious food to ensure birth of brilliant children who were full of values. Richik prepared one food item with Brahmin's mantras for a Brahmin child for his wife and another food with Kshatriya mantras for his mother-in-law for a Kshatriya child. After preparation, he went for a bath. Meanwhile, Satyavati's mother started thinking that her son-in-law had prepared better food for Satyavati. So, she requested Satyavati to exchange the food with her. Satyavati didn't find any difference between the two foods, and she fulfilled the desire of her mother. By the time Richik came to know about this, the two ladies had already taken the foods. He told his wife that she had done a great wrong. He wanted a Brahmin son, but now she'd deliver a fierce Kshatriya. On the contrary, his mother-in-law would deliver a boy who would be a learned scholar in spiritual sciences.

Satyavati wanted her son to be a scholar and not a warrior. She pleaded before Richik that her son be a scholar. Richik modified the effect of the mantras to the extent that her son would be a scholar in spiritual sciences, but her grandson would be a warrior. Satyavati's mother gave birth to sage Vishwamitra. Satyavati gave birth to Jamadagni. When

Jamadagni grew up, he married Renuka. Their youngest son was Ram and he became popular as Parasuram, because he kept the 'parasu' weapon with him. It is a weapon in the form of an axe.

Kartviryarjun was a powerful king of Mahishmati. As I had mentioned during the journey from Delhi to Jalandhar, Mahishmati was located in Madhya Pradesh at about 40 k.m. from Indore, on the banks of river Narmada. One day the king visited the ashram of Jamadagni. The sage received him very well, along with his soldiers, ministers and carriers. He provided a very delicious meal to his guests. Kartviryarjun found this surprising. He wondered as to how a poor sage could arrange so much food in such a short time. He asked Jamadagni the reason for it. Jamadagni told him that it was because of the divine cow that he had. The cow had supplied all the food. Kartviryarjun wanted to possess the cow. Jamadagni needed the cow because it provided him with things needed for religious sacrifices. Therefore, he refused to part with the cow. But king's soldiers forcibly took away the cow to Mahishmati."

He took a pause and cast a glance towards Kaushik with a question mark on his face. Kaushik satisfied him by saying, "It is a case of dacoity under section 395 IPC and names of the cattle lifters will be entered in red ink in the village crime note book."

We all laughed, as he resumed his story, "At the time of this incident, Parasuram wasn't present in their house. When he came to know about the incident, he became furious. He went to Mahishmati dressed like a sage but he was armed like a warrior, with his weapons, which he got from Lord Shiva. Kartviryarjun sent a huge army to fight Parasuram. But, Parasuram killed the entire army. Then the king himself came to the battle field. A fierce fight ensued. Parasuram was the winner, as he killed Kartviryarjun.

He brought back the cow to their ashram. His father was rather sad as he felt that Parasuram could have forgiven Kartviryarjun as there was always the need for a strong king at Mahishmati. He advised Parasuram to go for a pilgrimage. The latter went for a pilgrimage along with his four brothers. On return, they found that their father had been killed by Kartviryarjun's sons. Asking his brothers to take charge of his father's dead body, Parasuram rushed to Mahishmati with his weapons. In the battle that followed he killed the sons of Kartviryarjun. He killed many more of the warrior class. He got the earth rid of such Kshatriyas twenty-one times.

His anger upon Kshatriyas was for another reason as well. On one occasion, his mother Renuka went for a bath in a river. There she noticed king Chitraratha playing with his wife. She got infatuated towards the king. Realizing this, Jamadagni asked his sons to kill her. His four elder brothers refused to obey the order of their father. They were killed by Jamadagni through mantras. When his turn came, Parasuram killed his mother.

Being very pleased, his father offered him a reward. He begged for the life of his mother and brothers. Of course, he kept the pre-condition that his mother should not know that he was her killer. Jamadagni revived his wife and sons, though this sounds imaginary."

We were enthralled with the story of Parasuram. Mr Sharma drank some water and resumed the tale, "I've narrated the story of Parasuram with some purpose. Be it the case of Parasuram, Karna, Bhishma, Drona or Arjuna, you will find them earning consignments of rare weapons, along with lessons for using the same. It means that these powerful persons are chosen by some more influential person or persons for causing violence. We may call it terrorism sponsored by foreign forces. Remember that in the Mahabharata, the plight of these widows of Kshatriya kings slain by Parasuram was a matter of concern. On many occasions, they were forcibly raped by Brahmins."

At Ambala we took a break for lunch. A portion of the restaurant was used as a bar. People were taking beer openly, a proposition quite uncommon in Tripura. It became our issue of discussion during lunch. But, we tasted only lassi. We moved again towards Dehradun at around 3.30 p.m. By that time, our advance party had reached Narayangarh. They were moving roughly two hours ahead of us.

One good development in a span of a few days is that Anup Kumar has become an ardent listener of the stories narrated by Mr Sharma. At the same time, a good quality of Mr Sharma that is manifesting itself is that he never feels tired or irritated, despite his age. When we resumed our journey, Anup Kumar reminded him about Parasuram.

This time, he told the story of the other scion, Vishwamitra. He said, "Vishwamitra is associated with the creation of two great rivers, Beas and Sutlej which have formed the Doab area of Punjab. Jalandhar is a part of that area."

"Do you suspect Jarnail Singh Bhindranwale to be a descendant of Parasuram?" Kaushik put a question merrily. It caused laughter.

Mr Sharma reacted sharply, "I don't mean that, but people like Parasuram, or Bhindranwale haven't been born in a single day. Our society, to be particular, some opportunists, create them. Parasuram was a great human being. His motto was to keep the earth alive for birds, animals, trees, fruits and the entire nature with its beauty. But no one should support his genocide of Kshatriyas which was an act of terrorism and would invite serious punishment in a civilized society. Same may be true for Bhindranwale. We should hate the sin, not the sinner."

"I beg your pardon Sir, if it has hurt you", said Kaushik and added, "Sir, please continue with the story of Beas and Sutlej rivers."

"Pardon for what? You've not done anything wrong in bringing up this comparison. In fact, Bhindranwale was the Frankenstein created by some corrupt politicians", he stressed.

To change the topic, I said, "Sir, please continue with the story of the two rivers."

He regained his mood, "Right doctor! Punjab is a land of rivers. In fact, the state gets its name from the words 'Punj', which means five and 'aab' which means water. Thus the word

'Punjab' together means five waters. The five rivers—Beas, Sutlej, Ravi, Chenab and Jhelum make Punjab fertile.

Long, long ago, there lived a sage called Vasishtha. Vasishtha was a wise and learned Brahmin, one of the seven Rishis and a son of the God Brahma himself. The king Kalmashpad held Vasishtha in great esteem, and appointed him priest of the royal family.

Now, Vasishtha had a rival, the Sage Vishwamitra, the son of king Gaadhi. Vishwamitra was jealous of Vasishtha's great learning and wisdom, and honour given to him by the king. He wanted the position of the royal priest for himself. He decided to get even with Vasishtha.

The sage Vasishtha had a hundred sons. One day, Saktri the eldest son, came across king Kamalashpad and his followers. They were proceeding towards the same road. The king asked Saktri to move out of his way. But Saktri replied that being a Brahmin, he should get preference over the use of the path. The king was furious and he lashed out at Saktri with his whip.

Furious Saktri cursed the king: 'May you become an eater of human flesh!'

As luck would have it, Vishwamitra, in invisible form witnessed the incident. This gave him the chance that he had been waiting for. As soon as Saktri uttered his curse, Vishwamitra commanded a man-eating rakshasa to enter the king's body. The rakshasa did as Vishwamitra commanded, and immediately king Kalamashpad became a man eater. His first victim was of course, Saktri. Vishwamitra then caused the rakshasa in the king's body to eat and kill Vasishtha's remaining ninety-nine sons also. When Vasishtha heard of the death of his sons, he was devastated. He decided to kill himself.

He threw himself from the top of Mount Meru. But the rocks he fell upon became as soft as cotton. He plunged into a burning forest, but the fire didn't even singe him. He jumped into the sea with a rock tied around his neck. But the waves lifted him and cast him upon dry land."

He paused and looked towards Kaushik and asked, "What's the only offence for commission of which there's no offence, but mere attempt is an offence?"

Taking clue from the story, Kaushik quickly replied, "Attempt to commit suicide under section 309 IPC."

Mr Sharma was pleased with the answer, "Yes, there's no provision of punishment in the earthly world for committing suicide. But section 309 IPC could have prevented Vashishtha from making repeated attempts at suicide. He would have been in jail for the offence of attempt to commit suicide."

We felt delighted with the intricacy of the law, as he further unfurled, "Vasishtha then bound himself hand and foot with strong rope and jumped into a mountain river swollen with rain. The river refused to kill him, and, loosening his bonds, cast him vipash, unbound, upon its banks. From this, the river was given the name of Vipasha. We've seen this beautiful river, now known as Beas.

Finding that he could not kill himself, Vasishtha returned to his ashram in the forest. There he came across the unfortunate king Kalmashpad in the guise of man-eating rakshasa. The king tried to eat Vasishtha, but Vasishtha, through the strength of his powers, chased away the rakshasa from his body, and delivered the king from the curse. Vasishtha then ordered him to return to his kingdom to rule wisely and to pay Brahmins the respect that was their due.

Vasishtha then threw himself into another river, flowing swift and fast and full of crocodiles. But the river began to flow in a hundred streams and took the name of Shatadru. We call this river the Sutlej."

"Perhaps Vasishtha had a hermitage in Guwahati, Assam as well", I proposed.

Mr Sharma supported me, "You're right doctor, and I've once visited that ashram. But, Vasishtha seems to have been at the receiving end all the time. On one occasion, eight Vasus went for a holiday with their wives to a mountain tract where stood the hermitage of Vasishtha. One of them saw Vasishtha's cow, Nandini grazing there. Its divinely beautiful form attracted him and he pointed it out to the ladies. They were loud in praise of the graceful animal, and ultimately it was stolen by them. The youngest of the eight Vasus, Prabhas was the principal offender being instigated by his wife. They were cursed by Vasishtha and were subsequently born to the earth through Ganga. The incarnation of Prabhas was none other than our Bhishma."

"This will again be registered as a theft case", Kaushik declared without waiting for the nod from Mr Sharma.

"Since the offenders were punished by Vasishtha, we shouldn't reopen the case", Mr Sharma restrained himself from pronouncing other sections.

We expressed solidarity with him by remaining silent, as he went ahead with his story, "On the contrary, the sage Vishwamitra continued to get involved in activities which exposed his greed for power and authority. So, on one occasion, he was found engaged in great austerities and penance that would give him almost absolute power over the kingdoms of Earth and Heaven. He had successfully completed the requisite sacrificial rituals and was engaged in meditation and Yogic practices.

The king of Heaven, God Indra, was shaken to know about these efforts of Vishwamitra that could pose danger to his throne. Therefore, Indra decided to put obstacles in his practice of austerities and thereby break his Sadhana. Indra decided to use the weapon of lust. Accordingly, the most beautiful and ever youthful Apsara, Menaka, was sent from heaven to distract and seduce Vishwamitra. She descended down to earth from the heaven and tried to tempt Vishwamitra by various charming dances and songs.

After some efforts, Vishwamitra fell to the lure of her beauty and youthful attraction. They were married and the 'tapa' of Vishwamitra was broken. A beautiful daughter was born to them. The couple left the newly-born baby in a jungle, where it was guarded by a group of Shakun (Vultures). It caught the notice of one sage, Kanva. Since, the baby was guarded by Shakun, Kanva, named her as 'Shakuntala' and took her to his hermitage. Under his fatherly love and care, Shakuntala grew up as a simple but extremely beautiful lady.

But, the act of desertion of a new-born baby by Vishwamitra and Menaka was a great sin and totally unbecoming on the part of a sage of his stature. It would have attracted a case under section 317/34 IPC against the couple for desertion of an infant baby and they would have been sentenced to life imprisonment."

"Sir, the way you're narrating the story of Mahabharata is quite a lesson for me", Anup Kumar expressed his mind, "I've read the story of Shakuntala many times. Besides, I've seen its movie and drama. But it has never come to my mind that a serious offence had been committed."

"Probably you're now realizing the core issues like violation of human rights in Mahabharata", he said. "I don't know but when I read these stories, I found that people whom we admire for great virtues actually committed crimes, yet they remained scot-free. Consider the fate of the deserted baby Shakuntala. The absence of a mother's nurturing, love and handing down of traditions makes such girls vulnerable to child-marriage and pre-marital sex. This has happened in the cases of Kunti, Satyavati, Shakuntala, and so on.

As for Shakuntala, once the great king of the region, Dushyanta, happened to come near the ashram of Kanva on his way to a hunting expedition. He caught the sight of Shakuntala and lost his heart to her beauty and grace. The king proposed to Shakuntala and they were married secretly. Dushyanta stayed overnight and left for his capital city promising Shakuntala that he would soon send for her. He gave his precious ring as a memento to his wife cautioning her not to misplace it."

It was 5.30 in the afternoon and we were crossing a place called Jagadhari. We went ahead, as did Mr Sharma with his story, "In his busy schedule of affairs of the kingdom, the king Dushyanta forgot all about his love—Shakuntala!

It's simply unbelievable! How can one forget such an event unless he's very prone to extramarital affairs?

Shakuntala lost the ring given to her by king Dushyanta, and when she, in an advanced stage of pregnancy, went to the court of king Dushyanta, the latter refused to recognize her. Dejected and disappointed, Shakuntala left the court of the king for the forest all alone. There she gave birth to a beautiful son. She named him Bharata.

The union of this family was also equally dramatic. A few years later, Dushyanta realized his fault when the ring with the royal insignia was recovered from the possession of a fisherman by an honest official. It was reportedly recovered from the belly of a fish caught from river Sachi. Dushyanta also came to know about this. He went to the hermitage of Kanva. But, meanwhile it had shifted elsewhere.

The king was broken hearted and spent his years in isolation. He lost interest in food, hunting and games. He tossed in his bed with remorse. He cherished every minute of his days with Shakuntala. It kept him alive when he felt tortured.

After about eight years, he was invited to join in a distant war by one of his allies. On his way back, Dushyanta came upon a forest of exquisite beauty. He felt peaceful for the first time in years. His right eyebrow twitched, which was a good omen. Dushyanta rode on admiring the quietness of the land when he saw a hermitage at a distance. To his shock, he heard the growling of lions nearby. He got off his horse and walked gingerly to investigate the odd presence of wild animals near an ashram. He saw a little boy, as radiant as the moon playing with lion cubs as if they were kittens. The boy was fearless and extremely handsome.

An intense feeling of love came over Dushyanta as he came near the boy. He had never felt like this with a child before.

'Who are you?' he asked the boy, 'and, who are your parents? Who lives in this ashram in such a remote setting?'

The boy looked with curiosity at the stranger. He had never seen anyone so strong or dressed in such a costume. Before he could answer, a female voice called out: 'Whom are you talking to, Bharata? I've warned you many times to call if you see strangers.'

The voice, which betrayed concern, was familiar to Dushyanta. He stared in anticipation as a young lady appeared around the corner. She was dressed in simple costume of a hermit. Her face was calm as the full moon, but a tinge of sorrow hung around her like a cloud. She was Shakuntala. There were tears of joy in the eyes of everyone except Bharata. He felt only joy.

It's very inhuman that Shakuntala's father, sage Vishwamitra remained aloof when Shakuntala was in distress. In fact, her mother didn't remain totally aloof, as she rescued her and sheltered her in the hermitage of the sage Marichi."

When Mr Sharma completed his story, there was silence for quite a few minutes. We all would probably like to give a big hand to this beautiful lady Shakuntala for rearing her son Bharata despite hardship. It is from the name of Bharata that the name of our country is derived. He was the ancestor of the Kurus.

After Jagadhari, we reached Kaleshwar on Himachal Pradesh border. We crossed a road stretch of about 60 k.m. in Himachal Pradesh before reaching the hills of Uttarakhand. The place looked virgin, and in fact, it reminded me of the hermitage of Shakuntala, described by Mr Sharma a little while ago.

We were on the outskirts of Ponta Sahib. In Tripura, we're accustomed to Road Opening Parties (ROP) in the form of CRPF. Here we found nature's own army, our forefathers', the monkeys on the road side, sitting almost at equidistance from each other under the fading light. This ROP of the monkeys continued for almost eight to 10 k.m. along the hilly track, which seemed befitting for a nice hill station like Ponta Sahib. Probably there's some connecting road for Ponta Sahib City, as it didn't fall on our way.

Mr Sharma narrated the etymology of Ponta Sahib City, "It reminds us of the sacred memory of Guru Govind Singh, the tenth Guru of Sikhs. The city retains memorials of the martial guru in the form of his weapons and a majestic Gurudwara. The name of the city was derived from 'Paon' meaning 'foot', either because Guru Govind Singh set foot in this place, or according to an alternative story, because he lost an ornament which he wore on his foot called a 'Ponta' while bathing in the river Yamuna."

Despite our keenness to see this beautiful city, we had to move, as we felt the urgency similar to that of Robert Frost:

> The woods are lovely, dark and deep,
> But I have promises to keep,
> And miles to go before I sleep,
> And miles to go before I sleep.

In another one hour, we crossed the portion of the road in Himachal Pradesh to enter into Uttarakhand and near Dhalipur, we could establish contact with our advance team. They were in fact taking their dinner at a place called Jharjhara, close to Dehradun. Ultimately, we met our team at Jharjhara itself at around 8 p.m.

Jharjhara was on the foothills and a hilly river was flowing by its side. We stopped near a bridge. Some festival or country fair was probably in progress as we noticed chorus of announcements on a loudspeaker amidst Hindi songs and revolving of merry-go-rounds. We didn't get down from the vehicle and continued our journey, this time in a convoy. It took another one hour for us to reach the Indo-Tibetan Border Police (ITBP) Headquarters, Dehradun. On way we crossed through some narrow roads, populated by Mohammedans, evident from the presence of a mosque.

ITBP Headquarters, Dehradun is a beautiful complex having all modern facilities, spreading over probably more than one hundred acres, and its beauty has increased manifolds due to the presence of a huge lake. All the buildings and structures have come up around this lake. Mr Sharma, Anup Kumar, Kaushik and I have been accommodated in Tiger Mess while the others were placed in Sub-Officers Mess, and constable barracks. Though it summer, the climate is cooler as compared to Jalandhar. The average temperature is around 30°C.

It was breezy in the evening and we all felt very comfortable. After a quick bath, we took our dinner in the Tiger Mess and then witnessed an absorbing IPL match between Kolkata Knight Riders and Bangalore Royal Challengers played at Eden Gardens, which Dada's team won by five runs. We also listened about the background of Dehradun city from Mr Sharma:

> Dehradun is the capital city of Uttarakhand and also one of the oldest cities of the nation. It is situated at an altitude of 2200 feet above sea level. The valley of Dehradun situated in the Himalayan ranges, is bounded by Himalayan foothills to the north-east; the Shivalik Hills to the south-west; river Yamuna to the north-west and the Ganges to the south-east. The history of Dehradun dates back to the Vedic era. During this period, Garhwal Mandal of which Dehradun is a part was known as Kedarkhand. Legends say that Guru Dronacharya considered it an appropriate place for meditation and yoga. Hence, the valley was also known as Drona Ashram which means 'Abode of Drona'.

This sacred land is also associated with several Sikh Gurus. There are places of religious importance in and around Dehradun city like: Kedarnath, Badrinath, Lokpal, Hemkund Sahib, Narsingh Mandir, etc.

The present town of Dehradun was founded in the early 18th century by 'Guru Ram Rai', the elder son of seventh Sikh Guru, Guru Har Rai. He came here first and settled in village 'Dhamawala', which even today hosts the annual 'Jhanda Fair' on the fifth day after Holi in his memory. Thus, the name refers to his Dera or settlement in the valley, around which the present town gradually developed. A Gurudwara called 'Guru Ram Rai Darbar' was built in 1699 by Raja of Garhwal, Fateh Shah, marking this settlement.

Dehradun was once an independent kingdom, and a part of Nepal. Nepal lost Dehradun to England when India was colonized by England. Historically, Dehradun has remained part of the Garhwal kingdom. It's also known as 'Kedarkhand', founded by Ajai Pal, around 1400. He established the kingdom by capturing all the minor principalities of the Garhwal region, and the adjacent state of Tehri-Garhwal. Garhwal Kingdom continued till 1803, when Gurkhas invaded Kumaon and Garhwal.

❖❖❖

XIV

Today is our tenth morning. We met District Superintendent of Police, Dehradun Mr Rakesh Avasthi. He assured of all cooperation for the recruitment rally and immediately attached Inspector Dinesh Kumar, as our liaison officer. Dehradun is not a planned city and there's traffic congestion, but the facilities available at the Police Stadium are excellent. It's a huge stadium with a gallery on one side and the Police Hospital in the proximity. Dinesh Kumar, who's also the Subedar of Police Lines, promised all necessary assistance to Ajit Debbarma and his men.

Satisfied with the arrangement, we skipped lunch and left for Haridwar by 12.30. Roads are excellent, though very busy with traffic, mostly tourist vehicles. Driver Joginder said that before joining TSR, he had visited Haridwar from his hometown Gurgaon in Haryana on foot. They were in a group and it took them 15 to 16 days to complete the to and fro journey in winter. He further said that many people in north India undertook pilgrimage on foot, even at a very young age. I recollected the story of Shravan Kumar that I had read in my childhood, how he carried his blind parents from one pilgrimage centre to another.

We took lunch at a road side Punjabi dhaba. When we resumed our journey, we came across a road accident. Two youths on a motorcycle were run over by a truck. Seeing this, Kaushik commented, "There's a maxim on life these days: Life is nothing but a cigarette which starts with fire and ends with ash."

Mr Sharma reacted, "Well said, Kaushik! In respect of the Mahabharata era, this maxim can be drafted as: Life is nothing but a journey in mortal earth which starts with a curse and ends with a crime."

We got hints of a story, and so Anup Kumar requested him to elucidate. He explained, "Take the case of the Ganges which we're going to visit today. In the ancient age, there was a famous king Mahabhish of Ikshaku dynasty. After fruitfully completing sacrifice and rituals, he earned a place in heaven. Ganga, the daughter of sage Janhu was also a heavenly figure. One evening, gods were worshipping Brahma where Mahabhish was also present. Ganga also went there, and accidentally her clothes were blown away by air. All except Mahabhish bowed down their heads out of shame. But Mahabhish took a full glance at her youthful body candidly.

Brahma had also observed two of them for quite sometime and finally cursed Mahabhish, "You're not fit for heaven. You should take rebirth on earth and strive for heavenly life again."

Mahabhish wasn't unhappy with the curse, as also Ganga. Actually she had fallen in love with him at first sight. She decided to follow him to the earth. On the other hand, Mahabhish decided to be born as a son of a famous king called Pratip on earth. As she was following him, she came across eight Vasus, who were treated as gods, lying on the ground senseless and dejected. She stopped there and asked why they were so gloomy.

They had been cursed by sage Vashishtha to get birth on earth. She told them not to be worried since she was also going to the earth. The Vasus told her the story involving the Vasus and Vashishtha's cow Nandini. I've already described the theft of Nandini and her calf by the Vasus, yesterday.

Vashishtha's curse was that Probhasa, the Vasu who seized the cow, would live long in the world in all glory. But others would be freed from the curse as soon as they were born.

Sages who perform austerities acquire the power to curse, but every exercise of power reduces their store of merit.

"Thank God that sages like Vashishtha are no longer there" Kaushik declared, "otherwise it would have been difficult for common people like us to survive."

We laughed loudly. Mr Sharma carried on, "The Vasus felt relieved and approached the Goddess Ganga and begged of her: 'We pray to you to become our mother. For our sake, we request you to descend to the earth and marry a worthy man. Throw us into water as soon as we're born and liberate us from the curse.'

The Goddess granted their prayer, told them that she would descend to the earth to become wife of prince Shantanu, the son of emperor Pratip.

Here some deviation is noticed in the Mahabharata. In fact, after descending down to the earth, she fell in love with emperor Pratip. One day, Pratip was performing austerities on the bank of river Bhagirathi. On seeing him and pleased with his beauty and wisdom, she came out of water as a beautiful maiden and sat on his right thigh. The king with a surprise said: 'Charming girl! What's the purpose of your coming here? How can I please you?'

She replied: 'Great king! I love you and want to marry you. Turning down a willing girl like me will be a sin on your part.'

Pratip said: 'Darling! I'm a married man and I can't marry another girl. It'll be an act of adultery on my part.'

She replied: 'My Lord! I've come of a noble family. I'm Ganga and my father is sage Janhnu. I'm love-lorn. Don't reject me.'

King said: 'Sweet girl! I can't accept your proposal. But you've sat on my right thigh which is the place for my son and daughter-in-law. I'm assuring you that I shall get you married to my son.'

Ganga said: 'I accept your proposal with the condition that your son would never enquire about me, nor say any unkind word, or interfere in anything I do.'

Saying this, Ganga disappeared.

In due time, Mahabhish was born as a son to emperor Pratip, whom he named as Shantanu. When Shantanu became an adult, his father said: 'My son! Days back, one goddess came to me for bearing a child. If that maiden proposes to you for becoming her husband, you please agree to the proposal. Further, you always try to please her and don't interfere in anything she does.'

After crowning Shantanu as king, his father took retirement in the forest. King Shantanu was a passionate hunter. One day he was hunting on the banks of river Ganga. Suddenly he came across a beautiful maiden. His eyes stopped blinking and his feet grew roots. He gazed and gazed, drinking her celestial beauty. She returned his gaze. A bridge of love and light was formed between the two.

- Whoever you might be, a goddess or an apsara, a yakshini or naga, or human being; be my love and queen, and live with me.
- Yes, I would be willingly your wife and live with you. But, on certain conditions—that neither you nor anyone else should ever ask me who I'm, or where I come from. You mustn't stand in the way of whatever I do, good or bad, nor must you ever be angry with me on any account whatsoever. You mustn't say anything displeasing to me. If you act otherwise, I shall leave you then and there. Do you agree?

The infatuated king vowed his assent, and she became his wife and lived with him. They lived happily ever after, and the queen bore Shantanu a son every year for seven successive years. But she threw every newborn baby into the Ganges and drowned him by saying: 'It's for your good.'

Though stunned, Shantanu neither opposed, nor said a single word. He remembered his promise and dared not lose his dear wife. When the eighth son was born, and the queen carried him to the river to throw, the king couldn't help shouting: 'Stop it! Who are you to drown your own sons? How horrible!?'

She replied: 'Since you so desire, this son will survive and be your heir, but you've broken your promise. I can't be with you anymore. I'm Ganga, the daughter of Janhnu. The eight babies were the eight Vasus, fated to incarnate themselves as human beings under a curse. None but I could bear them, and then release the seven of them immediately from the human bondage. But, this last is cursed to live a long illustrious life.'

So saying, she disappeared, carrying her son Devavrata, as he was too young to be left behind with Shantanu."

We were at the outskirts of Haridwar, and the Ganges was visible with scores of people around her, all believed to be her children. Mr Sharma continued with his customary conclusion, "King Mahabhish was cursed by Brahma for an act which at best could attract the provision of section 509 IPC with the quantum of punishment for maximum of one year or with fine or with both for his gesture or act intending to insult the modesty of Ganga.

Interestingly, maiden Ganga didn't take cognizance of the stare from king Mahabhish; rather she enjoyed it. She followed him to the earth from heaven. But, the reason for her approach before emperor Pratip remains ambiguous and it displayed vulgarity on her part.

The yardstick for judgment was different in those days. In a similar situation, sage Bharadwaj enjoyed the naked youthful beauty of apsara Ghreetachi on the banks of river Ganges, which ultimately resulted in the birth of Dronacharya. But sage Bharadwaj was not punished.

Goddess Ganga had committed more serious offence under section 302 IPC by causing murder of seven new-born babies, in the name of liberation from bondage. These are gruesome murders for which she would have faced death sentence. By remaining silent on first seven instances, king Shantanu had abetted the offence, thorough act of omission. In the present day context, it would invite trial in the court for abetment of murder.

Shantanu returned to the capital with a sad heart after Ganga left him. But, he didn't allow this sadness in any way to affect his rule and administration. He ruled justly and well. People were happy and prosperous. Thus thirty-six years passed. One day, while Shantanu was chasing a deer on the banks of the Ganga, he noticed a strange phenomenon. At one place, he found the Ganges not flowing, and this puzzled him. Full of wonder and curiosity, he walked along the bank of the river, and saw a network of arrows shot and arranged into a sort of a dam. It was the handiwork of a handsome, hardy boy, his own son. But, he could hardly recognize his child.

Then there appeared Ganga and introduced Devavrata and handed over him to Shantanu saying: 'Here's your son, a brilliant scholar of Vedas, well versed in weaponry and other arts for becoming a prince.'

After blessing her child, Ganga disappeared."

But presently we were standing on her concrete cemented bank to see the sea of people waiting for evening prayers before Lord Shiva. Except constable Narayan and me, others have visited Haridwar earlier. People from all walks of life, especially the common masses from the cow-belt caught our notice. We sat down on the bathing ghat to observe the proceedings.

Mr Sharma narrated the mythological background of Haridwar, "Haridwar is the 'Gateway of Gods. It's also known as Mayapuri, Kapila and Gangadwar. The followers of Lord Shiva (Har) and followers of Lord Vishnu (Hari) pronounce this place Hardwar and Haridwar respectively. It's also a point of entry to Dev Bhoomi and Char Dham, viz., Badrinath, Kedarnath, Gangotri and Yamunotri. Archaeological findings have proved that terracotta culture existed in this region, between the periods 1700 to 1200 B.C. It is treated as one of the seven holiest places of the Hindus.

According to Hindu mythology, Haridwar is one amongst the four sites where drops of elixir of immortality, 'Amrita' accidentally spilled over from the pitcher, in which it was being carried away by the celestial bird Garuda, after the Samundra-manthan. These four spots—Ujjain, Haridwar, Nasik and

Allahabad—have today become places for Kumbha Mela celebration, once in every three years. Maha Kumbha Mela is celebrated after a period of twelve years at Prayag in Allahabad. It represents the kaleidoscope of Indian culture and civilization."

He also showed us the Brahma Kund at Har-ki-Pauri, meaning 'foot-step of Lord' where the nectar had fallen. We all took dip in the Ganges in the evening. The water was crystal clear and cool. After refreshing baths, we lit diyas (lamps) and floated them along with flowers in the waters to show solidarity with the devotees. We returned to our campus at around 9 p.m.

During the return, Kaushik cracked a joke, "Once a foreign couple visited India. They were atheists. But on returning home, the couple became believers in god."

We asked the reason. He explained, "They didn't find any semblance of governance in most parts of our country, yet the country was shining. So they became sure about the existence of some god who kept the country running despite so many inherent problems."

Mr Sharma asked Kaushik, "Do you have any more stock of jokes like this?"

He said this in a serious mode, which caused mirth amongst us. But Kaushik was clever enough and said, "Sir, your Sri Krishna in Mahabharata may be a duplicate person."

Anup Kumar instantly asked, "What?"

He replied, "Long back I read a story in a newspaper, that the Sri Krishna in Mahabharata was Vishnu alias Hari. Sri Krishna was more popular, particularly with the women folk. The Pandavas didn't know him by face. They were introduced to each other just after Draupadi's Swayamvara. Sri Krishna was the lover of Radha, and husband of sixteen hundred Yadav ladies. These ladies were the incarnations of rishis, saints and sages who wanted to see Lord Rama in Satya-Yug. Sri Krishna was proceeding towards Panchal from Dwarka to attend the Swayamvara of Draupadi. On the way, he came across Hari, basically a charioteer who had great knowledge about politics of the land. They became good friends. But unfortunately, Sri Krishna died on the way out of some ailment. Before dying, Sri Krishna told Hari to take his name and represent himself as Sri Krishna. This was how Sri Krishna became the charioteer of Arjuna during Mahabharata. After the Kurukshetra battle when Radha came across Sri Krishna, she refused to recognize him."

We liked the story, but of course with disbelief, and were impressed by the wit of Kaushik. It was half past eleven when we went to bed.

❖❖❖

XV

I received a call from Harleen at around seven in the morning on 10th May. She had taken leave for ten days and was going home tomorrow. But the interesting news which she gave me next was beyond my imagination. Mr Sharma advised her to meet Aman's parents at the earliest and to tell them about her plan. He also advised her to send the prayer under RTI only after her interaction with them. Aman's laptop should be recovered, even at the cost of any harsh treatment from them.

"So, it is going to be a tall order for you", I said. "But there may be some reasons behind his advice. After all, he's an experienced man in the field of investigation and laws."

She seemed like gathering up courage to face her future challenge. But I could not find suitable words to wish her success. Suddenly, I felt an urge to send her this SMS: "A robin red breast in a cage puts all heaven in a rage."

She acknowledged the SMS thus, "Thanks."

We came to the ground at around 9 a.m. The gathering was so huge that we had to move for about two k.m. on foot. Our men, led by Ajit Debbarma were there from seven in the morning with district police officials. In fact, they had shifted their accommodation from the ITBP campus to the stadium itself the previous evening. The gathering of more than 20,000 men from states like Uttar Pradesh, Uttarakhand and Delhi was waiting since last night. A large proportion of them were over-aged, mostly from Uttar Pradesh. They were claiming exemption for three years on the strength of OBC certificates. For the next three hours, we toiled hard to identify the over-aged candidates and to drop them at Dehradun Railway Station by buses arranged by district police administration. We completed distribution of tokens to the last of the 6,297 candidates by 8.15 p.m. Local police made excellent arrangements for illumination in the ground, which helped us in achieving our task. We returned to Tiger Mess sometime around nine in the night. I went for dinner after a quick shower.

After dinner we sat down in chairs outside, by the side of the lake. Anup Kumar reminded Mr Sharma about his unfinished story of the previous night about goddess Ganga.

He said, "I think, I've already described the role of goddess Ganga in the epic, yesterday. But it may be a coincidence that the company of celestial maidens made the male characters of Mahabharata crime-prone."

Kaushik guessed, "Sir, it suggests a long story."

"Yes, at times it is unending", he replied. "Besides, there's so much sex and vulgarity that you may not like these stories."

Anup Kumar reacted sharply, "If that is so, why do people like this epic so much?"

So, he explained, "Mahabharata is basically a flash-back story. You'll notice imitation of this in our modern day Bollywood films."

"You mean to say there's always an element of entertainment like movies", I suggested.

"Exactly! Doctor", he said, "you've used the correct expression."

"Sir, precisely for this reason", Anup Kumar made a point, "we like to listen to these stories from you. This gives our senses some delight. If you are not exhausted, you please continue."

"It's not the case; I can continue tomorrow and day after as well", he smiled, and started his story, probably after some readjustment. "Four years after Ganga had handed over his son Devavrata to his father; one day while roaming in the woods along the river Yamuna, Shantanu was assailed by a delicate and strange fragrance. Overwhelmed with the sweetness, he followed the fragrance.

It led him to a black-eyed beautiful girl, engaged in tying her boat. He'd kept his senses controlled ever since Ganga left her. But, the sight of this divinely beautiful maiden burst the bonds of restraint. He asked her to be his wife.

The maiden said: 'I'm a fisher-woman, the daughter of the chief of the fishermen. Will you please ask him and get his consent?'

Her voice was as sweet as her form. The father was an astute man. He said: 'She'll marry, as there can't be a better match than you. But there's a condition that she'll be made the chief queen and her son, and none else will be the heir to the throne after you'."

Shantanu was dumb-struck, thinking of his brave and god-like son Devavrata, whom he loved so much and had already declared as his Yuvaraj. He drove back to Hastinapura, sad and pensive. The love-lorn king languished in silence, but the matter remained buried in his breast. Seeing his father so distraught, prince Devavrata asked his father what was the cause of his anxiety?

But he could neither ascertain anything definite nor could he bear to see his father suffer in silence. The intelligent and imaginative Devavrata did not rest till he discovered the cause of his father's suffering. Finally he came to know it from the charioteer.

Devavrata, attended by courtiers and noblemen, went straight to the fisherman and vowed that the son of his daughter shall be the next king. But the shrewd fisherman pressed hard his condition and said: 'You are a virtuous prince and I'm sure you'll keep your vow. But how can I be sure that your sons too will keep your vow?

Then Devavrata with a scornful glance said: 'Listen! I give you my word in the presence of these courtiers and chiefs—never to marry. With me, my line would end, and I shall have neither sons nor grandsons. Now, are you satisfied?'

Immediately Gods rained flowers from above on Devavrata and exclaimed, Bhishma! Bhishma! The terrible vow resounded from all directions. He became known as Bhishma.'

Greatly pleased, the chief of the fishermen brought his daughter Satyavati and handed her over to Bhishma. He bowed before her, placed her in his chariot and hastened to his father. It mightily pleased Shantanu, and he out of gratitude towards his son granted him a boon—"Bhishma, so long as you wish to live, death won't harm you. You'll die only when it pleases you."

Shantanu and Satyavati were happily married. Two sons were born to them, Chitrangada and Vichitravirya. Young Chitrangada was crowned after his father's death. Then there ensued a fierce battle between Chitrangada and a Gandharba king. It continued for three years on the banks of river Saraswati, resulting in the death of Chitrangada. Now, the younger son Vichitravirya was crowned, and Bhishma acted as regent for Vichitravirya.

Here, Mr Sharma took a pause. Kaushik pointed out, "The censor board won't find any objectionable material in this!"

This led to a great deal of laughter and we decided to call it a day.

❖❖❖

XVI

I enjoyed sound sleep last night. Just after my bath in the morning, as I was leaving for breakfast, Harleen rang me up. She was calling up from Ludhiana, and was going to Ambala accompanied by her sister-in-law Khushpreet Kaur. I wished her all the very best. I also conveyed the information to Mr Sharma, but he did not react.

We arrived at the ground at around 8 a.m. Soon, we became busy with our task. One Dr P.N. Shukla from District Police Hospital assisted me and our staff. Things are more systematic, compared to Jalandhar. The conducive atmosphere made our task easy. We closed our medical counter at 6 p.m. After Dr Shukla left, I went to Kaushik who was taking chin-up tests.

Chin-up is the toughest test in this recruitment process. I have mentioned this earlier as well. Here, four candidates attend the test at a time. The timings, by making counts, are given by our ustads in their typical regional accent, which some times creates laughter. Often, this hilarity tickles to other candidates who are performing exercises on the beam. It is quite certain that some of them would be unsuccessful. Of course, candidates are given three chances, but initial failure affects their confidence. Sometimes, these ustads carry out mimicry of the performance of an unsuccessful candidate. Another noticeable point is the success of shorter candidates over the taller candidates. The reason may be the difference in gravitational force, which is more for bodies closer to the earth. The experience is more interesting in outdoor activities than it is for our medical tests.

While I was sitting with Kaushik, I suddenly received a call from Harleen. It was around 7 p.m. I went to a solitary corner to take her call. She was beaming with joy to narrate her experience of the day. She, along with her sister-in-law, had gone to Aman's house this afternoon. Contrary to their expectations, they were well accepted by Aman's parents. Especially his father, Baldev Sandhu was very cordial. Their old anger against her seemed to be forgotten. When Harleen disclosed the purpose of their visit and the new light given by Mr Sharma in respect of the death of their son, they were excited.

Uncle Baldev kept on repeating, "Puttar, why didn't this point of double-shots from the pistol come to my mind? I've handled fire arms for so many years!"

He was extremely repentant and unequivocally expressed that he was swayed by the words of Brigadier S.H. Yadav, Sector Commander, Bharatpur. According to him, when he visited Bharatpur on 3rd May 2006 to bring back Aman's body, Mr Yadav told him about his son's addiction towards women and wine.

He vehemently objected to Mr Yadav's claims by saying that his son could never go so astray, particularly because he had not been brought up in such a fashion, and his marriage was settled with a beautiful lady doctor. At that moment Captain Nilesh Rahane, a colleague of his son, showed a photograph which depicted Aman dancing with a lady in a rather intimate pose. Probably it was taken in a party. Baldevji was in a fix. Seeing his hesitation, Mr Yadav asked why Aman was still unmarried.

Uncle said: 'Sir I tried my level best during Baishakhi. But his fiancé didn't agree for the nuptial so hurriedly. She wanted to complete her MBBS.'

Captain Rahane said: 'That may be the reason why Aman became so frustrated after returning from home. He became addicted to liquor and other vices.'

Captain Rahane also gave uncle Baldev photographs of a few unknown girls. These were recovered from Aman's room.

Finally, the reason behind Harleen's harassment by Aman's parents was put in perspective. Now, uncle Baldev is sure that his son Aman was murdered. Certainly there's a deep-rooted conspiracy. He's eager to speak with Mr Sharma and meet him. Harleen and her sister-in-law are staying in Aman's house only. More importantly, Aman's laptop computer has been found. But it's not in an operative condition.

I gave her Mr Sharma's cell number and requested her to call at around 9 p.m. By that time, he'd be free.

I started singing to myself as I rushed towards Mr Sharma, "When the heart is hard and parched up, come upon me with a shower of mercy...."

Kaushik asked behind me, "Is anything serious, Doctor?"

"I shall bear the expenses of our dinner tonight", I replied, without paying any heed to the next question put by him.

Mr Sharma was taking physical measurement of the candidates. Still about 40 candidates were in the queue. As I approached him, he asked, "Is there any good news, Doctor?"

Seeing my glowing face, he stood up and took me to a distance. Then, without waiting for my answer, he said, "I knew it would happen like this. That's why I insisted that Harleen should visit Aman's house."

I narrated the happenings and requested, "I want to sponsor our dinner tonight."

- Bravo, Doctor! Please go ahead.
- Sir, will you mind if I keep drinks as well?
- Not at all, but I'm a teetotaller, please keep some soft drinks as well.

I returned to the mess by 8.30 p.m. and arranged the dinner. Mr Sharma, Anup Kumar and Kaushik came within another 20 minutes. By that time, my two other comrades also came to know about the reasons for the party tonight. They greeted me for helping Harleen out of her troubled situation. I said that the kudos should go to Mr Sharma. He was the person to point out the homicide angle in this case.

Kaushik said, "You're ignoring your own role, brother. You acted like a catalyst to ensure that she breaks her shackles and you shared her anguish."

Mr Sharma reacted by saying, "Commencement of journey is far more important than the proposition if we can complete it. At least we've made a beginning in this case; now we should make sincere efforts to help her out."

We assembled for dinner at Tiger Mess around 9.45 p.m. The bar is well-maintained. The collection is very rich. Almost all varieties are available. Kaushik took Scotch whisky. Anup Kumar and I took a glass of beer each. Mr Sharma took lemon-juice. He had a long discussion over telephone with uncle Baldev. As he finished, we all wanted to know the details.

He apprised us, "Baldevji has thanked me for the eye-opening. They've accepted Harleen as their daughter. He says that they've lost their son, but now they don't want to lose their daughter.

Today is a Sunday; Baldevji will send the prayer under RTI by Tuesday. He along with Harleen will visit Bharatpur on 14th May, Wednesday, for collection of the certified documents from the court. They'll also collect copy of records related to court of inquiry carried out by Black Panther Rifles Headquarters. Aman's laptop will be kept in safe custody, till they reach Bhubaneshwar on 29th May 2008. Baldevji and Harleen will meet us with the laptop at Bhubaneshwar. They would also bring whatever documents they can collect in the mean time. He also confirmed that the weapon used by Aman was a Browning pistol and two bullets were fired. Harleen is extending her leave while her sister-in-law is returning home tomorrow."

As he was telling us about Harleen's proposed visit to Bhubaneshwar, Kaushik cast a glance towards me with a smile. Here, Mr Sharma put a full stop on the Amandeep issue.

Instead, he resumed his story from the epic Mahabharata from where he had left yesterday night, "Today I shall narrate the story about the birth of Satyavati. Uparichar Basu was the king of Chedi and Girika was his wife. Once they planned to have sex to produce an heir for their kingdom. But the king couldn't spend time with his wife. He had to leave the palace and go to a far away spot in his kingdom to quell a rebellion. After accomplishing the task, he fell in love with the scenic beauty of the place. So he decided to take rest there for some days. But with spring setting in, all animals were into the act of reproduction. He also got restless, remembering his voluptuous wife.

He masturbated and caught his semen in a leaf. Planning not to waste it, he tied it to his pigeon. He sent the same to his wife, so that she could conceive an heir. So, off flew the pigeon with the semen. However, the pigeon was caught by an eagle and the leaf fell into the river Ganges. There it was eaten by a fish.

This fish was actually an Apsara Adrika, who had been cursed to live as a fish. As the semen went inside her, it gave birth to two fetuses—a girl and a boy. The fish was caught by a fisherman named Dashraj. When he cut the fish, he saw the two babies. He took both to the king Uparichar. The king kept the boy and gave the daughter back to Dashraj."

"Here also the Censor Board won't find anything objectionable", Anup Kumar commented.

"Objection, if any is overruled", Kaushik ordered. I also supported him joyfully.

So, Mr Sharma began, "The boy grew up to be the king of Matsya. The daughter grew up to be Satyavati, wife of king Shantanu. It is a beautiful story but certain facts are not logical. Apsaras are celestial maidens, basically keeps of gods. They're used for diplomatic purposes. Probably Apsara Adrika was aged and was spending her last days in the colony of fishermen on the banks of river Yamuna. It is also quite possible that queen Girika was barren. To cover the fact that the king had to visit other women to produce heirs, this peculiar story was concocted.

Alternatively, it is also possible that Adrika was used as a surrogate mother. In the case of Dronacharya's birth, we've witnessed a technique similar to test-tube babies of modern era.

The marriage of Shantanu and Satyavati is a case of bigamy and it would attract penal section 494 IPC. It prescribes punishment up to seven years and fine. Devavrata alias Bhishma would be charged as an abettor. The association of Satyavati perhaps compelled Bhishma to commit series of offences by the present day yardstick. However, it'll be a weak case, as Shantanu was practically a divorcee."

"Sir, don't worry about the Censor Board", Kaushik said, a bit rejuvenated, "since we're referring the matter to criminal courts, we shall tell the truth, and only the truth."

Enjoying the joke, Mr Sharma resumed, "Years rolled by. The prince Vichitravirya came of age and Bhishma thought of organizing his marriage. He came to know that the three beautiful daughters of the king of Kashi were going to choose their husbands in a Svayamvara. He took it as an insult because it had been a custom to marry daughters of Kashi to the princes of Kuru dynasty. He considered the three princesses—Amba, Ambika and Ambalika good enough for becoming Vichitravirya's queens. He stormed the place where the Svayamvara was being held and carried away the three maidens in the presence of various kings and princes, who had assembled as prospective bridegrooms.

Bhishma took the three brides in his chariot, and sped away towards Hastinapura, despite resistance, particularly from the mighty king Shalva. A terrible fight ensued between Bhishma and Shalva. But the latter was roundly defeated. Somehow, he managed to escape unharmed. The triumphant Bhishma entered the gates of Hastinapura and offered the three princesses to Vichitravirya as brides.

Just before the wedding ceremony, the eldest princess Amba told Bhishma that she had already chosen Shalva as her husband. In the Svayamvara, she would have garlanded him. Compassionate Bhishma immediately sent her to Shalva. But Shalva, defeated and disgraced by Bhishma, turned her away saying: 'Go back to Bhishma with whom you had gone'.

Meanwhile, the other two princesses, Ambika and Ambalika were married to Vichitravirya.

Here, Bhishma had committed a serious offence by the present day yardstick. He had committed an offence under section 366/494 IPC for kidnapping these three girls and compelling them to marry against their will and forcing Ambika and Ambalika to lead lives of bigamy. The first section prescribes punishment up to ten years' imprisonment and fine. The second section prescribes punishment up to seven years and also fine. Vichitravirya being a willing partner for these offences, would also face charges for abetting these offences."

"Everything is on record", it was Kaushik again, "so we can't save Bhishma and Vichitravirya, they've to face trial."

Mr Sharma with a smile proceeded with the story, "Amba returned to Hastinapura from Kashi and told Bhishma about what had happened. Bhishma tried hard to make Vichitravirya marry her too. But he categorically refused on the ground that Amba had already given her heart to Shalva.

Amba requested Bhishma to marry her himself. But how could Bhishma, the terrible-vow maker, do so? Bhishma again advised her to go to Shalva and to try her luck there. Proud Amba refused the advice initially, but finally when she went to Shalva in sheer desperation, she again received a blunt refusal.

This killed all her sweetness of nature and awakened in her heart a strong hatred and a desire for revenge against Bhishma. She went to the forest and narrated her plight to the ascetics. She met Parasuram, the great guru of Bhishma. He was aggrieved by her tragedy and promised to ask Bhishma to marry her. He called Bhishma and asked him to marry her. Bhishma told him about the terrible vow of remaining single for ever, and expressed his helplessness.

The disobedience of Bhishma made Parasuram very angry and a terrible battle raged between the two for days and nights. The battle was so intense that doomsday seemed to be approaching. Therefore, the gods intervened and stopped the fight. The Guru being mightily pleased with Bhishma's valour and the terrible vow, embraced him, but felt sorry for Amba.

Amba engaged herself in terrible penance. Sanmukha, the son of Lord Shiva, was pleased with her and appeared with a garland. He gave her that garland and said: 'Whosoever wears this garland will kill Bhishma.'

Amba, gratified with her penance and the garland, went from place to place in search of a warrior who could accept that garland and wreak vengeance on Bhishma on her behalf, but without any success. None dared to champion her cause. Finally, she went to king Drupada and told him her tragic tale. Drupada too refused to fight against the mighty Bhishma. Desperate Amba threw the garland round a pillar in Drupada's vast hall and departed.

Amba once again started the seven penances and continued with them for a long time. Lord Shiva appeared before her and said: 'Don't grieve and worry my child! In your next birth, you'll kill Bhishma and thus, you'll have your revenge.'

Amba lit a huge pyre and jumped into it to commit suicide. She was incarnated as daughter of Drupada. One day, she saw the garland hanging round a pillar in the great hall of her father. She took it down and wore it round her neck. It alarmed her father to see this but she placated him. Later on, she changed her sex to become a eunuch and was called Shikhandi.

The self-immolation of Amba would be treated as an offence—suicide due to abetment under section 306 IPC. The section prescribes a maximum punishment up to ten years and shall also be liable to fine. Bhishma would be the sole offender in this case."

"Bhishma had in fact accepted the punishment", said Kaushik, "as we all know Arjun and Sri Krishna duo used Shikhandi as a shield for killing Bhishma in the Kurukshetra battle. Bhishma refused to use arms against Shikhandi for he considered it beyond his dignity to fight a eunuch."

"Well said, Kaushik", Mr Sharma voiced his appreciation. "The lustful Vichitravirya enjoyed the erotic delights with his two young wives to his heart's content. But before long, he was afflicted with consumption and died.

Satyavati and Bhishma were stunned by this calamity. The fact that Vichitravirya died childless hurt them both all the more. The desperate Satyavati then turned towards Bhishma in the hope that he would continue the line of the Kurus. She requested Bhishma to marry one of the widowed queens in order to provide a son to the dynasty. But, Bhishma refused to do so, and reminded Satyavati of the terrible vow he had taken for her sake. Satyavati tried her best to persuade Bhishma. But he remained unmoved like a rock.

At that juncture, Satyavati remembered her island-born son Vyasa. This had happened before her marriage with Shantanu. She was in her teens, young and attractive. Her father found her a job on the banks of Yamuna river as boatwoman. She used to smell of fish. People tried to avoid her because of the smell emanating from her body. She was even called Matsyagandha, one who smells of fish.

She was still a virgin, when Parashar happened to meet her. Parashar was a great rishi who one day wanted to cross the river Yamuna. He asked Satyavati to take him across. It was around noon. The two of them were alone in the middle of the river. It aroused Parashar a great deal. He expressed his desire to have sex with her.

- I'm a virgin, and you're not going to marry me, are you? Moreover, I have such a filthy odour emanating from me, aren't you disgusted by that like all the other people?
- Oh beautiful lady, I can't marry you because I'm a rishi. If you give yourself to me, I shall, through my yoga and siddhi, restore your hymen. Moreover, I will give you such a sweet fragrance that it will attract people towards you from a yojana away.
- Thanks for the offer, but what'll you do if I get pregnant? What'll happen to the child?
- A son will be born from this union, and he'll be an adult as soon as he's born. He will be one of the most renowned rishis ever and history will remember him as Ved Vyasa or Krishna Dwaipanya, the dark island-born.
- However, it is still day time, what if someone sees us?

Parashar suddenly created darkness and told her: 'Take the boat to that island in the middle of the river.'

She complied with the instruction and took the boat to an island amidst foggy weather. In the delta of river Yamuna, Parashar played with the virginity of Satyavati for almost four hours. She felt pleasure but became senseless. When she regained her senses, she felt pain. She fell asleep and when she opened her eyes again, she found two men, not one, looking at her, lying naked. She tried to cover herself up, but the other man, who was one of the ugliest men she had ever seen, bowed to her, touched her feet and said: 'I'm your son, mother! Bless me. Father has told me to go and study the Vedas. But if you need me mother, just remember me and I'll come.'

Parashar left the place with Vyasa, leaving Satyavati alone. Finally, she went back to her father's home, her hymen restored and with no signs of her having had sex."

"It may be the ugliest part of the epic Mahabharata", I said, "son is witnessing mother naked, yet he doesn't think it necessary to give her a cloth, instead, he along with his father walked away."

"Certainly, this portion is objectionable", said Kaushik, "I think no Censor Board will allow this."

Anup Kumar also expressed solidarity with Kaushik and me. But Mr Sharma explained logically, "Satyavati told her father about the receipt of a new fragrance from the rishi. But, she left out all other details. She became Yojnagandha, one whose smell spreads for a yojana. Her smell and her beauty made many people ask for her hand in marriage. But her father refused them all. He knew his daughter was made for a better match. It soon came in the form of Shantanu.

It was blatant rape. Perhaps such violent sexual assault was hitherto unknown in the entire Mahabharata. In the modern era, sage Parashar would have suffered life imprisonment under section 376 of IPC.

Birth of an adult baby just after sexual intercourse is quite unreasonable. Even with the latest advancements in science, we cannot make out this. Thus, it needs to be explained in the present day context. From the circumstances, it is apparent that sage Parashar was a great magician. First he hypnotized Satyavati to create a misty atmosphere. Next, he offered her with some perfume to remove the fishy smell from her body and bring lotus fragrance. Probably she was suffering from some inferiority complex, out of her reported birth from inside the stomach of a fish. It was a psychological problem and the sage cured her easily. She was senseless for about four hours. Perhaps, sage Parashar called his son Vyasa to the river island of Yamuna when Satyavati was lying senseless, in pain and in trauma. Vyasa was certainly born long ago, considering his adulthood.

Parashar asked his son Vyasa to make Satyavati believe that he was born on that very day. Illiterate lady believed the story told by Vyasa, whose intellect knew no bounds, as was his physical ugliness. It is also possible that Parashar administered some oral contraceptives to Satyavati. As regards restoration of hymen, it would require proper medical examination to accept the claim.

Probably the same procedure of hypnotic magic and tricks was adopted for giving birth to two fully grown children of king Drupada, namely Dhrishtadyumna and Draupadi from sacrificial fire."

We decided to call it a day as it was half past eleven.

XVII

Today is 12th May 2008, Monday and we're hopeful about completing the rally at this venue by tomorrow. I've spoken twice during the day with Harleen to learn that they've sent almost all the petitions under RTI. She's overwhelmed with the affection shown by her uncle and aunt. Even they gifted her with new clothes.

Today we returned from the field early and were able to start our pre-dinner chatting by 9 p.m. Mr Sharma took feedback from me about the developments in Ambala. He asked me to tell Harleen to check the belongings of Aman meticulously.

As usual, Anup Kumar made the opening query, "Sir, is there any incident similar to the fate of Harleen in Mahabharata?"

Kaushik and I laughed loudly, "How could there have been a pistol in Mahabharata era?"

But Mr Sharma said, "At least one beautiful lady in Mahabharata had failed to marry her beloved. Her lover was murdered, though he was revived later on. Vyasa has narrated the beauty of many ladies in the epic. In the absence of photographs, we can only imagine their beauty. Intellect and personality of a girl also help a long way in enhancing her beauty."

Kaushik concurred, "These parameters are judged during beauty pageants these days."

Mr Sharma thanked Kaushik for the comparison, "This girl Devayani, whose story I shall narrate now was one of the most beautiful ladies, in my judgment. In ancient times, there was a bitter struggle between devas and asuras for the lordship of the three worlds. Both the groups had illustrious preceptors. Brihashpati was the guiding spirit of devas. The asuras relied on Sukracharya's profound wisdom. The asuras had the formidable advantage that Sukracharya alone possessed the secret of Sanjivani which could recall the dead to life. Thus, all those asuras who had fallen in the battle were brought back to life, time and again. They continued their fight with devas. Devas were thus at a great disadvantage in their war with their natural foes.

They went to Kacha, the son Brihashpati, and persuaded him to win the graces of Sukracharya and become his pupil. Once he acquired his confidence, Kacha was to acquire, by fair means or foul, the secret of Sanjivani. This would remove the great handicap of the devas. Kacha acceded to their request and set out to meet Sukracharya. He lived in the capital city of Vrishaparva, the king of the asuras. Kacha went to the house of Sukra, and after due salutation, said: "I'm Kacha, the grandson of the sage Angiras and son of Brihashpati. I'm a brahmachari seeking knowledge under your guidance."

It was the law that the wise teacher shouldn't refuse a worthy pupil who sought knowledge from him. So Sukra acceded and said, "Kacha, you belong to a good family. I accept you as my student gladly. By doing so, I shall also be showing my respect for Brihashpati."

Kacha spent many years under Sukracharya, rendering to perfection the prescribed duties in the household of his master. Sukracharya had a lovely daughter, Devayani, of whom he was extremely fond. Kacha devoted himself to pleasing and serving her with songs, dances and amusement to win her love, without compromising the vows of brahmcharya.

When asuras came to know of this, they suspected that Kacha's object was somehow to wheedle out of Sukracharya the secret of Sanjivani. They naturally sought to prevent such a calamity.

One day, Kacha was engaged in grazing the cattle of his master. The asuras caught him, tore him to pieces and cast his flesh to dogs. When the cattle returned without Kacha, Devayani was filled with anxiety, and ran to her father with loud lamentation: "The sun has set", she wailed, "still Kacha hasn't returned home. The cattle have come back by themselves. I fear some mishap has befallen Kacha. I can't live without him."

The fond father employed the art of Sanjivani and revived the dead youth. At once, Kacha came back to life and greeted his master with smiles. He told Devayani that as he was grazing the cattle, suddenly the asuras came there and slew him. How he came back to life he didn't know.

On another occasion, Kacha went to the forest to pluck flowers for Devayani, and again the asuras seized him and killed him, and pounding his body to a paste mixed it up in sea-water. As he didn't return that evening, Devyani went as before to her father. Sukracharya brought Kacha back to life by his Sanjivani and heard from him all that had taken place.

For the third time, the asuras killed Kacha and very cleverly, burnt his body, mixed the ashes in wine and served it to Sukracharya who drunk it without hesitation. Once more the cows returned home without their keeper, and once again Devayani appealed for Kacha.

Sukracharya tried in vain to console his daughter.

"Though I've again and again brought Kacha back to life", said he, "the asuras seem bent upon killing him. Well, death is the common denominator and it is not proper for a wise soul like you to grieve over it. Your life is all before you to enjoy, with youth and beauty and the goodwill of the world."

Devayani deeply loved Kacha; and since the world began, wise sayings have never cured the ache of bereavement. Devayani began to fast, telling her father, "Kacha was a blameless boy, devoted and tireless in our service. I loved him dearly, and now that he has been killed, life to me has become bleak and meaningless. I shall therefore follow in his path."

Sukracharya became very angry with asuras, and felt that the heinous sin of killing a Brahmin would weigh adversely on their fortunes. He employed the Sanjivani art and called upon Kacha to appear. By the power of Sanjivani, Kacha, dispersed as he was in the wine which was inside Sukracharya's body, regained life. But prevented by the peculiarity of his location from coming out, he could only answer to his name from where he was. Sukracharya exclaimed in angry amazement: "O Brahmachari, how did you get into me? Is this also the work of the asuras? Tell me the whole story."

Kacha narrated it all, in spite of the difficulty imposed by his position.

The noble-souled Sukracharya became angry at the deceit perpetrated on him through the wine, and proclaimed for the benefit of humanity: "Virtue will desert the man who through lack of wisdom, drinks wine. He'll be an object of scorn for all. This is my message to humanity, which should be regarded as an imperative scriptural injunction."

He then tuned to Devayani and said: "Dear daughter, here's a problem for you. For Kacha to live, he must rend my stomach and come out of it, and that means death to me. His life can only be brought by my death."

Devayani began to weep and said: "Alas! It is death to me either way—for if either of you perish, I shall not survive."

Sukracharya sought a way out of the difficulty. He said to Kacha: "O son of Brihashpati, I now see with what object you've come to me! I must bring you out to life for the sake of Devayani, but equally for her sake I mustn't die either. The only way is to initiate you in the art of Sanjivani so that you can bring me back to life after I have died when a way is torn out through my entails for you. You should employ the knowledge I'm going to impart to you and revive me, so that Devayani need not grieve for either of us."

Accordingly, Sukracharya imparted the art of Sanjivani to Kacha. Immediately, Kacha came forth from Sukracharya's body, emerging like the full moon from a cloud, while great preceptor fell down mangled and dead.

But Kacha at once brought Sukracharya back to life by means of his newly acquired knowledge of Sanjivani. Kacha bowed down to Sukracharya and said: "The teacher who imparts wisdom to the ignorant is a father. As I've come out of your body, you're my mother too."

Kacha remained for many more years under the tutelage of Sukracharya. When the period of his vow ended, he took leave of his master to return to the world of gods. As he was about to depart, Devayani said: "You've won my heart by your blameless life, your great attainment and nobility of birth. I've loved you long and tenderly, even though you were faithfully following your vows of brahmacharya. You should now reciprocate my love and make me happy by marrying me."

In those days, it wasn't an uncommon thing for wise and learned Brahmin ladies to speak out their mind with honourable frankness.

But Kacha said, "Darling, you're my master's daughter and worthy of my respect. I got back my life by being born out of your father's body. Hence, I'm your brother. It is not proper for you my sister, to ask me to wed you."

Devayani sought in vain to persuade him.

"You're the son of Brihashpati", she said, "and not of my father. If I've been the cause of your coming back to life, it was because I loved you and wanted you as my husband. It is not fit that you should refuse me who is sinless and devoted to you."

Kacha replied: "Don't seek to persuade me. You are enchanting, more so now than ever before. But, I'm your brother. Pray and bid me adieu."

With these words, Kacha gently disengaged himself and prepared to proceed to the abode of Indra, the king of gods.

The broken-hearted Devayani cried out in grief. She accused Kacha of using her to attain his goal. She cursed Kacha: "You'll never be able to use the craft of Sanjivani."

Kacha quietly listened and then spoke: "Devayani, it is wrong to curse me. I could have walked away without reviving your father. There's no doubt that my love was sincere. But, I also have a duty to perform towards my own people. Because of your unfairness to me, I'm cursing you. No rishi's son will ever marry you. I may still teach the craft of Mrita-Sanjivani to others, even though I may not be able to use it myself."

Saying this, "Kacha left for the abode of Indra, the king of Devas. Sukracharya gently led Devayani away. With passage of time, Devayani completely forgot Kacha. She once again became playful and lived happily with her father and her playmates in the city of Vrishaparva. Of her playmates, the most important was princess Sharmistha, the daughter of king Vrishaparva. Devayani ultimately married king Yayati, a Kshatriya, but of course after a series of fights with Sharmistha; this I may narrate on some other occasion."

We were mesmerised by the story of the beautiful lady, and sought critical analysis of this story from Mr Sharma.

He explained, "It's sad that Sukracharya hadn't taught the secret of Mrita-Sanjivani to asuras. In that case, he could have survived in this mortal world. Recent development of science ensures birth of animals even from somatic cell. I firmly believe that generation of human clones is possible. Sukracharya might have created clones of Kacha every time he was murdered.

As far as criminal interpretation is concerned, there would be three separate cases of murder and elopement of evidence under section 302/201/34 IPC against asuras who committed the offences. In connection with the investigation in all these cases, DNA finger printing on the remains of Kacha would be required for identification of the corpse. The asuras are likely to suffer death sentences for their participation in these heinous crimes."

Kaushik was silent for a long time, and so Mr Sharma asked him the reason for his silence. In his humorous way, Kaushik replied, "I'm thinking about sage Jamadagni, which category does he belong to; 'deva' or 'asura'?"

He was obviously referring to the story of Parasuram slaying his mother at the instance his father Jamadagni, and how she was brought alive by Jamadagni. Renuka couldn't even recognize her killer after she regained her life.

Mr Sharma replied, "This is a very tough question Kaushik. I think we should go for our dinner leaving it for the future generation to answer. But we shall honour the injunction imposed by Sukracharya on liquor."

XVIII

I spent the penultimate day of our stay at Dehradun in a holiday mood. My three companions remained busy in the ground. I took lunch in the house of my elder brother, Bhaskar Bhattacharjee. He's from Agartala and is serving as senior scientist in Forest Research Institute, Dehradun. His wife, Basabi and school-going son live with him. Bomkesh is a student of class-IX. Forest Research Institute is a huge campus spreading over more than 400 acres. It has almost all the plant varieties of the Himalayan region and a rich collection of flora and fauna. These species are known to me as I've read about them in Jim Corbett's books. I returned to the campus by four in the afternoon.

At about 5 p.m., Harleen rang me up in an excited mood. She had recovered a small note-book and photographs from the belongings of Aman. More importantly, the note-book contained some clues which might help us in proving the homicide. She said that the lady, with whom Aman was seen dancing in some snaps, was close to Captain Nilesh Rahane as well. In one photograph, the same lady was noticed in a compromising position with Captain Rahane. I advised her to keep these documents in safe custody.

My three pals returned sharp at eight in the evening. A few candidates were still left for viva-voce. I apprised Mr Sharma about the recovery of Aman's note-book and other incriminating documents. He expressed satisfaction over the progress.

During our pre-dinner gossip at around nine, Anup Kumar asked Mr Sharma, "Sir, what is the basis for you suspecting this case of Captain Amandeep to be homicide from the very beginning?"

Taking his time, he replied, "I've investigated many cases of fratricides. It is quite common in security forces, particularly in those areas where they fight insurgency. Rarely do the force personnel get leave. They remain away from home for months together. It causes family disputes. The boys leave their newly-married wives in their ancestral houses under the care of their parents or relatives. Due to invasion of western culture through cinema, television and electronic media, our society has become more open. As a result, many of these young married girls get involved in adulterous relationships, generally with male members of the family or with friends. Invasion of mobile phones also creates problem, many a times.

At the workplace as well, out of biological need, the boys get involved in extramarital affairs. Some times, they even visit brothels. This affects their economic affluence. They become psychological patients and irregular in their duties and a headache for their superiors. All these complications may at times lead to them committing the murder of their seniors or colleagues before committing suicide.

In Aman's case, he wasn't a married person. He was a commissioned officer. Aman could have easily enjoyed his married life after his fiancé secured her MBBS degree. Harleen never betrayed him, even during his tough days in Kashmir. His heydays were just round the corner. He was slated to join his headquarters at Jamsedpur, Jharkhand just after 'Operation Bikram'.

Bharatpur was not his field posting. He was practically passing his days without any assignment in view of the court of inquiry, following the two fire incidents in Black Panther Rifles' ammunition depots. It's unlikely that he was keeping a pistol with him. Even in the field, officers draw weapons from the kote only at the time of departure for some specific mission. So, I suspected it to be a case of homicide from the very beginning."

The theory of homicidal death of Aman became more and more convincing. He then switched over to his pet subject, the epic Mahabharata. Today, he narrated the story of sage Mandavya, "Vidura was the reincarnation of Lord Dharma. Mandavya was a great sage. He acquired strength of mind and knowledge of the scriptures. He lived in a hermitage in the forest on the outskirts of a city. One day, he was immersed in silent contemplation under the shade of a tree outside his hut. A band of robbers fled through the woods with officers of the king in hot pursuit. The fugitives entered the ashram thinking that it would be a convenient place to hide. They placed their booty in a corner and hid themselves. The soldiers came to the ashram tracing their footsteps.

The commander of the soldiers asked Mandavya: 'Did you see the robbers pass by? Where did they go?'

The sage, who was absorbed in yoga, remained silent. The commander repeated the question insolently. But the sage didn't hear anything. In the meantime, some of the attendants entered the ashram and discovered the stolen goods lying there. They reported this to their commander. All of them went in and found the stolen goods and the robbers who were hiding.

The commander thought: 'Now I know the reason why the Brahmin pretended to be a silent sage. He is indeed the chief of these robbers. He has inspired these robbers.'

He ordered the soldiers to guard the place, went to the king and told him that the sage Mandavya had been caught with stolen goods."

"Today's police also at times behaves like this", said Kaushik, "I think there's no fundamental change in the perspective of police at a certain level."

"You're right Kaushik", said Mr Sharma, "and this brings allegations of human rights violations upon police. The king was very angry at the audacity of the chief of the robbers in the guise of a Brahmin sage. Without trying to verify the facts, he ordered the wicked criminal to be impaled.

The commander returned to the hermitage, impaled Mandavya on a spear and handed over the stolen things to the king."

Mr Sharma looked towards Kaushik with a question mark on his face.

Kaushik said, "Here, the king is acting like a magistrate. So, he cannot be accused of violation of human rights, though the judgement was against the principles of natural justice. But as you've already narrated, the head of the police may face the charges for violation of human rights."

Mr Sharma expressed great satisfaction with the reply, and went ahead, "The virtuous sage, though impaled on the spear, didn't die. Since he was in yoga when he was impaled, he remained alive by the power of yoga. Sages who lived in other parts of the forest came to his hermitage and asked Mandavya how he came to be in that terrible situation.

Mandavya replied: 'Whom shall I blame?'

The king was surprised when he heard that the impaled sage was still alive and that he was surrounded by other sages from the forest. He hastened to the forest with his attendants and at once ordered the sage to be taken down from the spear. Then he prostrated at his feet and prayed humbly to be forgiven for the offence unwillingly committed.

Mandavya wasn't angry with the king. He went straight to Dharma, the divine dispenser of justice, and asked him: 'What crime have I committed to deserve this torture?'

Lord Dharma, who knew the great power of the sage, replied in all humility: 'O sage, you've tortured birds and bees. Are you not aware that all deeds, good or bad, however small, inevitably produce their results, good or evil?'

Mandavya was surprised and asked: 'When did I commit this offence?'

Lord Dharma replied: 'When you were a child.'

Mandavya then pronounced a curse on Dharma: 'This punishment you've decreed is far in excess for a mistake committed by a child in ignorance. Be born therefore as a mortal on earth.'

Lord Dharma, who was thus cursed by sage Mandavya, incarnated as Vidura. He was born to the servant maid of Ambalika, the wife of Vichitravirya."

We were delighted to listen to the story today, unlike the previous evening.

XIX

I skipped the morning session today, the D-day for our departure from Dehradun. Instead, I joined my companions at the ground for lunch in the afternoon. In the morning, I read *Code Name God: The Spiritual Odyssey*, written by Dr Mani Bhaumik, and then had a long chat with Harleen.

I informed her about our journey schedule tonight for our next venue, Dehri-on-Sone. We would like to visit Mussorie before that. She started laughing and asked me to be careful with the ladies.

- What's the secret of Mussorie? Why are you laughing?
- Sorry, whenever one speaks about hill stations, it reminds me of a story by our writer Yash Paul.
- Is it so fascinating?
- Yeah, you can call it fascinating; it is a story about a successful contractor, Shetty. He struggled hard to rise from extreme poverty. But in the process he couldn't manage time for his marriage. Once he was returning from a hill station and going to Amritsar via Pathankot. The road from the hills was closed due to incessant rains and landslides. A large number of vehicles with passengers were stranded at Pathankot.

While Shetty was waiting for the road to open at Pathankot station, he came across a beautiful young lady with her child Ballu. In the afternoon, when the road was cleared, Shetty hired a vehicle for Amritsar. He gave a lift to the lady and her son. In the course of the journey, Ballu became extremely friendly with him. The latter also tolerated all the playful misdeeds of the child. The young lady, Urmila also became affable with Shetty and she addressed him indirectly as his elder brother.

After proceeding for some distance, they again got stranded in the hills. He could manage only one room for the night's stay with Urmila and Ballu. She was a school teacher earning rupees sixty per month. Her husband Madan was also a poorly-paid employee. Urmila felt uneasy when Shetty ordered a lavish lunch for them, but she couldn't object. The caretaker thought her to be Shetty's wife. For dinner as well, lavish food was served. They spent the night in the same room, the man slept in an easy-chair on the veranda.

Circumstances forced them to spend another night in the same guest house. It was severely cold the next day. By that time they had become more genial and she proposed the marriage of her sister with him. But he didn't agree as he had already spent forty-eight springs alone. He was planning to spend the night on the veranda in the bitter cold. But Urmila persuaded him to stay inside the room. After initial hesitation, Shetty gave a pat on her back to go inside with Ballu while he slept on another bed in the same room.

The next day was sunny. The road blockade was removed in the morning itself. They asked each other if they slept well last night. Both replied affirmatively. The actual fact was that both had spend a sleepless night, yet they felt very fresh. While leaving, Shetty took a photograph of Urmila, in front of the cottage with her permission.

This interaction brought a sea change in her family life. She left her job as a school teacher. Her husband joined Shetty's firm as manager with a handsome salary. They cleared their debts in the market and bought back their house in Dalhousie. Shetty provided the entire amount. All these developments took place within a span of two months.

Ballu took admission in a convent after leaving his earlier school. Shetty, a bachelor with no close relatives, made a will bequeathing all his property in the name of Ballu with the condition that Urmila wouldn't conceive again. Shetty stays with them occasionally when he happens to visit Amritsar. But there's a thorn in this happiness. Whenever Shetty stays with them, Urmila has to wear clothes as per his desire.

It is true that Shetty hasn't married Urmila, but he loves her. He prefers the smell of oranges to a full square meal with pumpkin. Despite all the happiness and prosperity, Urmila feels that she's become a mistress of Shetty.

- It indeed is a charming story. But why do you cite this story? Where will you put me in this story?
- Actually it is one of my favourite stories. Since you're visiting a hill station, it just came to my mind.
- Its OK, Harleen, last night Mr Sharma told us a story from Mahabharata that bore resemblance to your episode with Aman.

"Really! Please tell me the story, at least the gist!"

- It's the story of Devayani and Kacha.

- I've read this story in Amar Chitra Katha. I don't think the story has much similarity with my case. Rather, I'm really impressed with the story of 'Na Hanyate', the book you've presented me.
- So you've read the story of Mircea Eliade and Maitreyi Devi. But 'It Doesn't Die' basically depicts the differences between European and Indian cultures, amid a tangle of mix-up between student and teacher, husband and wife, father and daughter, resulting in the girl Amrita succumbing to cultural constraints.
- In the Kacha-Devayani story, the boy was never a true lover. It was only Devayani who loved Kacha from the very beginning.
- OK, I agree with you. But tell me which portion of this book you like the most.
- The entire book is absorbing; especially the meeting between Amrita and Tagore is superb. The poet asked her to cool down and introspect over the past happenings. It is really an exceptional idea that the human mind can caste reflections like the crystal-clear water of a deep pond. What about you! How are you passing your time?
- Last two days I spend in the mess reading 'Code Name God' of Dr Mani Bhaumik except for some brief outings. The writer has tried to present the most complex issues of physics in their simplest form. But I failed to get the exact code of God.
- Is it so easy?
- May be it would be easy for you.
- Why?
- Have you already forgotten the meaning of your name? One who's absorbed in the Lord's love!
- So you still remember the meaning of my name, Dr Ashamanja.

- Actually my thoughts have become erratic ever since I read this book. No doubt the writer tried to describe the moments of creation of our universe through the Big Bang. But he could reach only to the millionth or trillionth of nano-second or may be closer to the zero. Yet he couldn't describe the zero position.
- It seems that there's a difference between our cultures, just like the cultural difference between Europeans and Indians, described in the book I've read. We, the Punjabis, try to remain happy with our present. But, the Bengalis prefer to analyse their past.
- It is a candid comparison.
- I think we should call it a day. I'm getting late. We're going to Bharatpur today. Aunty Jashmin Kaur is also accompanying us. Please tell Sharma Sir that we've completed our tasks at Ambala.
- What time are you leaving?
- Our train Amritsar Hazur Sahib-Nanded Express is leaving Ambala at ten. It'll reach Agra around 5 p.m.; from there we shall hire a taxi for Bharatpur. We would like to visit Pushkar as well.
- Best of luck. Take care.

At the Police Ground in Dehradun around noon, I found some candidates still in the queue. We took our lunch within an hour or so, and then started packing. Finally by four in the afternoon, our caravan left Dehradun for Mussorie. We moved slowly and cautiously along the hilly road in a cloudy weather. It took almost two hours for us to cover this single-lane road, stretching for approximately 40 k.m. I was thinking about the story narrated by Harleen in the morning. But fortunately for us, the cloud cover cleared after a light shower. In fact, Havaldar Akhilesh Kumar had correctly predicted the duration of the inclement weather.

We couldn't see much of this beautiful hill station due to time constraint. Still, we enjoyed the evening quite merrily. Almost all members of our team purchased some gift items. I purchased two shawls for my parents.

The utilization of land, especially the gorges at Mussorie needs special mention. The hotels are constructed on the narrow low-lying land located between hills. These are multi-storied structures with the top roof reaching the road-level and are used for parking light vehicles.

Descending from the Garhwal Hills was smooth. We came back to Dehradun, before proceeding for our next destination, Rampur for dinner. The road passes through Haridwar. But we didn't halt when we crossed the place around eleven. We paid respect to Lord Shiva from the vehicles only.

Driver Rafique Ansari had some knowledge about the road. So he led our convoy driving a bus, followed by our Gypsy and jeep. Up to Haridwar we moved along NH-72, and then took NH-74 up to Barmhera, reaching there some time after midnight. After that, I couldn't keep track of the road, till our arrival at Rampur 5.30 next morning adopting NH-87. Night journeys during, the summer season are very pleasing. We met very thin traffic, and went along slums and underdeveloped areas for most portion of our journey. At places, people were sleping in open areas on wooden cots. They, alongwith their domestic animals, used road side drains and barren places as toilets. Forest plantations also caught my notice at various places. These are mainly eucalyptus trees. Plants in Uttarakhand are in better health and more well-maintained, compared to Uttar Pradesh.

❖❖❖

XX

We made a brief halt at the CRPF Group Centre, Rampur on the morning of 15th May 2008, Thursday. It came into limelight during New Year's party this year, as some armed extremists entered into this campus to open indiscriminate fire from AK 47 rifles. They also hurled a grenade at the main gate.

But, the CRPF jawans hit back at the terrorists, forcing them to flee. One of the terrorists managed to enter the administrative block and killed three unarmed CRPF jawans. He however, managed to escape. In all, eight persons died in the gun-battle and five sustained injuries.

The entry point to this Group Centre doesn't seem ideal to me. There is a railway level crossing right in front of the gate. The railway track keeps quite busy. By the time we wait for strict security checks, perhaps imposed after the attack, two trains passed through the spot. A road for vehicles also passes close to the boundary of the campus.

The in-charge of the Group Centre, Suraj Bhan Singh was acquainted with Mr Sharma. He expressed regret for he couldn't remain present, as he was on tour. The accommodation was similar to that of Jalandhar. Every body was asked to freshen up and take rest as much as possible, and to assemble at the gate by 10.30 a.m. for resuming our journey.

I took a bath and a nice nap for about two hours. Kaushik rang me on the intercom at quarter to nine to call me for breakfast. Before leaving my room, I called up Harleen to get confirmation about their safe arrival. They reached hotel Laxmi Vilas Palace, Bharatpur, around seven last night. From Agra, they availed Gwalior-Udaipur Express instead of a taxi.

We resumed our journey at our scheduled time, and picked up NH-24 mainly passing through the plains of Uttar Pradesh to reach Barreilly within an hour. Here, an interesting thing happened. Joginder was playing a CD in his car. It was a collection of popular Hindi songs. As we were crossing the Bareilly market, the famous song, "Jhumka gira re, Bareilly ke bazar me jhumka gira re..." came in its own sequence. But it created a roar of laughter.

We talked about heroine Sadhna who featured in this dance. Our topic of discussion then revolved around heroines of films. Madhubala, Rekha and our Suchitra Sen were short-listed as all time best in terms of classical beauty. Names of Vaijayantimala, Wahida Rehaman, Meena Kumari, Parveen Bobby, Sharmila Tagore, Yogita Bali, Sridevi, Hema Malini,

Zeenat Aman, Madhuri Dixit, Urmila Matondkar, Vidya Balan and Divya Bharati also came up in the thread-bare discussion.

Despite his enormous contribution through hit songs and acting, Kishore Kumar came in for criticism for his indifferent treatment of his wife Madhubala, when she was suffering from cancer. Amusingly, the question of the best hero didn't come up. The discussion was quite lively, Anup Kumar and Kaushik being the storehouses of filmy gossips. Mr Sharma didn't contribute much except for his strong preference for Madhubala and Rekha.

He said, "You'll find lives of most of these film stars dissolute, though they may be acting in social films and playing characters that are holier-than-thou. Seldom one gets to see an unblemished married life led by a film star. Divorce, adultery, hobnobbing with the underworld, and many other activities unbecoming for common citizens has been their trademark."

"Sir, this is filmy Mahabharata", Anup Kumar suggested. "By the way, is there any similarity in the Mahabharata with our film industry?"

Mr Sharma giggled, "This is really a mixed bag for you. We've not come across any divorce in Mahabharata. Divorce may be a Western concept or the consequence of Muslim invasion in our country. One can compare niyoga system of getting progeny with widow marriage introduced by Raja Ram Mohan Roy, Ishwar Chadra Vidyasagar, Keshab Chandra Sen and other great men from Bengal. Living together or bearing children while remaining unwed is a rare event."

Anup Kumar asked, "Sir, why do you say that this is rare?"

He replied, "The birth of Vidura through a maid servant of Vichitravirya with sperm from Vyasa or the birth of Yuyutsu again through a maid servant from her union with Dhritarashtra when Gandhari was in her pregnancy are two notable examples. These offspring are termed as 'Anuloma'—through marriage between upper and lower castes. When the girl belongs to an upper caste and boy to a lower caste, it is termed as 'Pratiloma'. Dr Bhaumik may also agree that these offsprings are talented genetically due to gene variations and hybridization.

After a pause, he said, "In the beginning, on account of being born or created by Brahma, we all were Brahmins. Anyone could practise any profession without remaining confined to a particular one, like what we have adopted in our constitution. Brahmins performed any or all of the social functions as needed, without reservation, such as that of priesthood, ministering, teaching, military services, ruling, farming, trading and providing household services. Then, there came an age of specialization in profession. A class of professionals started practising only priesthood and teaching. Another class of professionals joined military and administrative services. Yet another took farming, while another engaged in trade and commerce. Finally, there was a class of professionals who engaged themselves in other than these four vocations."

"It's basically the process of evolution", I suggested.

"Yes, you're right, Doctor", said Mr Sharma, and he went ahead, "this practice passed from father to son and continued through generations. The initial fair distribution of labour later on gave rise to creation of four major varnas of Brahmins, Kshatriyas, Vaishyas and Shudras. Allegorically stated, the Brahmins were born of the mouth of Brahma, the Kshatriyas of his arms, the Vaishyas of his stomach and Shudras of his feet. The professionals who were originally classified according their roles in the society, later on, as a consequence, were categorized into assigned castes.

Castes, consequently, came to be determined and identified by birth. Initially there was flexibility in society. By virtue of his deeds, even a Shudra could be at par with a Brahmin or vice versa. Mandhata became a Brahmin by virtue of his penance. Similarly, Matanga and Valmiki belonging to lower caste achieved Brahmin-hood. Vishwamitra became a Brahmin from being a Kshatriya. The Kshatriyas later bifurcated into solar and lunar dynasties, depending on the presiding deity of the family being the sun or the moon."

Kaushik had been silent for quite some time, but now he reacted, "It seems that there was a democratic set-up in the beginning, just as it prevails today."

Mr Sharma accepted the idea, "In a sense you're right, in places where democracy is strong and age old, you'll not find the caste system. It is an outcome of neo-Darwinism, heredity and social bringing up. Monarchism, feudalism, division of labour, etc., act as catalysts for survival of caste system in our country. Fortunately for us, with the advancement in technology, the caste system is fading out gradually. Industrialization is traditionally associated with people belonging to the so-called lower castes. Increase in literacy rate has also acted as an impetus for eradication of this evil system."

"So, casteism is inversely proportional to literacy rate", I suggested.

He replied with a smile, "As a science student, you can formulate it that way. This may be the reason for higher literacy in states not ruled by kings from solar or lunar dynasty."

"But literacy rate in areas dominated by Muslims is even lower", Anup Kumar put up a query.

"Here, I shall not comment", said Mr Sharma, "I've very poor knowledge about the Koran. May be, our communists are right when they compare 'religion' with 'opium'."

Probably to change the topic of caste, Kaushik asked, "Sir, you narrated the evolution of caste system, but what about the institution of marriage?"

He reacted with a smile "Good question, Kaushik! Mahabharata depicts eight types of marriages. These are Brahma, Daiva, Arsa, Prajapatya, Asura, Gandharva, Raksasa and Paiśaca.

In Brahma marriage, a boy first completes gurukul, and then his parents approach the parents of a girl from a good family for marriage. In this form of marriage, girl's family doesn't give any dowry or jewellery to the boy's family.

Marrying a girl to a priest during a sacrifice is called 'daiva'. This type of marriage is considered inferior to that of Brahma. The third form 'arsa' is concerned with the rishis and the sages. In this form, the bride is given in exchange for two cows received from the groom. Here, the groom is a rishi, often rather aged.

In 'prajapatya', there's no tracing. Kanyadana is a part of it as in the Brahma ceremony. The difference is that in this case, the bride's father goes in search of a groom.

In the 'asura' type, the groom is in no way a match for the girl. But her father or relatives receive a good deal of money from the man who forces them to let her marry him. The marriage between Pandu and Madri may be treated as being of this kind.

The best example of 'gandharva marriage' is the marriage between Shakuntala and Dushyanta. It is a love marriage solemnized in a mandir or a place of respect clandestinely, may or may not be in the presence of witnesses.

In the 'raksasa' form, the groom battles with the girl's family, overcomes them and carries her away. The marriage between Sri Krishna and Rukmini is of this kind. Here, the element of clandestine love affair exists.

In paisaca, the girl's wish doesn't count, nor is any money or material given to her parents. She's seized against her will and her family is antagonized. The marriage of Vichitravirya falls in this category."

"So it is like universal sets and sub-sets in mathematics", I suggested.

"You're absolutely right, but you'll find fusion and intermixing between different categories", he made commented expertly, as we stopped for lunch at a dhaba just after crossing Shahjahanpur.

Initially, we intended to cover the distance of 715 k.m. between Rampur and Varanasi in a day, but after judging our progress, we changed the plan. Instead, we decided to make a halt at Lucknow, located at about 430 k.m. from Rampur. Accordingly, Mr Sharma approached the Police Headquarters,

Uttar Pradesh for arranging our accommodation. Soon, we got assurance of accommodation for the officers at District Police Guest House, Lucknow, and for others at the District Police Lines.

Our progress became slow due to poor condition of the road in patches. Our misery was further aggravated, as we couldn't pick up the exact link road for entering Lucknow City amidst load shedding and moved about 20 k.m., trying to find the right way. Finally, around 8 p.m., we arrived at Lucknow after crossing the Ganges. Electricity was also restored to allow us to have a full view of the illuminated city.

Lucknow was established by Laxman, the second brother of Lord Rama. Mr Sharma said, "The city was initially known as Lakhanpuri, slowly the name Lakhanpuri became 'Lakhknau' and then was named 'Lucknow' by the British. It is called the city of Nawabs. It is also known as the Golden City of East, Shiraz-e-Hind and the Constantinople of India."

We could take only a glimpse of the city. But Kaushik provided a real gem of an information. He asked, "Do you know there's an association between Lucknow and Tripura?"

All of us including Mr Sharma were clueless, till he answered, "Last Maharaja Bir Bikram Kishore Manikya Bahadur studied in Lucknow and his beautiful queen, Kanchan Prabha Devi hailed from this place. You may also find architectural similarity between our Ujjayanta Palace and old mansions of Lucknow."

We spent the night in Officers' Mess of Provincial Arms Constabulary (PAC) Battalion of UP Police. Our staff did not like the accommodation. They preferred to move further ahead after dinner. Considering the serious time constraints, Mr Sharma allowed the staff led by Ajit Debbarma to move by midnight, leaving us to follow them. We've to reach Dehri-on-Sone by the next day since recruitment is scheduled for the day after tomorrow.

❖❖❖

XXI

On Friday morning, we took early breakfast and left Lucknow by six for Varanashi through NH-56. Just at the start of our journey, Mr Sharma said, "Last night, I had a talk with Baldevji. They're getting copies of all documents relating to investigation of Aman's death from the court. Some force officials have also come to know about this new development. In fact, they've sent one retired ex-colleague to Baldevji just to create confusion in his mind. They have offered a proposal for conducting a shooting tournament in the name of Captain Amandeep Sandhu at their cost, on the condition that Baldevji should not try to get the case reopened.

Force officials are alleging that this action of Baldevji would tarnish the image of a disciplined force like Black Panther Rifles.

But, Baldevji was brave enough to categorically deny the proposal offered by his ex-colleague. He told him that though he had lost his son, but in exchange got a daughter in the form of Harleen. He didn't want to lose her. He wanted to see her happy. Admitting that he had committed lots of injustice upon her, he expressed his vow to amend it. In his words, "By God's grace, I've enough money, and with this I shall knock at doors of High Court or even the Supreme Court."

Mr Sharma further added that Aman was the best shooter in Black Panther Rifles. After his death, the force officials had proposed to run a shooting tournament in his name for the force personnel. They were in touch with the family for about six months. But later on, they abandoned the idea stating that Captain Amandeep didn't meet a heroic death, and it wouldn't be wise to sponsor a trophy in his name.

It was extremely hot outside. The temperature was hovering around 40°C. Unlike Punjab and Haryana, we saw a lot of people moving around, despite the scorching sun, covering their heads and ears with a gamchha (towel). We also took similar protection. We were crossing Amethi sometime after seven in the morning.

The very name of Amethi brought the name of our late Prime Minister, Rajiv Gandhi who was an MP from this parliamentary constituency, to our minds. Mr Sharma praised the vision of Rajiv Gandhi, especially his contribution towards revolutionizing communication technology in our country. Former Prime Minister, Atal Behari Vajpayee also received our acclamation for his project Golden Quadrilateral leading to the improvement of roads in our country. The benefits of this we're enjoying today.

We then listened to the Rajiv Gandhi assassination case from Mr Sharma. He narrated the same based on inputs from one of his seniors. The latter was a member of the Special Investigation Team (SIT), entrusted with the investigation. The story is now well-known to us, but it still sounds breath-taking when narrated by him, "Rajiv Gandhi arrived at Chennai on 21st May 1991, about two hours early. He then moved in a motorcade to Sriperumbudur. Along the way, he received garlands from many well wishers, Congress party workers and school children. At 10.10 p.m., the assassin, Dhanu approached him and greeted him. She then bent down to touch his feet and detonated an RDX explosive-laden belt tucked below her dress. The former Prime Minister and many others died in the explosion that followed.

It was a blind case. Many conjectures ranging from involvement of LTTE, Sikh extremists, internal conspiracy and so on came into consideration. By a mere chance, a local photographer Haribabu had captured the assassination on film. His camera and film were recovered from the site, though he himself had died in the explosion.

Prabhakaran, the chief of LTTE, masterminded the murder of Rajiv Gandhi. He alongwith his associates Pottu Amman and Amila, had hatched the conspiracy to kill Rajiv Gandhi. The seed of hatred in Prabhakaran's mind grew when IPKF handed over 17 key LTTE militants apprehended during its operation in Sri Lanka. Twelve of them consumed cyanide and killed themselves while being handed over. One-eyed Jack

Sivarasan was chosen to execute the plot because of his expertise in such killings.

Two or three squads sent by Sivarasan, landed in neighbouring Tamil Nadu across the Palk Straits under the guise of Tamil refugees. They took houses in Chennai and suburbs, made friends with local Tamil people and used them in killing Gandhi. Sriharan alias Marugan, a hardcore LTTE militant, arrived in Tamil Nadu through clandestine means. He befriended Chennai-based Indian Tamil woman Nalini, and married her.

When Gandhi's tour programme was made public, the five-member assassination squad met at Nalini's mother, Padma's place a day before the murder. The team arrived at Sriperumbudur and reached the venue of the election meeting ahead of time. Gandhi arrived there at 2200 hours and was blown to pieces within 20 minutes. Human bomb used by LTTE in the form of Dhanu carried 1 lb of plastic explosives packed with 10,000 metal pallets.

The trial was conducted under the Terrorist and Disruptive Activities (Prevention) Act (TADA). The designated TADA court in Chennai gave death sentences to all the 26 accused persons. This created a storm in India. Legal experts were stunned. Human right groups protested as the trial didn't meet the specified standards. On appeal to the Supreme Court, only four of the accused were sentenced to death and the others to various jail terms."

We remained simply spellbound. I confessed, "I don't know that such is the intricacy of law. In that case, it would be very difficult to punish terrorists."

"You're absolutely right", said Mr Sharma. "We're facing the same problem in Tripura. TADA is treated as a draconian law in Tripura. It had been decided by the State Government some time in 1993 not to register any case under TADA in Tripura. It is a question of ideology, and one can't question it. But this makes the task of police in Tripura harder to ensure punishment of accused persons involved in terrorism-related crimes. I personally feel that for dealing with organized criminals like extremists, some stringent Acts like TADA,

Maharashtra Control of Organized Crime Act, etc., are essential.

If necessary, suitable amendments should be introduced to prevent misuse of these acts. Everything is fair in love and war. We're practically fighting a proxy war, may be against our own men. But a good number of them are non-state actors. Remember, these elements are like gods for the police and security forces, they can see the police or the security forces, but the converse is seldom true. To fight with such asuras, police and security forces should be properly equipped, both in terms of legal empowerments and weaponry."

Anup Kumar said, "Is there any such suicidal attack in Mahabharata?"

Mr Sharma drank water, and then with his customary smile replied, "Probably the first suicidal attack in the history of mankind was upon Prahlad. This you'll find in our mythology. His father Hiranyakashyapu was a mighty demon king. After winning all the three worlds of heaven, earth and hell, he became very proud. He assumed that he could defeat even Lord Vishnu with his valour. He went to the extent of enforcing a law that everybody would worship him instead of gods and deities.

However, his little son Prahlad refused to accept his commands and continued to worship Lord Vishnu with complete devotion. Infuriated by this defiance of his son, he ordered his soldiers to throw him down from a hill. Praying passionately and having full faith in Lord Vishnu, Prahlad didn't retract from his word. True to his faith, Lord Vishnu rescued him at the last moment.

He was poisoned but the poison turned to nectar in his mouth. He was trampled by elephants yet remained unharmed. He was put in a room with hungry poisonous snakes, and survived. All of Hirankashyapu's attempts to kill his son failed.

Frustrated by these failures to kill his son Prahlad, Hirankashyapu invoked the help of his sister Holika. She had a boon that she could walk through fire unharmed. The wicked aunt agreed to the evil desires of his brother. She entered the fire with her nephew Prahlad. However, the brother and the sister forgot that Holika could only enter the fire alone or she would perish. Thus blessed by Lord Vishnu, the child Prahlad remained unharmed but Holika got burnt and died instantly. Holi is thus celebrated to commemorate the death of the evil aunt. The festival is named after her, and celebrates the new life granted to Prahlad for his devotion and faith."

"Sir, what about Bishkanya?" this time, it was Kaushik who queried.

He laughed loudly and said, "Bishkanya or venomous maids are not same as members of suicidal squads. They were like modern day prostitutes having HIV. They allured their victims to have sex with them and thereby caused their death.

In Mahabharata, we find the real presence of a suicidal squad in the form of Samsaptakas which ultimately caused the death of Abhimanyu, on the thirteenth day of Kurukshetra battle. Samsaptakas are the soldiers who have taken the vow to conquer or die, and never to retreat."

Then after a pause, he said, "It is again a lengthy story."

"Sir, today we don't have any time constraint", I said, "you can continue."

He resumed, "The battle began early in the morning with the Samsaptakas challenging Arjuna. They dragged Arjuna and his charioteer Sri Krishna on the southern front, far away from the scene of the main battle.

The Kauravas, led by Drona, challenged the other Pandavas to break a lotus battle formation known as Chakravyuh. Bhima led his forces, supported by Satyaki, Drupada, Dhrishtadyumna, Shikhandi, Ghatotkacha, Nakula, Sahadeva and many others. The fight began and the Kaurava army attacked Yudhisthira. The counter attack of Bhima and other generals were almost warded off by Drona's onslaught.

Yudhisthira found himself in a fix. Only Arjuna, Krishna, Pradyumna and Abhimanyu knew how to penetrate the Chakravyuh. Arjuna was fighting the Samsaptakas away from the scene. Therefore, Yudhisthira sent for Abhimanyu, the teenaged son of Arjuna and Subhadra. Abhimanyu was his only hope. He entrusted to him the formidable task of penetrating the Chakravyuh. He gladly accepted the heroic assignment. But he only knew how to penetrate the Vyuha, not how to extricate himself out of the web of the Vyuha. That was the only worry. So, they decided to follow Abhimanyu immediately after he broke open a passage in the Vyuha.

Yudhisthira blessed the youth, and he moved towards Kaurava lines. With lightening speed, he drove through the enemy formation breaking the unassailable Vyuha. Routing the enemy ranks, he stood in the centre of the Vyuha before Duryodhana. Alarmed Drona, Karna, Aswasthama, Kripa and others rushed to protect Duryodhana. Abhimanyu faced their combined attack undauntedly and single-handed.

The Pandavas generals had tried hard to enter the Vyuha in his wake, but the breach had closed immediately after Abhimanyu's entrance. They were barred by Jayadratha. He had sealed the opening and Bhima and others were rendered helpless. Lord Shiva had granted a boon to Jayadratha that allowed him to hold all the Pandavas, except Arjuna for one day. He made use of that boon. The Pandavas got horrified to think of the inevitable.

In the mighty battle that followed, Abhimanyu slaughtered ordinary enemy warriors and mighty heroes alike. He fought valiantly, single-handedly slaying several warriors who came in his way including Duryodhana's son Laxmana. Abhimanyu also killed Ashmaka's son, Shalya's younger brother, Shalya's son Rukmaratha and other great warriors. He destroyed 3/4th of an Akshouhini army single handed. He wounded Karna and made him flee. This made Dushasana faint in the battle field so that he had to be carried off by others.

The death of his beloved son Laxmana incensed Duryodhana. He ordered the entire Kaurava force to attack Abhimanyu. Abhimanyu then held the six Kaurava warriors Drona, Kripacharya, Aswasthama, Karna, Shalya and Bhorisravas, all together at bay. Ignoring all rules and propriety, the Kauravas attacked lone Abhimanyu all together. He met a heroic death in the process. Thus, the Kaurava force did make use of the suicidal squad Samsaptakas in engaging Arjuna from the main battle field and thereby succeeded in killing a warrior of the stature of Abhimanyu."

❖❖❖

XXII

We crossed the Ganges at Varanasi around half-past twelve. The Ganges looked really beautiful at this place. Kaushik had been to Varanasi before. He showed us various ghats like Dashashwamedh Ghat, Shivala Ghat, Manikarnika Ghat, Scindia Ghat, Man Mandir Ghat, Lalita Ghat, Mansarowar Ghat, Darbhanga Ghat, Tulsi Ghat, etc. Tulsidas wrote Ramcharitmanasa at Tulsi Ghat. Most of these ghats, numbering approximately 100, were built when the city was under Maratha control.

Before lunch, we visited Dashashwamedh Ghat and Vishwanath Temple. Local police helped us, but I felt very sad to notice the presence of scores of policemen and security forces. The officer on duty apprised us of the terrorist attack on the temple by the terrorist group Laskar-e-Kahab in March 2006. It took the life of 28 persons. In November 2007, Varanasi again witnessed a bomb blast in the civil court, resulting in the death of 20 people and injury to over 100 people.

It is a congested place, and introduction of several gates with frisking by cops along a zigzag path made the things even clumsier. In churches and mosques, we don't find any restriction to entry. But in Hindu temples, there will always be a narrow passage for entrance and haggling by the priests. The same thing is observed in Durga Puja pandals at Agartala in many areas. There, it is manmade congestion of human traffic on the pretext of crowd control.

We received VIP treatments from the cops on duty on disclosure of our identity. Perhaps, such favour is absent in other religions. I interpreted the opportunity to be a part of social dynamics.

We purchased some souvenirs and left Varanasi for Dehri-on-Sone after lunch at around 2 p.m. Visiting Varanasi made us feel good. Anup Kumar asked Mr Sharma, "What's the story behind the name of Varanasi?"

He dived into the depths of his wisdom and replied, "According to American writer Mark Twain, Varanasi is older than history, older than tradition, older even than legend, and looks as old as all of them put together. It is believed to be the oldest living city in the world, the abode of Lord Shiva and Parvati.

The present name Varanasi has its origin in the two tributaries of the Ganges—Varuna and Asi, which flank its northern and southern borders. Banaras or Benaras, as it is popularly known, is only a corruption of the name Varanasi. The ancient name of this city is Kashi, as you'll find its reference in Rig-Veda. Through the ages, Varanasi was variously known as Avimuktaka, Anandakanana, Mahasmasana, Surandhana, Brahma Vardha, Sudarsana, Ramya and Kashi."

I was thinking about Munshi Prem Chand, who hailed from this place. He continued, "The culture of Varanasi is closely associated with the river Ganges and the river's religious importance. The city has been a cultural and religious centre in north India for several thousand years. The Banaras Gharana form of Indian classical music developed in Varanasi. Many prominent Indian philosophers, poets, writers and musicians resided in or still reside in Varanasi, including Tulsidas, Kabir, Ravidas, their Guru Swami Ramanand, Trailanga Swami, Munshi Prem Chand, Jaishankar Prasad, Acharya Shukla, Ravi Shankar, Girija Devi, Hari Prasad Chaurasia, Bismillah Khan, and many more."

I was recalling a story written by Munshi Prem Chand in the backdrop of Varanasi. Seeing me lost in thoughts, Mr

Sharma said, "Doctor, you've been keeping quiet for quite some time. Have you received any call from Harleen?"

Kaushik and Anup Kumar laughed. I felt a little embarrassed. I said, "Thanks, for reminding me about her. But, I've not received any call from her since yesterday morning. I'm thinking of something else."

He said, "Don't worry! She's fine. In fact, I've had a talk with Baldevji. They have completed their task at Bharatpur. More importantly, they have received the copy of Aman's post-mortem report, the seizure list and photographs of the place of occurrence. In the seizure list, apart from the recovery of one pistol with two empty cases, the seizure of one magazine with 10 rounds are mentioned. They're moving to Ajmer this afternoon by Ala Hazrat Express. Probably, they're now visiting Keoladeo National Park, Bharatpur."

"Sir, does it corroborate homicide?" asked Anup Kumar.

"Yes, my dear", he said with certainty, "it confirms that two shots were fired on the temple region. Now, it can be conclusively declared that Aman was murdered on the night of 2nd May 2006 at Bharatpur."

"Sir, we should listen to Dr Bhaumik", said Kaushik, "he was actually thinking of something else."

Mr Sharma said, "You're right Kaushik, Dr Bhaumik was trying to say something. Actually, I wanted to share the good news that I heard from Baldevji", and then turning towards me, he asked, "Doctor, tell us what you were thinking."

- I was trying to recollect a short story by Munshi Prem Chand on the backdrop of Varanasi, which I had read a long back.
- Prem Chand had written many stories on the backdrop of Kashi; tell me the central idea of the story.
- It's something about the return of a nonagenarian man from abroad to his homeland.
- Bravo doctor, bravo, you've indeed called up a master-piece of Prem Chand.

We all were spellbound at the intellect of this gentleman, as he recited, “Prabhu mere avagun chit na dharo.”

- Yes, this bhajan was sung by the principal character in the story.

It’s actually a bhajan by Surdas; meaning Lord, heed not my faults, which was nicely used by Prem Chand in his story—‘Better than Heaven’. It’s a story about a man from Varanasi who left his motherland voluntarily at the age of 30 to try his luck at doing business in America. He attained peaks of success there and earned substantial wealth. He succeeded on the family front as well, having got married to a beautiful lady, who bore him five healthy sons. His well-settled sons gave him beautiful grand-children also. At the age of ninety, suddenly a desire to visit his motherland seized him.

It was the pre-independence period and the Britishers were ruling our country. He landed in Bombay by ship. The first thing which caught his attention was that the sailors at the port were clad in dirty half-torn coats. Soon, he noticed foreign cars and lavish life of Englishmen. As he travelled by train from Bombay to his native place, he felt deep pain to find the rich heritage of flora and fauna on either side of the track missing. His native village was totally changed and it had become the abode of Englishmen. The villagers too, appeared changed to him. They preferred speaking about police stations, courts, etc. He even noticed a native being punished with lashes by a policeman in red cap.

He didn’t find any of his childhood friends. The place where he used to go for his morning walks had become a primary school, filled with malnourished students. At once he realized that he had not come to visit this India.

With utter frustration and fatigue, he sought shelter before five villagers one after another, only to be refused each time. The fifth man gave him a handful of groundnuts, which he couldn’t hold as he was trembling with pain. Finally he planned to spend the night in a Dharmshala. But there also he suffered setback, as he found the dormitory occupied by rich people. It had become a den for gambling, adultery and drinking, with no space for poor countrymen.

He decided to spend the night somehow sitting by the side of a drain and return to America again. At around three in the morning, he noticed 15 to 20 aged persons, clad in white dhotis with pots in their hands leading towards the Ganges singing, "Prabhu mere avagun chit na dharo...."

At once, he joined them leaving his coat and trousers. He travelled the six miles stretch to the Ganges with them with joy and took great pleasure in bathing in the Ganges. He built a hut and spent his remaining life on the banks of the Ganges. At last he got his motherland, which had more value than Paradise for him.

We were mesmerized by the story. Mr Sharma broke the silence, "This is precisely the reason for which old people prefer to stay in Kashi. You'll find lots of widows from Bengal staying at temples and colonies in Varanasi."

❖❖❖

XXIII

Soon we took NH-2 for moving towards Dehri-on-Sone.

"Sir, have you ever heard of 'Dehri-on-Sone', earlier?" Kaushik put the question to Mr Sharma.

- No, I came to know about this location only after the announcement of the itinerary of the recruitment rally.
- We're fortunate that Anup Kumar is from this area.
- Yes, I'm a native of Bihar, but not exactly from Dehri.

In the next half an hour, he told us about the Dehri-on-Sone. Dehri is a Hindi word. Traditionally it was called Dehri Ghat. Its new English name is 'Dehri-on-Sone', which means on the banks of Sone river.

According to another popular version, Dehri means 'Temporary Dwelling or Shelter'. In the ancient age, there was a tradition of construction of temporary shelters in Bihar for spending time in summers. Britishers made Dehri or Kuthy on the bank of river Sone and accordingly, the name 'Dehri-on-Sone' surfaced.

It is a municipal town in Rohtas district of Bihar. Approximate area of Rohtas is 4,000 square k.m., with three subdivisions—Sasaram, Dehri and Bikramganj. Sasaram is the district headquarters. The population of the district is about 25 lakhs.

Sasaram is a place of historical importance. Sher Shah's father was a Jagirdar of 500 horses of Sasaram. Sher Shah received all his expertise and training in administration from his father at this place.

The headquarters of 2nd Battalion Bihar Military Police (BMP), where we're going to conduct the recruitment rally is located in Dehri. The district has a variety of landscapes within a small area. It has flat plains running alongside the Kaimur Range and Rohtas Plateau. The Sone river is a tributary of the Ganges originating in Madhya Pradesh. The Kaimur Range is an extension of the Vindhya Range.

It has a mixed population with a Hindu population of about 80 per cent and the rest is comprised by Muslims, Christians, Buddhists, Jains and non-believers.

"You've given us a fairly good idea about Dehri-on-Sone", I said to Anup Kumar, "but I shall tell you a story of an eminent singer and recipient of Padma Shree, who was born in Dehri-on-Sone".

"Is it Manna Dey?", Kaushik guessed.

"No, not Manna Dey, the singer is a lady", I replied.

"Is she Gangubai Hangwal?", this time Mr Sharma guessed.

"No, she's not Hangwal. She's a Bengali lady", I said.

"Is she Suchitra Mitra?", said Anup Kumar.

"Yes, it is Suchitra Mitra", I confirmed. "Was it just a guess?"

"Yeah! I've seen her face on TV, in 'Mile Sur Mera Tumhara', that beautiful song on national integration", Anup Kumar explained.

"This is first-hand information for me", Mr Sharma said.

"You'll find it in her autobiography 'Mone Rekho'", I said, "and it's certainly a story to be remembered. She was born in a train. Her parents were enjoying holidays with her elder brother and probably, two elder sisters, at Dehri-on-Sone in early 1920s. While they were returning from Dehri in train, her mother was beset by labour pains. It happened to be an express train which didn't stop at all stations. There was no system of pulling emergency chain in those days. Her father became restless. Her brother was by the side of her father. He was wearing a black coat. The young boy had filled both the pockets of his coat with some stone chips and small bottles collected as souvenirs from Dehri.

Necessity is the mother of invention. Her father, who was a writer by profession, wrote a letter on a piece of paper 'My wife is seriously ill. Please arrange a halt for this train at the next station.' This letter was inserted in a bottle collected by her brother and with a weight attached in the form of a stone-chip; it was thrown from the running train onto a station platform. It worked as the train made a non-scheduled halt at a beautiful station, which came next amidst a 'Shal' forest. The name of the station was Gujandi. She was born at that station. That was the reason why her parents and family members gave her nickname 'Gaju'."

"Gujandi is a hill station in Jharkhand now", said Anup Kumar, "it is 6 to 7 k.m. from Koderma, at a height of more than 1,200 metres above sea-level. Gaya and Bodhgaya are also located close by. One can go from Sasaram as well."

"I believe Gujandi was in news in the recent past", said Kaushik, "the Maoists blew off the railway tracks at Gujandi."

Anup Kumar confirmed the information given by Kaushik.

Mr Sharma said, "Koderma produces 60 to 65 per cent of the world's mica. The entire Chhota Nagpur belt which constitutes Jharkhand is very rich for mining. One may find a correlation between Maoist upsurge and mineral reserves in India.

One reason for Maoist activism is the lack of development in these areas despite mineral resources. The economic condition of local people engaged in mining remains unchanged. Here you'll find illegal mining running parallel to public sector mining. The illegal miners are a major source of fund for the Maoists.

The black money, which these people have amassed, may be hundred times more than the loan waiver given by banks to poor farmers. The Maoists take advantage of this deprivation of common masses to allure them to join their hands. Maoists can't survive without the help of rich and influential people. They hold control over political, social, administrative and even religious activities in these areas. This privileged class always becomes richer and the poor poorer. You may find this absent in Tripura. Corruption is there in Tripura, but the development is all-round along with upliftment of the downtrodden. This is the reason why extremists are finding it difficult to induct people of Tripura in their organizations these days.

This is my assumptions in respect of Maoists. I want to verify this through interaction with the local people, in next few days."

At about half past five in the afternoon, we crossed Kudra and moved towards Sasaram. The road's condition is quite bad, compared to Delhi, Haryana, Punjab and even Uttar Pradesh. We found people working on the road in patches. Traffic was very thin. Only a long queue of stationary trucks facing towards Uttar Pradesh caught our notice. We found no habitation on either side of the road, running alongside Kaimur Range and Rohtas Plateau.

We took the directions over the telephone from our advance team. They had reached their destination a few hours back. Unlike the north-west, twilight was fast approaching here. The darkness was further aggravated by load-shedding.

"Maoists can kidnap us very easily, from this road", said Kaushik.

"Maoists will never do this". Anup Kumar replied with authority.

"How can you say with such certainty?" asked Mr Sharma.

"Sir, you've come here to give jobs to the local boys and that too from another state", Anup Kumar explained. "They'll never disturb you. But they'll certainly try to loot your firearms."

His reply convinced us, but we remained apprehensive about our security for the next few days.

Our boys greeted us with emergency lights and candles when we reached Second Battalion BMP Campus around 7 p.m. We were accommodated in a guest house named 'Indrapuri' that belong to the irrigation department. It is located about 5 k.m. from BMP Campus near the barrage on Sone river. That night, we were fortunate to get electricity for about two hours.

Care taker Mishra and cook Sahuji were properly briefed by Anup Kumar, in Bhojpuri dialect about our status and the reason for our visit. We expressed our desire to eat fresh fish from Sone river. Sahuji fed us in a homely atmosphere with excellent recipes. Our emergency lights were of no use. It is difficult to charge the same in roughly two hours for which electricity persists, that too at irregular intervals. So, we favoured kerosene lanterns and candles. However, we enjoyed sound sleep in the 'Andhar Puri' in breezy weather, despite the hot summer. I deliberately didn't use the term 'Pret Puri' for 'Indrapuri', as I had not encountered any ghosts.

XXIV

We faced a tough challenge in tackling a gathering of more than 20,000 people at BMP Ground, on 17th May 2008, Saturday. Local police was allowing the candidates to the ground through a narrow gate, after preliminary screening. Had they done this impartially, there would have been no chaos. But soon, they started showing favour to some candidates. This was objected to by the candidates who had been standing in the long queue since morning. Agitated candidates started shouting from behind, resulting in a pandemonium. Police resorted to mild lathi charge, and started blaming us for keeping only three counters.

The situation improved considerably after the arrival of the local SDPO. Mr Sharma asked him to entrust the law and order duty to some responsible officer with instructions to carry out the task impartially. He also showed him the video-footage of the morning's happenings. Local police acceded to our request, helping us in smooth distribution of the tokens. By 3 p.m., we could leave the ground.

The morning however began with a promising note. I got a call from Harleen at around six. She was in a jovial mood, in the company of uncle Baldev and aunty Jasmin. They had arrived at Ajmer last night at around nine, and took rooms at Hotel Puloma on Station Road, Ajmer. They would visit Ajmer Dargah in the morning and Pushkar in the evening, and return to Ambala, day after tomorrow. She also gave confirmation about the documents they had collected from the office of subdivisional magistrate, Bharatpur.

The four of us attended a dinner at a restaurant in Sasaram hosted by Shri Himanshu Ranjan, SP Rohtas, in the evening amidst load shedding. Mr Ranjan managed a restaurant with generator back-up with utmost difficulty. He was accompanied by his wife, two children and a family friend, Mr Kamal Singh, a freelance photographer. We enjoyed their company. Discussions revolved round the comparison of facilities available in towns and villages of Bihar and Tripura. We agree that the infrastructural facilities available in villages and towns in Tripura are far better than Sasaram and Dehri.

Kamal Singh praised our Chief Minister, Sri Manik Sarkar highly, especially his honesty. We felt elated and thanked him for his compliment towards our CM. He also praised the honesty and sincerity of present Chief Minister of Bihar, Sri Nitish Kumar. Mr Singh is a native of Hazaribagh. When he learnt that we would be next visiting Ranchi for a recruitment rally, he invited us to his house. Hazaribagh would be en-route to Ranchi. Mr Sharma thought for a while and asked for our views. Since the distance between the two venues Dehri and Ranchi is the least, and we've kept two days as reserve in between the completion of rally here and the commencement at Ranchi, Kaushik and I nodded in favour of acceptance of the invitation. It was decided that we would visit Hazaribagh on 22nd May 2008, for one night's stay. Anup Kumar wouldn't accompany us. He would leave for his native place, Bhagalpur on completion of rally at Dehri to bring his two kids to Ranchi for a trip.

We came back to Indrapuri around ten to find the area still engulfed in darkness. We sat down in the courtyard of the guest house. One Mohit Kumar, superintending engineer of the irrigation department joined us. He is in his mid-fifties and is staying in the same guest house. I was under the impression that only the young generation of officers from Bihar and Uttar Pradesh deleted their surnames to conceal their caste identity. But after interaction with Mohit Kumar, I had to change my view. By the way, he's a Brahmin. He apprised us of some fascinating facts about the Indrapuri barrage. It happens to be one of the longest dams in India. It provides irrigation to entire western and central Bihar.

He gave us a grimy picture of the industrial sector at Dehri. Till 1980, Dalmianagar, located close to Indrapuri was one of the major industrial cities in India. It had sugar, vegetable oil, cement, paper and chemical factories. But now these are closed. Interference from the local mafia in the form of dacoity and extortion, led to the downfall of this place. Incidents of kidnappings have increased manifold, forcing local businessmen to move out of the district.

One reason for this is the nexus between local politicians and criminals with tacit support from the police. We went to bed around midnight.

❖❖❖

XXV

I rang up Harleen around half-past six on Sunday morning. They had visited Moinuddin Chisti's Dargah yesterday morning and Pushkar Lake in the evening. Today, they're again going to Pushkar for worshipping Brahma.

We spent an extremely busy day carrying out different tests of the candidates cautiously under trees. We had to bear up with the 'Loo' from morning eleven to five in the afternoon. Several cases of false personifications had been detected. In most of the cases, the candidates had replaced their photographs in the application forms. Mr Sharma sent two such cases with complaints to the local police. In one case, a local police official was also found to be involved.

Our experience of previous two venues helped us to carry out our task fast and with accuracy. My medical unit also worked like a well-oiled machine to meet the challenge without assistance from local administration. The bottom line is that despite adversity of nature, our achievement during the day was satisfactory when we retuned to our guest house.

But, at Indrapuri, things were not found to be in order. At first, no attendant was visible. After some time, cook Sahuji surfaced, followed by caretaker Mishra. They were in a state of panic, and looking for somebody. They tried to show normalcy, once they saw us. Mohit Kumar also appeared in the courtyard. The following story came out.

At around noon today, an elected member of the Legislative Assembly visited Indrapuri guest house with about fifty associates. On their advent, Mohit Kumar and Mishra ran away. They asked Sahuji to prepare their lunch. Sahuji demanded money for the food, which they didn't like. Finally, they ate whatever was available. They even took away some towels from the guest house, and left just before our arrival. Mohit Kumar said, "This is a regular affair with elected representatives here, irrespective of party affiliations."

We offered some money to Sahuji, but he refused to accept, stating that we had already given sufficient advance. But I'm sure that these three people are starving since the hooligans ate up whatever was available.

We then passed the time by listening to enjoyable stories from Mahabharata from Mr Sharma. He explained the marital status of the Pandavas and the Kauravas in the epic. The interaction was less intense today, despite the ample presence of inflammatory materials. He went on, "Yudhisthira had another wife Devika, apart from Draupadi. Devika was the daughter of king Govasana of the Saibya tribe. He had one son from her called Yaudhya.

According to another version of Mahabharata, Yudhisthira's second wife Devika was an incarnation of Shyamala. The latter was the wife of Yama. In accordance with yet another variation, Yudhisthira's second marriage happened during the Pandavas' final pilgrimage, when they stopped at a place called Dharmapuri. There, a merchant approached him with a proposal of marriage for his young daughter, Suhani. She was Oriya. As per prediction of astrologers, the moment she got married, she would die. She was delaying her marriage for this reason. At the same time, it was against tradition to keep the daughter unmarried like that. So her father decided to get her married to Yudhisthira, hoping that it would bring good fortune for her.

Yudhisthira agreed, and so the marriage was solemnized. At the marriage ceremony, Lord Yama's agents came to collect Suhani as per the prediction. They were challenged by Arjuna and roundly defeated. When Yama himself appeared; he too was defeated by Arjuna and tied up. On the request of Suhani's father, Arjuna freed Yama on the promise that the latter wouldn't visit the place again. Later, Yudhisthira told Suhani to go the Kapilasa hills and wait for him to return. Unfortunately he never returned, for the Pandavas left the earth at the end of their pilgrimage."

"This is a totally new story for me", Kaushik reacted.

"This you'll find this in the Oriya Mahabharata, written by Sarala Das", said Mr Sharma. He proceeded to describe the marital status of other Pandavas, "Bhima had three more wives, apart from Draupadi. He married Balandhara, the daughter of the king of Kashi. She bore him a son, Sarvaga. He also married Hidimba and the sister of Shishupala. According to folktales in Rajasthan and Orissa, Bhima had married a Naga woman. When the Kauravas tried to poison him and drown him in a river, he was saved by Ahuka, a Naga, and taken to the empire of the serpents, where he got married. Bilalsen was born from that union, and he played a role in the war later on. In some variants, Bilalsen alias Barbareek, is mentioned as Ghatotkacha's son. Hence, he's the grandson of Bhima, not his son.

Similarly, Arjuna had three more wives Ulupi, Chitrangada and Subhadra in addition to Draupadi. Arjuna married the Naga Ulupi, the princess Chitrangada of Manipur and finally Krishna's sister Subhadra during pilgrimage. But in Tamil version of the Mahabharata, he married a total of seven women. One of them was a warrior woman called Ali who refused to marry him. But Arjuna was so obsessed that he sought Krishna's help. Krishna turned him into a snake and he slipped into Ali's bed at night and frightened her to become his wife. This would certainly invite a cognizable and non-bailable case under section 376/494 IPC for committing rape by deceit and bigamy. He would have suffered capital punishment. Here, Krishna probably acted as snake-charmer to frighten the girl with his pet snake and to force her to have sex. Krishna would be charged for abetment.

The marriage with Subhadra needs some elaboration. Once, Arjuna stayed in Dwarka with Krishna, his best friend.

Krishna's elder brother Balarama, the king of the land, gave a warm welcome to Arjuna.

One day Arjuna caught the sight of Subhadra, Krishna's sister, and fell in love with her. Balarama however had selected Duryodhana as Subhadra's future husband. When Krishna foresaw the situation, he indirectly suggested to Arjuna to elope with Subhadra, saying that a Kshatriya like him should never beg to win his lady-love. He should win her by force. So, Arjuna borrowed Krishna's chariot and forcibly took away Subhadra, when she was returning from the temple.

On receiving this information, Balarama flew into a rage and called for Krishna before waging war against Arjuna. He guessed that the abduction must have been committed with the connivance of Krishna.

Balarama burst out at Krishna, 'It is disgraceful to tolerate the misdeed of Arjuna, your best friend. I could never have imagined that a royal guest like him will return our favour with such a mean act. What do you have to say before we go after Arjuna?'

Krishna heard the allegations attentively and spoke in a pacifying mood, 'Brother Balarama, isn't it a matter of pride for us to be related to the Pandavas? They'll be our strong allies. Arjuna is invincible, and if we're defeated, it'll be more disgraceful. I'll suggest that we honourably call Arjuna back and arrange for a royal marriage between Subhadra and Arjuna.'

So, Arjuna and Subhadra got married at Pushkara in the presence of royal guests. Once again, it is a case of neo-Darwinism, survival of the strongest. But in a democratic environment, it could have invited a case under section 366/494 IPC against Arjuna for the offence of kidnapping as well as bigamy. He would have suffered imprisonment of ten years with fine and seven years' jail term with fine for the second offence. Krishna would also have suffered same quantum of punishment for abetment under section 366/494/114 IPC."

"One thing is clear that the Pandavas visited the north-eastern states", said Kaushik.

"How are you so sure?" asked Mr Sharma.

"Because all these wives like Chitrangada, Hidimba and Ulupi retained their sons with them, and they didn't move with their husbands", replied Kaushik. "This practice is still in existence in these states."

"You're right Kaushik!" said Mr Sharma, "and probably it is the reason for the dislike by the tribals of these places towards the people of the mainland. In these marriages, the Pandavas faced initial resistance. The Manipuri classical dance which depicts the love story of Radha and Krishna is probably an indication of the arrival of the Pandavas and their culture in this part of our country.

Nakula had two more wives in addition to Draupadi. One of them was Karenumati, daughter of Shishupala. The latter was a Chedi king. He also married the princess of Madra.

The last of the Pandavas brothers, Sahadeva had three more wives other than Draupadi. He married Vijaya, princess of Madra, apart from marrying Bhanumati, a Yadava princess.

He also got married to Jarasanadha's daughter Bhima. This marriage has some interesting background. Her father died in a fight with Bhima. Jarasanadha's son, also named as Sahadeva, accepted Yudhisthira as their lord and sovereign. He then proposed the marriage of his sister named 'Bhima' with the second Pandava, Bhima. But Bhima asked his brother Sahadeva to get married with Jarasanadha's daughter, Bhima.

On the Kaurava front, the track record is unblemished, as far as polygamy is concerned. The reason may be heredity and the environment in which they were brought up.

Duryodhana had married only once. His wife Bhanumati was the daughter of Bhanuman. She was in fact the sister-in-law of Bhima. She was called 'Satiratna' in Mahabharata. She was an ideal wife who was ready to sacrifice anything for the happiness of her husband. This, she had demonstrated during the marriage of Subhadra. She nodded in favour of the marriage of Subhadra with Duryodhana when Balarama had proposed the match. But, the marriage didn't take place as Arjuna kidnapped Subhadra and got married to her.

However, Dhritarashtra got involved in an adulterous relation with a maidservant engaged in looking after him when Gandhari was pregnant. Their union gave birth to Duryodhana's step brother Yuyutshu. This would have invited a case under section 493 IPC for cohabitation, with provision for imprisonment upto ten years.

Lastly, Karna had two wives, one was called Vrushali, daughter of a charioteer. His second wife Supriya was Bhanumati's friend. At her request Karna, married Supriya. It is not known if it was with or without the consent of his first wife Vrushali. He had a decent married life. But, this bigamy would have been costly for him and would constitute an offence under section 494 IPC. He should have suffered punishment of upto seven years' jail term and fine."

I rang up Harleen just after dinner at around 10.30 p.m. To my pleasant surprise, I found that she had boarded a bus to go from Ajmer to Ludhiana. She said that they had utilized the time in the morning to visit Pushkar. But in the afternoon, the weather was too hot to stay outside. So they decided to leave Ajmer in the night itself by bus. She hinted something else, which had prompted uncle Baldev to change his plan of journeying by train. I recited William Blake:

> Every Night and every Morn
> Some to Misery are born.
> Every Morn and every Night
> Some are born to Sweet delight,
> Some are born to Endless Night.

❖❖❖

XXVI

We remained extremely busy at the ground on the third day of our stay at Dehri. I completed the medical tests of the candidates. Physical measurements and verification of documents were also complete. But, considering the detection of false personification cases, we decided to carry out physical measurements and verification of documents once more, at a later stage of the rally. The progress of physical tests was also satisfactory.

On the way back to our guesthouse around five, we visited the local police outpost to enquire about the threat perception from Maoists. We met the SHO, Sub-Inspector Satyadev Jha. He informed us that during the last three months, only one incident of kidnapping by Maoists was reported from his jurisdiction. But, adjoining Aurangabad, located on the other side of Sone river, had been worst affected by leftwing extremism. He also advised us not to keep weapons and assured of security coverage around Indrapuri.

After return to Indrapuri, we all took a bath. At around 7 p.m., we went to Sone Bridge. Which was at a waking distance. The water level of Sone was very low. Practically the river-bed was exposed.

We found some fishermen with their boats. Anup Kumar talked with them in their mother tongue and arranged for a boating excursion. It was a nice, pleasant trip for about half an hour under the moonlight. We used two boats, but none of the boatmen was ready to take money from us. We were further indebted when Anup Kumar took pieces of 'litti' from them. It is a typical Bihar food item, prepared from wheat filled with chana and sattu by roasting the same on charcoal fire.

The sand of Sone river is very precious. The other day Mohit Kumar was praising it to the skies. Royalty from this is a good source of revenue for Rohtas district. I took a look at the sand, against the moonlight. But I failed to detect any speciality, except for its purity. It seemed reddish in colour.

The depth of the river-bed from the bank is about a hundred meters. It was quite an exercise for us to reach the cemented embankment. The weather was breezy and pleasant. Anup Kumar floated the proposal of spending the night on the barrage, as guests of Mohit Kumar. He would be on night duty at the barrage from 10 p.m. onwards. Traffic along the road was very thin. We came across only two motorcycles crossing towards Aurangabad from Dehri side. On one motorcycle, a girl was riding as pillion with her lover. This sight prompted me to start thinking about Harleen.

As if by telepathy, I received a call from Harleen, giving confirmation about their return to Ludhiana. I told her about our experience of boating on Sone river. Her experience had been mixed. The officials at subdivisional magistrate's office, Bharatpur were very cooperative. They provided the requisite documents without any hassles.

The centre of attraction at Bharatpur is Keoladeo Ghana National Park. Unfortunately, they found the water body and marshlands dried up. The authorities tried their sincerest best to keep the park alive by pumping water from bore wells. Even then, they were fortunate enough to see some sambhars, nilgais, rabbits and a few local birds.

They reached Ajmer on Friday night. Next morning, they went to Khwaja Moinuddin Chisti Dargah in Ajmer. The dargah was very crowded with devotees, mainly Muslims, even in this off season. Two big containers of food, each of which could feed about 20,000 to 25,000 people had caught their attraction.

Spending the day time in Puloma Hotel, they went to Pushkar by bus in the evening. The bus ride took about forty minutes. Pushkar has series of temples, each having a religious myth. Beauty of the place increased manifold due to the presence of three natural lakes within a radius of eight to nine kilometres. According to mythology, lotus flowers from Lord Brahma's hand fell in these three places in Pushkar area, resulting in creation of these lakes.

The Senior Pushkar is the place where the lotus fell first. Hotels are located around this lake. Middle Pushkar has a small Hanuman temple and a very old banyan tree. Junior Pushkar has a small Krishna temple. Pushkar's entomology is that Brahma threw the Pushpa (flower) with his Kar (Hand).

Harleen said, "We were sitting under the banyan tree at Middle Pushkar in the evening. Suddenly, all the bells started ringing. It created an electrifying atmosphere combined with bhajans and resonance of sound of bells. We enjoyed this for quite some time.

On returning to the hotel, we discovered that our room key was missing from the key board. At first, we thought that the key might have been taken by some attendant for changing water. But this wasn't the case. We found the room unlocked and the keys inside. Our belongings were disturbed, though nothing was lost. The miscreants could have taken valuable articles, which they didn't. Suddenly I realized that the purpose of the visit by the thieves was something else. Thank god, the documents related to Aman's death are still in our possession!

Next morning, we took a taxi and moved around Ajmer and Pushkar. But, we curtailed our tour after locating Captain Nilesh Rahane in the crowd in civilian clothes. He slipped away on seeing uncle Baldev. This made us, especially uncle, very anxious."

I went a little away from my comrades while talking to Harleen. When I came back, Mr Sharma said, "I believe everything is well on the other front."

The other two laughed which I ignored and said, "Yeah, Harleen has returned to her house at Ludhiana accompanied by her one-time critics, uncle Baldev and aunt Jasmin."

"This of course is good news", Sharma responded, "I didn't expect the reunion of the two families so fast. Hats off to Harleen, for the courage shown by her!"

I told Mr Sharma about the incidents at Ajmer and Pushkar. Mr Sharma remained silent for a few minutes and then said, "There seems to be a deep-rooted conspiracy behind the murder of Aman. Rajasthan Police may not be able to deal with the case. Baldevji may have to file a writ petition in the Rajasthan High Court for investigation by the CBI. Anyway, tell Harleen to remain very cautious till they meet us at Bhubaneswar."

All of us suddenly became serious. Perhaps to break the shackles, Mr Sharma asked, "What's the name of the hotel Dr Bhaumik, you just mentioned?"

- Sir, you mean to say, the hotel where Harleen stayed with her uncle and aunt in Ajmer?
- Yes, of course!
- Hotel Puloma at Station Road, Ajmer.
- Do you know who Puloma was?
- I've absolutely no idea. Is it related to your Mahabharata?
- Certainly, and you'll find this reference, at the beginning of the epic.

"I thought, probably it is a reference to Pulwama district of Kashmir", this time, it was Kaushik who reacted.

"I don't know the background of Pulwama district of Kashmir", said Mr Sharma, "but this name Puloma is certainly related to the Mahabharata. Puloma was a beautiful lady. She was the wife of saint Bhrigu who was the son of the self-existing Brahma. His son was saint Chyavana.

Before marriage, she was deeply in love with a person of Rakshasa origin, also named Puloma. But her father gave her in marriage to Bhrigu. Their priest, Agni solemnized the marriage. Bhrigu left his homeland with his newly-wedded wife after marriage. He built a hermitage on the banks of Ganges.

Rakshasa Puloma was mad with rage at losing his beloved Puloma. Wandering aimlessly, one day he came to the hermitage of Bhrigu. Puloma was in the hut though Bhrigu wasn't there at that time. She was pregnant. Their family friend, aged Agni was there to look after her. She entertained Rakshasa Puloma with fruits. Seeing her, he was a little doubtful whether she was his beloved Puloma or not. So, he asked Agni about her identity. Agni was in a fix whether to disclose her identity or not. Finally, Agni decided in favour of telling the truth.

On being confirmed about her identity, Rakshasa Puloma abducted her. But, it had so happened that on the way, she delivered her son Chyavana. The myth is that at the mere glance of the new-born baby, Rakshasa Puloma was burnt to ashes. Brahma rescued Puloma and her son Chyavana. She returned to her husband with her son and narrated the incident.

Bhrigu became angry with Agni and he cursed him to remain as eater of everything forever. Invention of fire or Agni is a boon for mankind. But fire is a destroyer as well. According to Hindu mythology, this destructive character of fire was due to the curse of Bhrigu."

"Here also, some case will be attracted", said Kaushik.

"No, I hasn't attach any section to this case, as Rakshasa Puloma met his death", said Mr Sharma, "it'll only attract the case of an unnatural death. My belief is that Rakshasa Puloma committed suicide, the moment he realized his fault. He practically became a psychic."

It was 10.30 in the night and so we returned to the guesthouse for our dinner.

❖❖❖

XXVII

On 20th May, we left our guesthouse very early. Before that, I spoke to Harleen and asked her to remain extremely cautious these days. I also apprised her about the preference given by Mr Sharma towards entrusting the investigation of Aman's death to CBI.

We spent the whole day in the ground conducting written and oral tests. Apprehending possible mischief from miscreants, taking advantage of the load-shedding, we didn't carry out any tests after dusk. So, we returned to Indrapuri guest house by six in the evening.

During our evening gossip at the guesthouse, Anup Kumar arranged special Behari food Litti and Chatni through Sahuji alongwith tea. I told Mr Sharma about my conversation with Harleen earlier during the day. I put a point before him, "Sir, one thing I don't understand! You're a police officer from the state, yet you prefer a CBI investigation!"

- It is just like you referring patients to hospitals outside the state, for better treatment.
- But, investigation of a case can never be equated with treatment of a disease. Moreover, in the latter case, you can go anywhere as per your choice and budget.
- Police is a state subject. The investigation of cases, and even fighting problems like Maoism are the responsibility of the concerned state government.

But the diversity and complexity of this case is enormous. First of all, it'll be difficult for the state government agencies to ferret out clues from within the force's establishment. There's every possibility of a deep-rooted conspiracy, involving some big shots. The initial investigation itself is very sketchy. In such circumstances, only a central investigating agency like CBI may do some justice. I am sure that from Black Panther Rifles headquarters, there would be pressure for pushing the case to a departmental enquiry or a court martial.

Just at that moment Mohit Kumar joined us. He said, "Hope I've not disturbed you."

"Not at all!" said Mr Sharma. "We're discussing about the lack of responsibilities and the inconsistencies in the manner in which state governments are tackling problems like insurgency. You may also throw some light upon the issue, particularly Maoism. This you're facing in your state."

We felt extremely pleased with the cleverness with which Mr Sharma changed the topic of discussion. Mohit Kumar seemed elated for being chosen by Mr Sharma for answering this question. In India, such middle level officers sometimes possess in-depth knowledge about social dynamics.

He provided vital information about the merger of Communist Party of India (Marxist-Leninist) with People's War Group (PWG) of Andhra Pradesh in adjoining Jahanabad, Bihar sometimes in 1998. Since then, most of the Naxalite factions had further come under a single umbrella, known as 'Maoism'.

Appreciating him for his wisdom, Mr Sharma said, "Tell us about the method of operation of the Maoists."

Mr Kumar obliged enthusiastically, "They generally don't harass local people, so long as they continue to get their support, and can conceal their identity from the police and security forces. They would commit crimes away from their places of stay. Money seems to be no problem for the Maoists in Bihar and Jharkhand as they have earned several hundred crores as levy from big businessmen. They would not touch employees like us."

"Have you ever come across any Maoist?" Kaushik asked.

"On quite a number of occasions, in my village in Jahanabad district", said Mohit Kumar, "and, at least once in Dehri during the last winter. I was doing night shift at the barrage. They were six in number, on three motorcycles wearing jackets. They called me by name and asked me about police movement, and finally went towards Aurangabad. Two days later, I came to know that Maoists had blasted the Nadaul railway station on the Patna-Gaya section, Danapur Division. Their intelligence network is very strong."

Anup Kumar said, "Nadaul is not far away from this location, hardly 50 to 60 k.m."

"They're like Robin Hood for the villagers", said Mohit Kumar, "but in today's society, people have to go out of their native places in quest of knowledge, livelihood and earning for future. The moment one goes out of his village, he comes under the scanner of Maoists. In case of any raids by the police or security forces on their dens, they'll catch him and hold Kangaroo courts, after the departure of the police. Heavy penalty will be imposed upon him. They may even kill him in front of villagers, claiming him to be a police informer."

"Which are the areas that are affected by Maoist activities in Bihar?" Kaushik made a query.

"Apart from Rohtas and Jahanabad districts, the other major affected districts are Patna, Aurangabad, Gaya, Buxur, Saharsha, Khagaria, Banka, Jamui and may be a few more", said Mohit Kumar.

"I'm fortunate that my Bhagalpur is not affected", Anup Kumar confessed, "in fact I've not come across any Maoist incident in my life time. We remain deployed along the international border only."

"You're right in one sense", said Mr Sharma. "But international border with Nepal along Bihar and Uttar Pradesh is the hub of Maoist activities. It is treated as a red-corridor. I believe SSB and ITBP are entrusted with guarding the Indo-Nepal border."

"Yeah!" said Anup Kumar, "as the name suggests, Indo-Tibetan Border Police (ITBP) mainly guards the border with China. As Nepal is a friendly country and there's no concept of passports, vast portion of our border with Nepal practically remains porous. Maoists avail of this situation to extend their activities."

"I've seen in newspapers recently that in approximately 220 districts spreading over twenty states of India, Naxalites are active. In terms of geographic area, it covers almost 40 per cent of our land. Maoists are active in states like Andhra Pradesh, Bihar, Jharkhand, Orissa, Maharashtra, Chhattisgarh, Madhya Pradesh, West Bengal and may be even Karnataka", said Mohit Kumar.

"Mr Kumar is absolutely right", said Mr Sharma, "Maoists are a major threat to internal security in India. They've approximately 20,000 armed cadres in addition to 50,000 regular cadres."

"What are the reasons for their growth", Kaushik asked.

"Reasons would be many", said Mohit Kumar, "and perhaps you've realized by staying here for the last 4 to 5 days. Have you seen any development work?"

"Compared to my state, hardly any development work has caught my notice", Kaushik replied.

"You're very correct!" said Mohit Kumar. "In the last twenty years, not a single brick has been fixed. The condition of electricity, well, you've gathered enough experience already."

"Yes, these shortcomings get aggravated", said Mr Sharma, "in the absence of democratic decentralization. We've not noticed any Panchayat activity here."

"You've detected the disease properly," an elated Mohit Kumar responded.

"But Sir, your formula doesn't hold good in case of West Bengal", said Kaushik. "In spite of elected Panchayats, many districts of Bengal are facing the Maoists problem."

"Thanks for raising this question, Kaushik", said Mr Sharma, "things are little different in Bengal. One reason for the survival of Panchayat system in Bengal is bipolar politics for more than thirty years. When the party in power is sure about its success in Panchayats, it goes in for election to these local bodies. But the political equation is rapidly changing in West Bengal. With the increase in strength of the opposition, there's resistance to the very existence of the Panchayati system. Even small corruption issues are blown out of proportion. There are about sixty odd Panchayats in Lalgarh, Midnapore. More than half of these are presently closed. This is total anarchism. If the Panchayat Pradhans or members are corrupt, they should be booked and punished under appropriate section of laws. Closure of Panchayats is not a solution.

Remember the beginning of Lalgarh agitation. The initial issue was police atrocities in the aftermath of Shalbani bomb blast. Is it not bizarre that a district police superintendent had to beg for forgiveness before the masses for a lapse not committed by him. That too, before the allegation was even proved.

We've also faced similar situation in Tripura. Extremist groups, especially the National Liberation Front of Twipra

(NLFT) used to bring allegations against TSR of atrocities upon the tribals. These allegations get fuelled following some incidents of arsons, alleged to be committed by TSR personnel in the aftermath of losing their comrades in extremist attacks. We suitably punished the TSR personnel involved in such incidents after identifying them properly. This apart, we've brought a humane touch in TSR through better police-public relationship. This is providing us good dividends. We've not faced a single major allegation of human rights violation against TSR for almost a decade. This paves the path of our success against the extremists in Tripura."

"I don't think police officers in our state carry out such in-depth analysis", Mohit Kumar expressed his doubt.

"Actually to meet such a law and order situation, there should be proper infrastructures", said Mr Sharma, "state police forces need immediate modernization to meet this challenge."

We called it a day around midnight.

❖❖❖

XXVIII

We finished our task at Dehri-on-Sone as per our target on 21st May 2008, Wednesday afternoon. So we allowed our staff to visit Sasaram in the evening. We're leaving Dehri for Hazaribag tomorrow morning after early lunch.

I rang Harleen in the evening. I told her about our travelling plans for tomorrow. We shall reach our next venue Ranchi, the day after. She started laughing, the moment I uttered the word Ranchi.

- Please visit the mental asylum at Ranchi.
- Do you think I'm a mad?

- Not at all! But as a medical officer, you should visit this premier mental hospital.
- Thank God, you've not diagnosed me as mad! But frankly speaking, I may be mad for you!

She took the gesture positively and started laughing again. This time I couldn't find any reason for the mirth.

- There's a story involving this mental hospital. Just after independence, our first Prime Minister Jawaharlal Nehru once visited this hospital. He introduced himself to the inmates. One of the inmates responded by saying that for the first time, everybody calls himself the Prime Minister only! Actual identity will be exposed only after a few days' stay. The inmate treated Nehru as a new patient!
- I think it's a joke.
- That's for you to judge. That's why I've suggested that you visit this hospital.
- OK, I shall try to enquire. But what about the treatment for my madness!
- This I shall prescribe after examining the patient physically.

I felt relaxed, and recited Browning:

Dear rose, thy term is reached,
Thy leaf hangs loose and bleached:
Bees pass it unimpeached.

In the evening, Sahuji served fish pakoras with tea. They were marvellous. Sahuji disclosed the secret of the recipe to Kaushik. Sahuji worked in a hotel in Boubazar, Kolkata for almost ten years before joining this service. Perhaps, this Bengal connection inspired Anup Kumar to ask Mr Sharma, "What's your analysis of the Singur problem?"

This question put him slightly off-guard, as he replied, "See, I'm not an inhabitant of Bengal, though I'm a Bengali. One senior officer told us an interesting story during our basic training. It is the story of an IPS officer. After his induction in Indian Police Service, he was allotted the Bengal Cadre. He was a Jat, from Haryana. His father was a farmer and illiterate. When he was leaving for West Bengal, he sought blessings from his father.

His father said that he didn't know much about bureaucracy, but one thing he'd advice his son and that is not to argue with Bengali people, and always keep them at distance. Singur is a vivid example of this argumentative Bengali character."

We all laughed, as he explained further, "Perhaps, you still remember the story of the 'Miller and the Donkey', you read in your childhood."

We remained silent. He went on to describe, "Once upon a time there was a miller. He had a donkey. He decided to sell his donkey. One day, he and his son left their house for the market with the donkey. It was a hot day. Initially, the miller was riding the donkey while his son followed him on foot. Seeing this, the pedestrians started saying, 'Look, the father is enjoying the ride leaving his son walking under the scorching sun. He's so inhuman.'

The miller was deeply moved by the criticism. He at once got down from the donkey and asked his son to ride. After sometime, some other pedestrians started saying, 'Look, the young boy is enjoying the ride forcing his aged father to toil.'

This proposition was also not suitable for them. They decided to ride the donkey together. After sometime, some other people noticed them. They said, 'Look, how cruel this miller and his son are! They're riding this poor donkey together.'

The miller and his son were in a fix. Finally, they decided to carry the donkey on their shoulders by tying a bamboo with its legs. Seeing this, the pedestrians started laughing. They were very close to the market and crossing a bridge. They were just about to lower their load. But the donkey got off balance and fell into the river below, and died eventually."

I tried to link this story with the Singur problem. But I didn't find any similarity. Seeing me confused, Mr Sharma asked, "What's the moral of this story?"

Kaushik replied in a flash, "One who tries to please everybody can please nobody."

"Right" he said, "we the Bengali people basically live like the miller. We try to please everybody and in the process, fail to please anybody. There are too many conflicting interests in Singur, which I shall touch upon; inference can be drawn by you yourself.

In the 1950s, West Bengal was one of the most industrialized states in our country. Industrial plants in Durgapur, Asansole, Kalyani, Howrah and Calcutta had come up during this period. But the disturbance in 1960s and 1970s in the form of militant trade-unionism, Bangladesh War and of course Naxalite movement slowed down the industrial development. Consequently, states like Maharashtra, Gujarat, Punjab, Tamil Nadu and Karnataka attracted industrial investment and experienced tremendous growth.

The present government established in 1978 introduced land reforms and was successful in giving a boost to agricultural production. But as a matter of fact, the growth in agriculture would be always less than the industrial growth, and its impact would be nullified due to increase in population. The population density in West Bengal is probably one of the highest in our country. Moreover, agriculture is an expensive occupation now days. It has become difficult for the small farmers to bear the expenses of fertilizers, seeds and irrigation. The situation gets aggravated by repeated floods and draughts. Suicides by farmers in our country are an indicator of this. Only the big farmers or community farming can survive this onslaught. Government tries to compensate the loss suffered by the farmers through soft bank loans, National Rural Employment Guarantee Scheme, etc.

But for job opportunity, particularly for the educated unemployed youth, one has to adopt the path of industrialization. Realizing this candid truth, the state government has made all out efforts to invite investments in industry."

While we were listening to Mr Sharma, there was pin drop silence and we didn't even notice when Mohit Kumar joined us, till the latter said, "You've depicted the exact story of Bengal."

He accepted the acclamation and continued, "Now, I will just point out the salient points of these conflicts. For industrialization, one needs a good brand and Tata fulfills this criteria. Tata was shown four or five different locations and they preferred Singur under Hoogli district for establishing a small car factory for manufacturing Nano. This would be the cheapest car in the world.

To take advantage of Land Acquisition Act, 1894, Tatas went for acquisition of about 1,000 acres of land through the state government. A good number of land owners were not actually staying in the location. Perhaps for that reason, the state government agencies underestimated the possible resistance. The land holdings of the farmers are small with insufficient yields to sustain their families. Majority of the land owners gave consent while a good percentage didn't.

They claimed that they'd get more compensation, had the deal been struck directly with Tata. The interest of behind-the-scene actors like competitors of Tata from the automobile sector is also a factor, apart from politicking of Bengali people."

Anup Kumar said, "The dealing of the issue by West Bengal police is pathetic. Consider the firing at Nandigram, there was absolutely no professionalism."

Mr Sharma remained silent.

Kaushik said, "The two cases are not similar; at Nandigram there was no conscious effort by the government to acquire land."

This time Mr Sharma broke the silence, "I think we shouldn't discuss Nandigram since it's a sub-judiced issue. But I'm highly impressed by the remarks of Anup Kumar about the lack of professionalism, on the part of West Bengal police.

About a year back, I came across a senior police officer from West Bengal in an in-service training. He was holding a very important field posting. His jurisdiction included Nandigram.

Just out of curiosity, I asked him about law and order situation in his area. To my utter surprise, he replied that the previous night, Maoists had robbed an outpost in his jurisdiction. I was completely at a loss and couldn't imagine how the gentleman had left his state after such a serious incident!"

I asked, "Sir, I've not seen it in the newspapers!

He replied, "You would not find such news in newspapers and practically the police can do nothing in this area."

Then he went on to describe the topography of the area. One can't approach Nandigram without crossing numerous canals. Even during the British rule, Nandigram police station was captured by freedom fighters and kept under seige, for quite a number of days.

I didn't comment. He narrated the technological advances made by West Bengal police. I preferred to listen as the latter was senior to me in rank. But, I cherish a feeling that the technological advancement gives an opportunity to some malingerers to evade duty. You'll find numerous examples of this if you open your eyes."

We all cackled, and left for dinner, as it was eleven in the night.

❖❖❖

XXIX

We witnessed a little drizzle at Dehri on the morning of our departure on 22nd May. While serving bed tea, Sahuji said, "I've never witnessed shower during the month of May at Dehri, in the last ten years. It is by yours grace only that this spectacle has happened!"

I thanked him for the good words, and his service during the last six days.

Harleen rang me up at around seven. As usual I narrated to her our gossips of last night. She started laughing. But this time, I've learnt the secret of her laughter. Obviously, she has some story in her mind. So I pressed her.

- It is just a joke. It has come to my mind from Mr Sharma's observation about the argumentative Bengali race. The story dates back to independence period. It is about three families, one from my race, Punjabis, one Marwadi and one from your race, Bengalis. They were refugees from Pakistan. Each was provided with ₹ 1,000 as financial assistance for rehabilitation, just after partition. In those days ₹ 1,000 was highly valued. After 25 years, a survey was carried out to ascertain the status of these families.
- This is something really interesting.
- The Punjabi family had purchased a farm house and a couple of cattle. They're now well-settled with one of their sons serving in armed forces. Their family can be treated as upper middle class. They deal in lakhs.

The Marwadi family on the other hand had invested the entire money in business. Despite initial adversity, they're very rich and have at least three shops in prime locations in Rajasthan. They deal in crores.

The Bengali family had purchased books for ₹ 800. The remaining money was spent for purchasing pens and note books. They're now living in a small cottage with their well-educated sons and a daughter. In terms of earnings, they deal in thousands.

- I'm a bit confused. Is it a compliment or criticism for the Bengali people? The Punjabi family is in the advantageous position.
- How?
- Because the second generation Punjabis have picked up the characters of Marwadis, like your brother, who's in business. At the same time, they're getting

educated like Bengali people. Vivid example is Dr (Miss) Harleen Bedi.

- In that sense you're right. The Bengali people can't yet come out of their shackles. Still their need is so simple—a small cottage, a small job, books and the latest addition, a laptop.
- You've studied a lot about Bengalis!
- How can I ever ignore Bengalis? Especially these days, when a Bengali knight is tormenting my dreams.
- Any further clue about the knight?
- The Don Quixote will soon visit an asylum.
- OK, I shall try to take the assistance of Mr Sharma to identify the knight who dares to spoil the sleep of my fair lady!
- Convey my best wishes to him and your other companions.
- Is there any further nugget about Bengalis in your pocket?
- I know the story of Bengalis from Bengal only, not from Tripura. One thing you can tell Mr Sharma that the flats which are coming up in Kolkata would be beyond the reach of Bengalis.
- Thank you, Dr (Miss) Harleen Bedi for such critical dissertation of Bengalis.
- Credit should go to Dr Chauhan, my boss; he attended a dinner in our house yesterday. He might be in turn indebted to his friend, Dr Jayanta Mallik.

By the way, the Bengalis, especially the new generation, are not so puritan. At least they've learnt how to venture out of the confines of their four walls.

- Thanks for your candid observation, but this may be the reason for the lack of cohesion amongst Bengalis. In a sense, it is another form of partition, a drifting away from the binding force of the nucleus.

- Best wishes to Dr Ashamanja, for presentation of this new theory of social-dynamics.

I recited, 'Women and Roses':

Dear rose, thy joy's undimmed,
Thy cup is rub-rimmed,
Thy cup's heart nectar-brimmed.

❖❖❖

XXX

We reached Hazaribagh by around 2 p.m. Kamal Singh received us at the stand and took us to DVC guesthouse located in the heart of the town. Our supporting staff were accommodated at the district police barrack. The journey from Dehri to Hazaribagh had been rather pleasant, passing through green areas, almost for the entire portion of the journey. The distance is about 55 k.m. We moved half the distance along NH-2 upto Bashi, and then through NH-33.

Hazaribagh, the town of a thousand tigers, is a health resort. With depletion of the tiger population, the literal meaning of 'Hazaribagh' has been changed to 'city of a thousand gardens'. We found a beautiful garden around a pond in the heart of the city. But there were no flowers as it was the off-season. We decided to see the Hazaribagh before going for dinner to Kamal Singh's house. Driver Rafique Ansari, being a native of this place, became our guide. As advised by Kamal Singh, we didn't move far away from the Hazaribagh municipal area. This was on account of the Maoist threats. We skipped our programme to visit Canary Hills and Hazaribagh Wild Life Sanctuary. Instead we moved around the market area and visited Hazaribagh District Jail from outside.

Mr Sharma said, "It is a historical jail of India, freedom fighters like Dr Rajendra Prasad, Jay Prakash Narayan and many others arrested during the Quit India Movement in 1942, were kept in this jail. Escape of Jay Prakash Narayan from this high security prison is one of the legends of the Indian Independence Movement."

"So, it is an Angrej ke jamane ki jail", Kaushik commented, mimicking *Sholay*.

He replied, "The place itself is historic and associated with Santhal rebellion and first battle of Independence in 1857. We shall listen to the stories from Kamal Singh, this evening."

We took snacks at a restaurant, in a Muslim-populated area and enjoyed great hospitality. The city has a sizeable Mohammedan population. Our staff took early dinner and went to see movies in two groups.

We found Kamal Singh waiting for us at seven when we reached his house on foot. Built by his father late Mahendra Singh, it is a big palatial building. His father worked in Dhanbad coal fields. The arrangements for dinner were excellent, and I'd say lavish. Kamal Singh had invited two of his friends, Jaswant Singh and Pradip Kumar. The former is a journalist with a local daily, while the other is a professor of political science at Vinoba Bhave University, Hazaribagh. The interaction between Mr Sharma and Mr Kumar, especially on the history of formation of Jharkhand state, was quite lively. Kamal Singh and Jaswant Singh also contributed at times. When we came out of the house of Mr Singh at half past eleven, I had a fair idea about 'the land of Ulgulan'.

Jharkhand state was created on 15th November 2000, on the birth anniversary of Birsa Munda, the legendary Santhal hero. The Santhals are the largest tribal community in India who live mainly in the states of Jharkhand, West Bengal, Bihar, Orissa and Assam. There's also a significant population of Santhal in Bangladesh and Nepal.

The Santhali script or Chiki is a relatively recent innovation. Till the twentieth century, the Santhals used Latin/Roman, Devnagari and Bengali alphabets. Chiki doesn't share any of the syllabic properties of other Indian scripts such as Devnagari. It uses 30 letters, 6 basic vowels and 3 additional vowels.

The Santhali culture has attracted many scholars, anthropologists and Christian missionaries for decades. Unlike many other tribal groups of Indian sub-continent, the Santhals have preserved their native language, despite waves of migrations and invasions such as those by the Aryans, Huns, Mughals, Europeans and others. Santhali culture is depicted in the paintings and art works in the walls of their houses.

The Santhals may earn a place in the Guinness records for maximum number of armed revolts. Their resistance and sacrifice of masses against the might of the British Government is unparalleled. Prominent amongst these are Mal Paharia revolt, Santhal revolt under the leadership of Tilka Manjhi, Munda revolt in Tamar under the leadership of Bishnu Manki and Maiju Manki, Chaur revolt, Munda revolt in Palamu under the leadership of Bhukan Munda, Ho upspring, Oraon revolt under the leadership of Budhu Bhagat, Santhal Hul under the leadership of Sidoh and Kanoh Murmu, Sardar movement under Munda tribes and of course, Munda Ulgulan revolt under the leadership of Birsa Munda.

Adivasi armed revolts and resistance are characteristically different from other contemporary instances of struggle for independence. They used bows, arrows and other traditional arms against fire arms. Their struggle was for freedom, natural justice, identity and traditional rights over land, forest and water. They adopted the tactics of guerrilla warfare. They fought against the British army and their sepoys, police, Zamindars, money lenders and government administrators.

Birsa Munda is treated as a legendary Bhagwan here. He was a tribal leader and a folk hero, belonging to Munda tribe. His name is taken with great respect as one of the freedom fighters of the Indian struggle for independence against British colonialism. He was born on 15th November 1875 on a Thursday. He was named, after the day of his birth, according to the then prevalent Munda custom. By the time he was in his 20s, his activities in the tribal areas of Jharkhand state (earlier Bihar) had already begun to worry the British establishment to a considerable extent. He was finally caught by the British when he was just 25 years old. He died soon afterwards under mysterious circumstances in Ranchi Jail.

Permanent zamindari settlement of 1793 added to the woes of adivasis. Obviously, adivasis didn't have faith in sepoys and feudal lords, who led the 1857 war of independence. Yet, 1857 war of independence in Jharkhand broke out at Hazaribagh on 30th July when Santhals rebelled against the East India Company's government, broke the jail and freed the prisoners. The Hazaribagh Deputy Commissioner fled to Barhi. Hazaribagh became free.

The credit for mobilizing the Santhal adivasis against the Company's government goes to Shekh Bhikhari. He himself was a Zamindar of 12 villages. Later, he became dewan of Khatanga State of Tikait Umrao Singh. Both of them were patriots. They closely followed the war of independence which had begun in other parts of the country. They encouraged the sepoys of Ramgarh army battalion to revolt. The foreign officers and loyal sepoys were defeated in Chutupalu Ghat.

In this process, beginning on 30th July 1857 within a few months, large areas of Hazaribagh, Ramgarh, Ranchi and Palamu of present day Jharkhand were liberated from the British rule. But, the freedom fighters couldn't sustain at the local level due to disunity, absence of central command, lack of trained armed personnel and ammunitions.

By 1858, the war of independence in the area of present Jharkhand was ruthlessly suppressed by the British army. Two hundred Santhal rebels in Hazaribagh and hundreds of sepoys were executed.

In 1857 feudal India, the declared objective of the war of independence was to re-establish the Mughal emperor to the Delhi throne. At the local level, the freedom fighters wanted to establish their native rule and maintain their feudal social system and cultural identity. The First War of Independence was naturally led by feudal lords.

The concept of parliamentary democratic system in India came by the end of the nineteenth century with the growth of industrialization and formation of national bourgeoisies. The role of the working class, their ideological and political struggle came much later.

Kaushik and I remained silent listeners, as Mr Sharma exchanged his views with Prof. Pradip Kumar. Kaushik put a last question before our Hazaribagh friends, "What's the reason for the Maoist upsurge here?"

Jaswant Singh said, "Let me answer this question. Jharkhand is famous for its rich mineral resources starting from uranium, mica, bauxite, granite, gold, silver, graphite, magnetite, dolomite, fire clay, quartz, feldspar, coal, iron, copper, etc. The coal available here is one-third of the total coal reserve in India while copper accounts for one-fourth of the entire reserve in our country. Forests and woodlands occupy about 30 per cent of the state. Barring the north-eastern states like your Tripura, it'll be the highest in India.

Yet, after 60 years of independence, we fail to provide the indigenous inhabitants with the three basic needs—food, clothing and shelter. Very seldom, can the adivasis avail the benefit of forest products from their land. Sometimes, the overly-stringent provisions of the Indian Forest Act, curtail even eco-friendly practices of the tribals."

Mr Sharma said, "It is a Herculean task. Our state government is very interested in induction of boys in our elite Tripura State Rifles (TSR) from this area. Precisely, for this reason, we're going to Ranchi for conducting a recruitment rally. Please encourage the youths, especially tribal boys from your state as well as from adjoining Orissa and Chattisgarh to make use of this opportunity."

Jaswant Singh assured proper coverage of the recruitment rally in the local media.

❖❖❖

XXXI

On 23rd May, at around 10.30 a.m., driver Rafique Ansari invited our entire team for early lunch at his house before departure around ten. The food was delicious. We enjoyed fried rice with chicken followed by some sweet as per Muslim custom.

We covered the distance of 77 k.m. from Hazaribagh to Ranchi along the NH-33 in two hours. But, after entering Ranchi municipal area, we faced repeated security checks. We could reach the district police lines, Ranchi at around 1.30 p.m. only. Mr Sharma contacted the District Superintendent of Police, Ranchi over his cell phone. He in turn arranged all our accommodation. One hardcore Maoist had escaped from police custody that day itself. The reason for stringent police checks could be guessed.

We, the officers, got accommodation in the circuit house, Ranchi while our staff stayed at district police lines. The circuit house is a new building that is air-conditioned. At the same time, it is the hub of political activities in Jharkhand. The rooms are occupied by the politicians of various political groups. The lobby and dinning halls are filled with their supporters. I apprised Harleen about our safe arrival.

It is our fourth venue for recruitment. Our support staff has become expert by this time in handling the various tasks. We decided to have a look round the city. Anup Kumar hadn't yet returned from his house.

At the second crossing from our place of stay, we found a big cultural festival of the Bengalis in progress. We had to stop our vehicle due to a traffic jam. The gathering was huge. We had a look around the stalls. The organizers had displayed the rich Bengali culture. One minister of Jharkhand also adorned the dais amidst chorus of Bengali recitation, songs, dances, etc. After spending an hour or so in the company of this sizeable Bengali population, we went to see the market area. The city looked nice and vibrant. We returned to the circuit house by half past nine.

❖❖❖

XXXII

The attendance at the ground was less compared to other venues, on the opening day. We returned to the circuit house a bit early, after distribution of tokens. We first roamed around Ranchi city, and by 7 p.m., assembled in Mr Sharma's room. In this circuit house, we can't use the lobby for our evening discussions. It remains busy with VIP visits. Anup Kumar has arrived today with his two lovely kids. Daughter Ankita is studying in Class III and son Ayush is studying in KG-II. Mr Sharma provided him with the Maruti Gypsy and made his duty in the field optional.

We enjoyed the IPL match between Delhi Daredevils and Mumbai Indians played at Feroz Shah Kotla in Delhi. The home team won the match.

After the match, Kaushik reminded Mr Sharma about his promise to tell the story of chemical weapons used by Arjuna. He thanked Kaushik for remembering, and begun, "It's my presumption, and you may not find any explanation anywhere, as this had happened before the Kurukshetra battle. After Yudhisthira lost the second game of dice in Hastinapura Assembly with Shakuni, the Pandavas suffered thirteen years' exile, including one year's incognito. The Pandavas with their wife Draupadi spent the thirteenth year in Virat's court in disguise. It was the last day of their hiding. Ever since the beginning of the thirteenth year, the spies of Duryodhana had been busy searching for the Pandavas.

Kichaka was the chief of army of Virat kingdom. Incidentally, he was the brother of queen Sudeshna. He was brutally murdered by Bhima for his sexual harassment of Draupadi who was serving as personal companion and serving-maid of Virat queen, Sudeshna. She posed herself as Sairandhri, wife of a Gandharba. Realizing the involvement of Sairandhri behind the murder of Kichaka, the queen told her to leave the city immediately. But Draupadi stayed back, saying that her Gandharba husband would be in a position to take her back soon. The queen Sudeshna acceded to this request. She was terrified at the murder of her brother.

According to another version of the Mahabharata, after the death of Kichaka, his brothers, one hundred and five in number, told king Virat that because of Sairandhri, Kichaka was killed. So, she should be burnt with Kichaka in the same pyre. King Virat acceded to their pressure, and ordered in favour of sati. Draupadi was dragged to the burning place of Kichaka by his brothers. She was tied to the pyre. Just when the Kichaka brothers were about to set fire to the pyre, Bhima arrived there. He uprooted a tree, and using the same as weapon, he killed all the Kichaka brothers.

From the death of Kichaka, Duryodhana could make out that the Pandavas were hiding in the Matsya kingdom of Virat. So he, along with Karna, worked out a plan to attack Virat kingdom with their ally, king Susharma of Trigarta, and others. Their intention was to recognize the Pandavas before the stipulated period of exile. In that case, they could send the Pandavas back to exile for a fresh term of thirteen years, as per the condition of the game of dice. They decided to rob Virat of his cattle wealth if they failed to locate the Pandavas.

The Kaurava army led by Susharma attacked Matsya from one side and captured Virat's cattle. Both the armies clashed. Virat's chariot was surrounded by the enemies, and he was taken captive.

Bhima rallied the routed force of Virat and attacked the enemy. He got Virat released and captured Susharma. But, Yudhisthira told Bhima to take pity on him and let him go. Disgraced and humiliated, Susharma returned from the field. Virat praised Bhima alias Valhalla and his brothers. They spent the night on the battlefield talking merrily. The people in the capital city were making preparations to receive the triumphant king and his army.

In the meantime, Duryodhana attacked the capital from another side. They captured cattle in thousands, and pushed towards Virat. The cowherds ran in panic to the city to seek protection. There, they found only prince Uttar.

Prince Uttar said to them, "I can defeat and drive away enemy. But I need a charioteer."

Arjuna was hiding in the royal palace as an eunuch with pseudo name Brihannala. He was engaged as music-cum-dance teacher in king's harem. He heard Uttar's words and told Draupadi to approach the princess Uttara to allow him to be a charioteer. Draupadi, in the guise of Sairandhri, spoke to the princess on Arjuna's behalf. Prince Uttar agreed to use Brihannala's services as a charioteer.

Arjuna knowingly donned his armour in a very awkward fashion and with a hesitation. This made the royal ladies laugh heartily. Princess Uttara and her maidens laughed, they said, "Brave Brihannala! Bring pretty garments for our dolls from the battle field."

Soon, they were both speeding away in their chariot to the battlefield. On reaching there, Uttar saw the large Kaurava army and his courage failed. He grew nervous and frightened. He requested Arjuna to take him back to the city. Arjuna encouraged him by saying, "Be fearless. You're a Kshatriya prince. People will laugh and mock at you if you turn your back now. Even the ladies won't spare you."

But, terrified Uttar jumped down from the chariot. He ran back towards the city. Arjuna chased and caught him. Then, he sped to the burial ground, where his weapons were kept concealed. These were kept hanging high up a Sami tree in a bundle, shaped like corpse. Arjuna made prince Uttar climb up the tree to take the bundle of weapons down. The bundle was brought down. It was untied. Uttar stood wonderstruck on seeing such shining weapons, and asked, "Whose are these?"

"These belong to the mighty Pandavas."

"But, where are they now?"

Then, Arjuna revealed their identity to Uttar. This revelation made the prince bold and fearless. He welcomed Arjuna, and took the charioteer's seat. Arjuna blew his famous conch and twanged the Gandiv.

Duryodhana said, "This is Arjuna, we've discovered him. He'll have to go in exile again for twelve years."

"The period of exile is already over", said Bhishma after calculating the time.

In the meantime, Karna attacked Arjuna and a fierce but decisive battle raged. The sky was overcast with sharp arrows, sent out by the opposing warriors. Arjuna shot his arrows in all directions with great precision. The Kaurava army had to retreat. It amazed Drona, Bhishma and all. Soon, Arjuna came up to Duryodhana and forced the latter to give up. Bhishma, Drona, Ashwasthama, Kripa and others didn't fare any better. Actually, Arjuna had employed a magic weapon which made them all fall down unconscious on the battlefield. While they were in that condition, he snatched away their garments. The seizure of the clothes of the enemy was the sign of decisive victory in those days. The cattle had already been recovered.

After a pause, Mr Sharma said, "We all know the subsequent developments and the marriage of princess Uttara with Abhimanyu, the son of Arjuna. But why did Arjuna fail to use this magic weapon in the Kurukshetra battle?"

Kaushik and I guessed the answer. But we remained silent, allowing him to conclude, "Obviously, it wasn't a conventional weapon. It was probably barred in those days for use in battles. From the effect of the weapon, one can draw the inference that it was a *Chemical Weapon* which Arjuna couldn't dare to use again. Mahabharata is extremely silent on this."

We express solidarity with the logic put forth by Mr Sharma.

❖❖❖

XXXIII

We're leaving Ranchi for Bhubaneshwar any time tomorrow. Our initial few days here were very dull. Suddenly, it has become rather tense since yesterday, the 26th May 2008.

District police had earlier cautioned us not to venture outside the Ranchi municipal area, because of threat from left-wing extremists. We visited the shopping malls quite a number of times. As prescribed by Harleen, I was interested in visiting the Central Institute of Psychology, Ranchi.

Finally, we managed time on 26th May 2008, Monday evening. It is a huge campus, spreading over a very large area. It was established by the British in May 1918, exactly ninety years back, under the name 'Ranchi European Lunatic Asylum' with a capacity for 174 patients. It catered to the needs of the European mental patients only. It got affiliation to the University of London for Diploma in Psychological Medicine examination in 1922. Presently, it is a pioneering institute not only in our country, but in the entire world in the field of psychosurgery and neurosurgery, occupational therapy, clinical psychology and electro encephalography (EEG), neuropathology, use of lithium and chlorpromazine in psychiatry, sophisticated cerebral angiography, pneumonia encephalography, air ventriculography, myelography, etc. The Mental Health Act of India, 1987 was drafted here.

While I was collecting this information accompanied by Kaushik from officials, Mr Sharma, who was standing a little away from us, received a phone call. He became agitated. This, we had never witnessed before.

Kaushik went to him and asked, "Sir, is there anything serious?"

He disconnected the call. By that time, I also joined them. He said, "Dr Bhaumik, I think we should return to the circuit house."

So we got into the vehicle. He instructed Joginder to drive back to our place of stay. Inside the vehicle, he remained silent and thoughtful. Within an hour, we returned to the circuit house and went inside his room. By that time, he had regained his normal composure and ordered coffee for us.

He then said, "I used to receive some calls from unknown callers ever since I've taken this assignment. This, I generally ignore. Most of these calls are related to recruitment rally, requests from known circles."

There was a little interruption for serving coffee and snacks, "The cell phone has one advantage. You can see the telephone number from where the call has been initiated. You've the liberty to overlook it if it is not from your preserved directory."

He gave a pause and asked Kaushik to see if anyone was around our room to listen to our discussion. The latter investigated, both from the front and the rear door, the possible way of invasion of this room to ensure secrecy.

Mr Sharma started again, "This evening, when you and Kaushik were busy talking to the officials of the Psychiatry Institute, I received a call from a landline number. I didn't attend to it immediately. When I received the call the second time, I looked at it carefully. It was a local landline number. I responded.

The caller was a tribal youth. He was aware of our movements, as he said: Sharmaji, aplok abhi shayad Ranchi pagal khana ghumke dekh rahain hai. Main apka shubh chintak hoon. Ap logon ko marne ke liye maovadi ke pass supari pahunch gaya hai. Jab tak aplog Jharkhand main hain, thora sambhalkar chalna.

> [Mr Sharma, perhaps you're presently visiting the Lunacy Centre of Ranchi. I'm your well wisher. The Maoists have received funds for killing you. As long as you're in Jharkhand, please be cautious.]
>
> *Maovadi se hamari kya dushmani? Ho sakta hai, aap najdeek se hamain dekhkar phone kar rahen hain.*
>
> [What's our enmity with Maoists? It's quite possible that you're speaking from somewehere close by, just seeing us.]
>
> *Asal me Maovadiyon ke sath app logon ki koi dushmani nahi thi. Lekin jin logon ke sath ap log dushmani ko anjam de rahein hain, woh log maovadiyon par kafi dabav dal rahein hain ap logo ke khilaf kuchh karne ke liye. Wo log hamein paise ka lalach dikha rahe hain.*

[Actually you've no hostility with Maoists. But the persons whom you're challenging are friends of Maoists. They're creating pressure upon Maoists to harm you people. They're alluring us with money.]

Ap kaun hain?

[Who are you?]

Main bhi maovadi hoon. Lekin main nahi chahta hoon maovadi log aapke khilaf kuchh karein, Mera rishtedar bhi TSR me naukri karta hai. Aap logon ko kuchh hone se bahali radd ho jayegi.

Jo log apke khilaf ham ko bharka rahein hain, wohi log ap logon ke chalne firne ki khabar bhi de rahe hain. Idhar ke police ke sath kuch bat mat kijiyega. Kripaya mera number gopaniya rakhiyega. Aur ek bat, kal aap logo ke Hundru Jal prapat dekhne ki bat hai na? Udhar mat jaiyega.

[I'm also a Maoist. But I don't want that the Maoists should take any action against you since my relative is also serving in TSR. In case of any mishap against you, the rally will be postponed.

The persons who are instigating us against you are providing details about your movements. Don't share anything with the local police. Please keep my telephone number secret. Probably you're planning to visit Hundru Falls tomorrow. Please don't go there.]

"My god, they knew our programme about visiting Hundru Falls tomorrow", Mr Sharma said to himself.

Ap hamesha apna phone on kar ke rakhiyga. Koi jaruri bat hone se phone karunga.

[You please keep your cell phone on at all times. In case of urgency, I shall ring you.]

Mr Sharma thanked him for the information. We could realize the gravity of the situation. The entire development was the outcome of Harleen episode. But we stopped our discussion as Anup Kumar entered into the room with the kids. Ankita and Ayush appeared very happy after visiting Pahari temple, Durga Bedi, Jagannathpur Temple, Jain Mandir, Nakshatra

Van, Fun Castle, Crocodile Farm and Aqua World. Ankita, the elder of the two was narrating details of her visit to the house of Team India Captain, Mahendra Singh Dhoni at Ranchi. We went for dinner together. After dinner, Anup Kumar went to his room with his children. Kaushik and I came to Mr Sharma's room again for discussion.

He said, "The person or persons who are behind the murder of Aman have access to the Maoists. In all probability, force personnel are involved in the murder of Captain Amandeep. How do force personnel get acquainted with Maoists? It is really a tough question to answer!"

Kaushik said, "Sir, everything is possible. Have you forgotten the association of a security force personnel with the banned National Liberation Front of Twipra (NLFT) in our state?"

Mr Sharma said, "In that sense you're right, everything is possible in our country. Sometimes, I feel sceptical about incidents, like arrest of Laskar-e-Toiba (LET) activists in metro cities, on the eve of our national functions. The citizens are not apprised with the follow up actions. This may be a ploy on the part of corrupt bureaucrats to create pseudo threats, and to woo the forces out of the actual threat areas."

I said, "This reminds me of a science fiction I read a long time back. It was regarding the use of robots in war field, written in the backdrop of the cold war era between NATO and WARSAW countries.

The tussle between USA and USSR resulted in the Third World War which continued for several years. Both the groups used robots as their soldiers. The robots were fighting for them on the surface of the earth. People took shelter in underground bunkers to witness the live coverage of battle outside through CCTVs. They couldn't come out, as the environment outside became polluted and not suitable for human habitation. War continued for years together and common people turned restless. Some of them started peeping out of the bunkers to take an on-the-spot assessment of war outside. But, they didn't notice any confrontation outside. Soon, some more people came out. To their utter surprise, they discovered that the war had stopped. The robots of both the sides had signed a peace agreement many years back. They were befooling their creators by feeding old battle pictures."

"So, you compare the cops with robots!" said Mr Sharma. "Well, I like the story very much, Doctor. During my attachment with Black Panther Rifles, at the beginning my career, I noticed one thing. The average educational qualification of the jawans is deliberately kept very low. I asked our course co-ordinator about the reason behind this. He made an honest confession: 'An educated man can never fight valiantly like an illiterate. So, the educational qualifications of jawans are kept low, and they're provided with their weekly doses of liquor. This makes them apathetic to other needs of life, and they behave like your robots'."

"Sir, probably this is the legacy of the British colonial system", suggested Kaushik.

"You're right", said Mr Sharma, "but things are changing rapidly. Now, battles can be fought with non-state actors. Besides, the role of policemen is quite different to that of armed forces."

"But why did the Maoists spare us, at our previous venues?" I said.

"My god, that would have been a serious catastrophe for us", replied Mr Sharma.

"I think", Kaushik said, "by the time, the persons who engaged the Maoists for causing harm to us sent their feelers to them, we had left Indrapuri. It may also be possible that operatives of their confidence among Maoists are active in Jharkhand only."

Mr Sharma said, "We should be very cautious in future. Our movement plan should remain confined to the three of us or at best, we may share it with Anup Kumar."

Kaushik said, "Sir, two is a company and three is a crowd. Upto Bhubaneshwar, you should only know about the timings and movement plan. We've full faith in you."

I also supported Kaushik. On the reference of Bhubaneshwar, Mr Sharma said, "Please tell Harleen tonight itself to cancel their train tickets for Bhubaneshwar tomorrow. Request them to travel by air. I shall also tell Baldevji accordingly."

I nodded my head in affirmation. Coming out of his room, looking at the moon, I recalled some lines from Wordsworth:

> What fond and wayward thoughts will slide
>
> Into a lover's head!
>
> 'O mercy!' to myself I cried,
>
> If Lucy should be dead!

It was half past eleven when I rang Harleen. I apprised her of the development. She informed me about the arrival of uncle Baldev and aunt Jasmin to their residence that evening. She would board the train from Ludhiana with uncle Baldev the next afternoon. Aunt would stay back in Harleen's house. On getting my instructions, she assured me that she would follow the instructions of Mr Sharma. I felt lucky that we had the advantage of cell phones these days, unlike Wordsworth. I shared the thoughts of Housman:

> But if you ever come to a road where danger
> or guilt or anguish or shame's to share.
> Be good to the lad, who loves you true,
> And the soul that was born to die for you
> And whistle and I'll be there.

❖❖❖

XXXIV

Harleen confirmed the cancellation of their railway tickets. In the process, they've suffered a loss of about rupees six hundred. Now they're using the Indian Airlines flight from Ludhiana to Delhi for 28th May 2008 scheduled at 9.15 a.m.

From Delhi, they will board the connecting flight of Indian Airlines to Bhubaneshwar on the same day at 11.20 a.m.

As for us, we've three alternative routes, first through NH-75 from Ranchi-Khunti-Band Gaon-Chandradharpur-Chaibassa-Jainitgarh to Orissa border, Second through NH-33 from Ranchi-Bundu-Chandil-Jamshedpur-Mahulie—Juntion with NH-6 near Baharagora and the third, through NH-23 from Ranchi-Berosisai-Gunta-Palkot-Kolebira-Simdege—Orissa border. Mr Sharma has chosen NH-33 for obvious reasons of safety. We shall cover a little more distance to avoid Maoist threats.

Anup Kumar sent back his children to his residence by train. A relative came from Kolkata to take the kids. It is a wise decision, for it would be difficult for the kids to undertake such a strenuous journey. But, Mr Sharma delayed the start. Finally, we took departure at five in the afternoon in a convoy of three vehicles with our armed personnel on guard.

I counted days on my finger. Exactly 20 days after our last separation, I would meet Harleen. In the intervening period, the love god has provided enough favourable variations to bring the two thirsty souls closer. I recited from Browning:

> Dear rose without a thorn,
> Thy bud's the babe unborn:
> First streak of a new morn.

❖❖❖

XXXV

The journey from Ranchi to Bhubaneshwar was eventless. We reached Bhubaneshwar on May 29, Thursday at around 9.30 a.m. Harleen and Baldevji greeted us at the CRPF Group Centre Bhubaneshwar. Harleen looked marvellous in a pink salwar kameez and dupatta. She looked like a blooming flower. Her sad aura which I had noticed at Jalandhar was almost gone. The first words she said to me were, "Hope, you've had a pleasant journey. When did you take dinner?"

"The journey was quite comfortable", I replied, "and the dinner was more memorable."

She looked at me with a question mark on her face. Mr Sharma and Baldevji hugged each other as if they were known to each other for years. To remove her confusion, I said, "It was a small locality, a little short of Jamshedpur where we had dinner at around eleven. Suddenly, Kaushik asked the shopkeeper the name of the place. The latter replied: 'Ghatshila'.

We were stunned, and repeated the question, "What's the name of the place?"

Shopkeeper replied again, 'Ghatshila'.

For Bengalis, Ghatshila, the work place of eminent writer Bhibhuti Bhusan Bandopadhay has been like a pilgrimage. So, we enquired about the hut at Ghatshila where the writer used to stay, amidst nature. To our utter surprise, we detected that the cottage was at a walking distance from the restaurant. The shop-owner gave us a guide. We visited the cottage immediately with delight. We took our photographs, keeping the cottage in the background, with immense satisfaction."

Harleen said, "It may be the real character of Bengalis. They're ready to starve for the sake of literature. But, we the Punjabis prefer to give priority to satisfy the other need of our life, the need of our stomach. Get fresh quickly for breakfast."

We four went to our respective rooms. Our support staff got accommodation in sub-officers' barrack. They were asked to get ready for the trip to Puri by 3.00 in the afternoon.

We're treated as guest of Harleen here. She is a medical officer, and at the same time, an assistant commandant of CRPF. The breakfast was excellent and I took an extra alu paratha.

After breakfast at around 11.00 a.m., Harleen took a CRPF jeep and left the campus with Mr Sharma and uncle Baldev for the State Forensic Science Laboratory (FSL),

Bhubaneshwar, Orissa. The Cyber Laboratory is located in the same complex. It is is one of the best equipped in our country. More importantly, the in-charge of the State FSL, Dr Alok Pradhan is a personal friend of Mr Sharma. He has agreed to take up this case of retrieving data from the laptop last used by Aman. It could be possible only due to a personal request by Mr Sharma. Both of them had stayed in the same hotel during a Police Duty Meet at Bangalore, 5 to 6 years back. Since then, they have remained in touch with each other.

However, before visiting State FSL Orissa, they would first visit a court of the notary at Bhubaneshwar to get an affidavit made. There should be a declaration containing inter-alia all the facts related to this laptop, on a non-judicial stamp paper of suitable denomination. Thereafter, they would hand over the same to Dr Pradhan. It is expected that they would join us by lunchtime.

I took a good nap in my room and woke up on receiving a call from Harleen around 1.30 p.m. They would be late in returning to the campus, as they had just completed the task at the notary. She requested me to take lunch with my other comrades, otherwise we would get late for Puri. Instantly I replied that none of us would accept this proposal and we would wait for them. Finally, they came at quarter to three and we took lunch hurriedly.

Mr Sharma decided to stay back at the Group Centre, with uncle Baldev to study the incriminating documents and photographs recovered so far. We also wanted to stay back. But he discouraged us, saying that he would like to do the job alone.

So the rest of the party, along with Harleen, left in the mini-bus for Puri at around 3.30 p.m., with one Havalder Nilesh Panda, from CRPF Group Centre as our guide. This is the first time our team is moving without Mr Sharma. Harleen took a seat by my side, as usual. Our staff became curious about the nature of our relationship. Some information about the enquiry related to the death of Aman had perhaps percolated to them through driver Joginder and constable Narayan. But, they're in a fix whether it is her urge for unfolding the mystery of the death of her lover, or her new found love which has brought her from Jalandhar to this place.

I asked Harleen, "Tell me what happened this morning".

- It was quite an encounter, with the advocates and their clerks! I've never visited a court before. Seeing me, everybody thought it might be a case of marriage registration. But, they couldn't ascertain the combination. After finding Mr Sharma and the CRPF vehicle, they suspected the bride-groom was from the Bengali community, serving in the security forces. Someone even taunted 'Macha Khaibi Ilishi, Ghaita Polici.' Everybody wanted to have us as their client.
- Thank God I wasn't there, otherwise they would have started pulling my leg. Finally, how did you manage?
- We came back to our vehicle; Mr Sharma rang up Dr Pradhan and sought his help. Dr Pradhan in turn talked with a senior advocate of the Bhubaneshwar Bar, Abhishek Pattanaik and gave him our cell number. The latter called us to his room by sending a junior. He was also convinced; with the reasons cited by Mr Sharma to prove Aman's death was homicide.

Her eyes became wet, as she took the name of Aman. But soon she recovered and said, "Sorry!"

- It is ok; it only proves the depth of your love towards captain Amandeep.
- As suggested by Mr Pattanaik, the reason for choosing State FSL Bhubaneshwar has been explained in the affidavit. Bhubaneshwar has been selected for our mutual convenience. Besides, it is easy for me to stay at CRPF Group Centre, Bhubaneshwar as I am an employee of CRPF. Uncle Baldev has filed this affidavit, as my close relative and the father of the deceased.
- The process is so tedious!
- Yeah! The process is very cumbersome. We're presently engaged in private investigation. So, we've to prove our bona fide intent. After the affidavit, we

met Dr Pradhan at State FSL and gave him Aman's laptop. We also deposited rupees five thousand as fee for the examination. The report is expected within 4 to 5 days. Till your return from the next venue Nellore, uncle and I shall stay here only.

- Tell me about the note book of Captain Aman. Once you had mentioned this in a telephonic discussion.
- Actually, Aman may not have been the possessor of the notebook. It may have belonged to Captain Rahane. Interestingly, it contains the telephone numbers of at least two girls, whose photographs were recovered from Aman's custody. They may be call girls. Aman is no way associated with them. The notebook doesn't contain the handwriting of Aman. In one photograph, Captain Rahane is found in an intimate position with the same lady, with whom Aman's intimacy was claimed.
- I think Mr Sharma will be able to throw more light on this issue.
- What about your well-wisher from the Maoists? Did he ring again?
- I think he's still in contact with Mr Sharma. He didn't tell us anything about him after that day. But Mr Sharma once said that because of an adivasi boy, we were saved this time. He's hopeful about solving this mystery.

By the way, there was an abduction near Hundru falls. Two Bengali tourists were kidnapped by suspected Maoists. They were released unharmed the very next day.

Harleen expressed a sigh of relief and sat further close to me. We were speaking to each other intensely in low voices, indifferent of the life outside. We came out of our stupor when our vehicle stopped at Shakshi Gopal temple. A very few numbers, led by Anup Kumar and Kaushik, got down from the bus to see the deity. Harleen and I remained seated. When the bus started again, Kaushik asked guide Nilesh, "Pandaji, it seems to be in a very bad shape. I found it well-maintained last time when I visited in 2000."

Nilesh replied, "Sir, entire Cuttak is badly affected by floods this year. Probably flood water has caused the damage. But it is one of the oldest temples of Lord Krishna in India."

Kaushik enquired, "Do you know the story associated with this temple?"

"Why not sir!" Nilesh said like a professional guide.

"Then tell us the story for our enlightenment", said Kaushik.

He started his story in Hindi mixed with Oriya. The gist of the story was like this: "Once two Brahmins from Vidyanagara of south India went out for a pilgrimage to northern India. After a long time, they reached Vrindavana, the sacred place of Lord Krishna. They visited holy places together and eventually, arrived at a great temple of the Gopala. Gopala is Lord Krishna in his eternal form as a cowherd boy. The beauty of the Gopala stole away their hearts. They remained there for three to four days.

One of those Brahmins was elderly and from a high class family. The other was poor and from a low class family. The young man, out of love and respect, had delivered menial services to the elderly man. The elderly Brahmin was so grateful for his reverential attitude that he announced his intention to hand over to the young Brahmin his daughter in marriage."

The young man immediately objected, "Sir, I'm not at all a suitable bridegroom for your daughter. You're well-educated and very rich. I'm without a decent education and have no wealth. Furthermore, your wife and sons won't certainly agree to it."

The elderly Brahmin insisted, "My dear boy, I'll give you my daughter. Don't doubt me in this regard; just accept my proposal!"

The young Brahmin replied, "If you really have decided to give your young daughter to me, say so before the Gopala Deity."

In those days, it was the custom to honour any promise made in front of the Deity. So, entering the temple of Lord Gopala and before the Deity, the elderly Brahmin said, "My dear Lord, please witness that I've promised to give my daughter to this boy."

Then the young Brahmin addressed the Deity, saying, "My dear lord, you're my witness. I shall call upon you to testify if it's necessary later on."

Weeks passed by and finally the two Brahmins returned to Vidyanagara. After a while, the elderly Brahmin remembered his promise. With some anxiety he called all his relatives and friends. He told them what he'd promised in front of Gopala Deity. They were all very disappointed. They said, "When people hear of this, they'll crack jokes and laugh at you. If you give your daughter to that boy, we shall give up all connection with you."

Indeed, his wife and sons even threatened to commit suicide. The elderly Brahmin said, "How can I undo the promise! That too, a promise made in a holy place! If I don't give my daughter to the young Brahmin, he'll call Gopala as witness."

His son replied, "The Deity may be a witness, but He's in a distant country. How can he come here to depose against you? Simply say that you don't remember what you said. I shall take care of the rest."

The next day, the young Brahmin came to the house of the elderly Brahmin. But his son took a stick and chased him away. The young Brahmin then called the village people together. They in turn summoned the elderly Brahmin to their meeting place.

"This gentleman promised to hand over his daughter to me in marriage", explained the young Brahmin.

The elderly Brahmin said that he could remember nothing of what had taken place. His son stood up and said, "While touring various holy places, my father carried much money. Seeing the money this rogue decided to take it away. He gave my father poison, which had made my father mad. Now he claims that my father promised to give him his daughter?"

The young Brahmin pleaded his innocence, "I told this gentleman that I wasn't a fit husband for his daughter, but he insisted. He made his promise in front of the Gopala Deity. I've asked the supreme Lord to be my witness".

The elderly Brahmin immediately said, "If Gopala personally comes here to bear witness, I shall surely give my daughter to the young Brahmin."

The son also agreed.

With full faith in Gopala, the young Brahmin started at once for Vrindavana. On arrival, he narrated everything in detail to the Deity, "My dear Lord, I'm not thinking of becoming happy by getting the daughter as a bride. I'm simply thinking that the Brahmin has broken his promise. This is giving me great pain. You're very merciful and you know everything. Therefore, kindly be a witness in the case."

Lord Krishna spoke, "I've never heard of a Deity walking from one place to another."

The Brahmin replied, "That's true. But how's it that you're speaking to me? My dear Lord, you're not a statue; you're Lord Krishna Himself. !"

Lord Gopala smiled, and said, "My dear Brahmin, just listen to me. I shall walk behind you. Don't try to see me by turning around. As soon as you see me, I shall remain stationery at that very place. You'll know that I'm walking behind you by the sound of my ankle bells. Cook one kilo of rice daily and offer it to me. I shall eat that rice and follow behind you."

The next day, the Brahmin started for his country. Gopala followed him. The Brahmin became very pleased to hear the tinkling sound of Gopala's ankle bells. Everyday, he cooked first class rice for Gopala to eat. The Brahmin walked and walked in this way until he eventually arrived outside his village. Then he thought, "I shall go to my home and tell all the people that the witness has arrived."

Thinking this, he turned to look back, and saw that Gopala was standing there, smiling. The Lord said, "Now you can go home. I shall stay here and shan't leave."

When the village people heard of Gopala's arrival, they were struck with wonder. They went to see the Lord and offered their respectful obeisance to him. Everyone was very pleased to see Gopala's beauty. Thus, in the presence of villagers, Lord Gopala bore witness that the elderly Brahmin had indeed offered his daughter to the young Brahmin. Soon afterwards, the marriage ceremony was duly performed.

When the king of that country heard of this wonderful story, he also came to see Gopala. He constructed a nice temple for the Lord. Some time later the Deity of Lord Gopala was moved from Vidyanagara to the town of Cuttak in Orissa. This is the story of Shakshi-Gopala.

There was pin drop silence in the bus when Nilesh was narrating the story of Shakshi-Gopala. Everyone enjoyed the story. Here, Harleen asked me an interesting question, "What'll be the explanation of Mr Sharma to this story?"

I giggled, as in the span of one month, Mr Sharma had cast a great influence upon me, "May be he would say that the Deity was lifted by the young Brahmin from Vrindavana to Vidyanagara. Like, it was shifted from Vidyanagara to this place in Cuttak. May be he would consider registration of a theft case."

She erupted into laughter. Anup Kumar and Kaushik who were sitting one row in front of us also started laughing. Kaushik said, "You're absolutely right, Doctor!"

Obviously, he was mimicking Mr Sharma. I accepted the compliment smilingly and said to Harleen, "I know another story, somewhat similar to this. It is a story of two friends, from a village close to the woods. One day, one of them went for pilgrimage, leaving his only horse in the custody of his friend. After return from pilgrimage, he requested his friend to return the horse. But his friend flatly denied that he had ever taken any horse from him. Actually he had sold the horse to some one else.

The owner of the horse went to the Qazi for redress. Qazi asked him, "When did you hand over the horse? Is there any witness to the event?"

He mentioned the date and the time, but couldn't cite any witness.

- Where did you hand over the horse to your friend?
- Inside the forest, Sir.
- Is there any mark of importance at the place of transfer?
- Yes sir, there's a big 'Neem tree' at that place.

Qazi expressed satisfaction and fixed a date for hearing the case. On the day of hearing, both the parties arrived at the court at the scheduled hour. Large number of villagers also assembled, as spectators to see the trial of the case. The Qazi took up this case first. He asked the owner, "Go immediately to the place under the 'Neem tree', where you had handed over your horse to your friend. Call the 'Neem tree', to come here for deposition."

The owner replied, "Sir, how can a 'Neem tree' come to the court for deposition?"

Qazi said, "Don't worry; I've had a talk with the 'Neem tree'. He agreed to appear in the court for deposition. You just go there and invite the tree for deposition. It'll follow you."

The owner left the court, a bit hopelessly towards the forest to invite the 'Neem tree'. Meanwhile the Qazi started hearing other cases. In the intermittent period, he asked the other friend if it was time for his friend to return to the court with the 'Neem tree'. The accused replied that 'Neem tree' wouldn't come, but his friend may be expected to return by that time.

Just at that moment, the appellant returned to the court. He said, "Sir, as per your instruction I went to the spot, touched the 'Neem tree', and requested it to come for deposition in your court. But it didn't respond."

Qazi said with a smile, "The Neem tree' has already made its appearance in the court, and made its deposition."

There was a murmuring in the court out of bewilderment. The accused person also objected.

Qazi told the accused friend, "You've correctly judged the distance of the 'Neem tree' from the court. You've even told us about his expected time of arrival to the court by visiting the spot, under which your friend had handed over his horse to you, before proceeding for pilgrimage. How can you tell all this if you're not associated with this episode?"

The accused friend couldn't find any option other than to confess his guilt.

- This is really excellent stuff from the Qazi.
- There's another version of this story of 'Shakshi Gopala'. While following the young Brahmin, Lord Gopala sustained injury. Something sharp pierced into his bare feet and he stopped to extricate the sharp object. As the tinkling sound of Gopala's ankle bell stopped, the young Brahmin looked back and the Lord became a statue.

It is quite possible that the villagers of Vidyanagara didn't believe in the beauty of the Deity of Gopala witnessed by the two Brahmins at Vrindavana. So, they asked the young Brahmin to bring a replica of the Deity. Otherwise, a sensible person like him wouldn't marry a girl after such humiliation.

- I still believe you need treatment at CIP, Ranchi.

Our vehicle stopped in front of the Jagannath temple. The brother of our guide, Nilesh is a priest of the temple. He handed us over to Naresh. We went inside the temple barefoot, leaving our shoes in the vehicle.

Situated on the east coast in the state of Orissa, it is one of the four holiest places in India as per Hindu mythology. The other three places are Sringeri, Dwaraka and Jyotirmath. A pilgrimage to Puri is believed to liberate a person from the cycle of rebirths. The focus of attention is the huge Jagannath (Lord of the world) temple dedicated to Vishnu. It was built during the reign of Anantavarman Ganga in the twelfth century. About 6,000 priests and attendants served menially. The most popular festival of Puri, the ratha-yatra, takes place in June/July every year. A huge canopied car, on which Krishna is enthroned, is pulled through the streets on thick ropes by hundred of pilgrims. The feast commemorates Krishna's journey from Gokula to Mathura. The main chariot is followed by two smaller ones, carrying Krishna's sister Subhadra and his brother Baldeva. After seven days, Krishna returns from the Gundicha temple, his Aunt's place in an equally spectacular procession.

It was 5.30 in the afternoon. Naresh hurriedly took most members of our group for worshipping Jagannath. Driver Rafique Ansari, Harleen and I enjoyed the architecture of the temple. In particular, what remained a mystery for us was how the flag was hoisted on the peak of this huge temple. It is equally difficult to understand how the walls of this temple, especially the upper portion, are painted so intricately.

We went to the sea beach at around six, and in the process missed the sunset. But the beauty of Puri beach under the fading light invigorated us, and the waves let no one feel bored. The beach was very wide and it became more pleasant with bubbling activities after sunset amidst presence of thousands of tourists and hawkers whose number was probably endless. Harleen and I sat down on the beach side by side, silently enjoying every moment of the evening as our other comrades were busy in shopping. I didn't know what Harleen was thinking, nor did I wish to ask about her feelings. I was sure that she was equally satisfied, seeing nature in one of its purest forms.

But I was comparing the vastness of Lord Jagannath with the sea god in front of us. A short while ago, a Muslim, a Sikh, and may be a non-believer weren't allowed to enter the temple due to prohibitions imposed by the priests. I recollected the story of Puri, written by Mark Tully in his book *India's Unending Journey*. The columnist of BBC has given a vivid description of the plight of young women from Bengal who visited this place for pilgrimage with the Pandas, and how they were forced into prostitution.

These priests didn't see the injustice when the Devas stole away nectar after the churning of the ocean, depriving the

Daityas. Initially the deal was fair; rather the Daityas were put up to the difficult task of holding the poisonous head of the king of serpents, Vasuki, who allowed him to be used as rope for churning, with Mount Mandar as a churning stick.

Now what's the guarantee that Lord Jagannath would give justice to poor people? Especially to those who belong to the lower strata of the caste system. When I started thinking like this, the sea seemed to me the dearest, like Harleen.

We returned to the Group Centre at Bhubaneshwar at around 9 p.m. Uncle Baldev and Mr Sharma received us. They looked extremely satisfied. We, the quartet, Harleen, Anup Kumar, Kaushik and I quickly went to our respective rooms to change and then met again for dinner within half an hour.

At dinner, Sardar Baldev, a retired Captain in his mid-sixties was at his personal best. He was truly amiable. The centre of attraction was his affectionate behaviour. He was especially kind to me. I felt at home. We enjoyed the dinner, and the specially-prepared fish, in particular was excellent.

After dinner, we sat down in the garden in front of the mess, under the clear star-studded sky. Mr Sharma gave hints about the progress of our ongoing quest for revealing the mystery behind Aman's death. He said, "This afternoon, I've gone through the documents and photographs. One number 291709, on the back side of a photograph which apparently looks like a telephone number, enchanted me very much. It is the photograph in which Captain Rahane is found in proximity with a girl, with whom Aman's intimacy was assumed."

Here, Harleen intervened, "I've also seen this, and probably this is the only handwriting which may be that of Aman. Inside the digit '0', face of a lady was sketched. I didn't like that."

"You've relieved me to a great extent", Mr Sharma said, "I also feel that these figures were written by Aman only. It apparently looks like a telephone number, rather a BSNL landline number, as it starts with the digit '2'. But these days, most of the towns and cities have seven or eight digit telephone numbers. Moreover, no STD code is associated with it."

He took a pause, and then began, "It puzzles me, and I tried to solve the mystery. Suddenly, I recollected my recent talk with a source. He was giving me a telephone number for contact over telephone in Hindi.

I recited the Hindi pronunciation of this number on the paper, which sounded like: 'Do Nau Ek Sath Shunya Nau'.

The person who had written this number, obviously tried to communicate some message. Then, I started thinking about the sketch inside the digit '0', which Dr Bedi had mentioned a little while ago. I first thought it to be a sketch of a young lady. Then I asked myself why it could not be the 'sketch of a mother'.

So, I substituted 'Shunya' with 'Ma'. The Hindi pronunciation of the number then became, 'Do Nau Ek Sath Ma Nau'. The intention of the writer became clear to me."

Kaushik, who was silent, suddenly opened up, "Sir, do you mean to say, 'collusion between the two'?"

"Excellent Kaushik!" said Mr Sharma, "Perhaps, you've uttered the right words. The death of Aman was outcome of a conspiracy. It was hatched by these two persons, Captain Rahane and the lady in the photograph with him, and their associates.

If I believe my source in the Maoists circles, and certainly there's no reason for disbelief, there's a racket in the Black Panther Rifles, involving smuggling of ammunitions to the Maoists."

'What?' Anup Kumar reacted with surprise, and he repeated the last words of Mr Sharma.

"Yes, Mr Kumar!" said Mr Sharma, "when I first heard this from my Maoist source, I was also surprised like you. Then I correlated the sequence, leading to the death of Captain Aman. Remember, the two fire incidents in the two ammunition depots of Black Panther Rifles in a span of three days during Operation Bikram. It is true that in summers, particularly in Rajasthan, such accidents can happen. But after perusing the notebook, which in all probability belonged to Captain Rahane, I got the major clue. I detected the telephone number of the PCO from where one of our Maoist well-wishers rang me the other day. The nexus between the murderer of Aman and Maoists became crystal clear to me. These incidents of fire in ammunition depots are arranged just to destroy the scope for stock verification, and thereby causing elopement of evidence."

Anup Kumar didn't know about the incident of the CIP, Ranchi, and looked with surprise towards Kaushik and me. Kaushik narrated the incident of 26th May 2008 to him. I related to him the incident of abduction of two Bengali tourists from a jeep, on their way to Hundru Falls on the following day and their subsequent release without causing any injuries. Obviously, they were abducted in a case of mistaken identity.

Mr Sharma said, "Tomorrow morning at 6, we're leaving for Vishakapattanam. I've taken the photocopies of all relevant documents, which I would like to study further. I'm expecting some specific clues from Aman's laptop. Harleen and Baldevji will stay here till our return from Nellore."

We called it a day on a satisfying note around midnight. But my mind was engulfed with the thought of impending separation, which forced me to take shelter under 'Godmother':

I give her sadness and the gift of pain,
a new moon madness and a love of rain.

❖❖❖

XXXVI

Harleen and uncle Baldev stood in the lobby to see us off, when we left Bhubaneshwar for Vizag sharp at 6 a.m. on 30th May. I was in a total stupor for about an hour, as I was recalling the pleasures of her company last night. I felt guilty for not requesting Mr Sharma to invite her to join us, with uncle Baldev upto Nellore, for they would have to pass 5 to 6 days at Bhubaneshwar practically without any assignment. I also forgot to give her the gift I had purchased from Ranchi. For doing this, I would get the chance after returning from Nellore.

I came to my senses as our vehicles stopped near Chilka Lake. The location is just 2 k.m. from NH-5 and it is a part of Khurda District. Chilka is the largest coastal lake in India. The lake was formed due to the silting action of the Mantei River. This river drains into the northern end of the lake, and the northern currents in the Bay of Bengal have formed a sand bar along the eastern shore leading to the formation of a shallow lagoon. We took our breakfast at a restaurant on the north shore of the lake.

The area of the lake in this dry season is around 900 square k.m. It'll increase by about 20 per cent during the rainy season. Kaushik calculated that the area of Chilka would be one-tenth of our Tripura state. We resumed our journey at around ten.

We moved non-stop along the NH-5 till our stoppage for lunch at Srikakulam in Andhra Pradesh around 2 p.m. In the process, we crossed places like Chettrapur and Brahmpur of Orissa, and Ichchapuram, Palasa, Tekkali and Narasannapeta under Andhra Pradesh. The condition of the road, barring some patches, in Orissa, was bad, compared to Andhra Pradesh. One can make out the difference easily.

Our vehicles were held up in a traffic jam at Orissa—Andhra Pradesh border near Ichchapuram. We moved along the coastal areas of Orissa and Andhra Pradesh. From Chilka onwards, manufacturing salt by blocking the sea water during night tide in the fields, and then drying the water in the sun, caught our notice. Pisciculture is also popular in Orissa. The people of both the states are hard working. Inside Andhra Pradesh, as we proceeded further south, alongwith pisciculture, the practice of poultry, floriculture, horticulture, etc., caught our notice.

Our general topic of discussion centered round the saga of Andhra Pradesh in curbing the activities of People's War Group (PWG). The following points came out during our discussion in which Mr Sharma was again the principal contributor:

- → Andhra people always give a clear mandate; this empowers the government in power to deal with such issues firmly and with authority.
- → According to researchers, the intensity of Left Wing extremism in Andhra, at its peak period was evaluated as level-1, on a scale of maximum level-5. So, the task was easier.
- → The economic development in Andhra Pradesh is significant, both in terms of quality and quantity. This ensures dissociation of common masses from the insurgents.
- → Panchayati Raj System in Andhra Pradesh is functioning well and this ensures decentralization of power to the marginal population.
- → Andhra doesn't have any international boundary with any foreign country and as such the outside influence is minimum.
- → Structural formation of Andhra Pradesh police is one of the best in our country, and the elite force like Gray Hound Commandos raised by the state police also paves the way for curbing PWG activities.
- → The very presence of SVP National Police Academy at Hyderabad, Andhra Pradesh and regular interaction of the police officials from Andhra Pradesh with the top hierarchy of police, judiciary, civil administration, politicians, and the press through various seminars help in improving the performance of Andhra Pradesh police. These seminars and vertical interaction courses are just like pulse polio immunization programme for police personnel; they raise the level of performance of police personnel in fighting against insurgency and especially raise their efficiency in dealing with organized crimes.
- → PWG is basically an urban insurgency and it is to the credit of Andhra police that they don't allow the

insurgents to make use of the terrains of eastern ghat hill ranges, except of course the Godavari delta region.

- → As compared to other Maoist infested areas in other states, Andhra Pradesh has comparatively less mineral resources in adjoining forests; consequently, the possibility of constant supply of funds from illegal mining is missing. For generation of funds, PWG has no alternative other than resorting to extortion, kidnapping, dacoity, etc., which causes loss of sympathy from the common masses.
- → Better road connectivity in Andhra Pradesh reduces the reaction time for police to act on information received by them.
- → Advance electronic infrastructure has helped Andhra Police to reach affected people in quick time and to carry out psychological operations.
- → Andhra Pradesh police is the pioneer in the entire country as far as use of cyber information, technical surveillance and computerization of police network are concerned. This has made the task of police easy.
- → Presence of the advanced Forensic Science Laboratory at Hyderabad is directly helping Andhra Pradesh police to conduct quality investigations. One proper investigation can prevent commission of at least ten crimes.
- → Impact of colonization by the Britishers is less in Andhra society; consequently old social values, indigenous leadership and local strongmen still exist is Andhra Pradesh. It is difficult for the PWG to break this legacy.
- → People of Andhra Pradesh are truly educated and have a cosmopolitan outlook. They've the advantage of a common language in the form of Telegu.
- → Average slope of the affected areas along with forest cover are a contributing factor for insurgency. In Andhra Pradesh, these are in favour of the

police/security forces, compared to other Maoist infested states.

- → Andhra people display high levels of social psychology, political culture, social ethics and common decency for making democracy work.
- → Marginal population develops linkages outside geographic limits as it forms into the politico-legal structure of the country. The standard of living in tribal areas in bordering states like Chhattisgarh, Orissa and Jharkhand is so awful and alarming that the PWG activities would continue in those areas, till homogeneity is achieved.
- → In a study in Dantewada district of Chhattisgarh, it has been revealed that 98 per cent of Maoists are Adivasis. Percentage of Adivasis, who have been the most deprived class for ages vis-à-vis the general population, is a determining factor that governs their increased interest in Maoist activities. Probably this ratio is adversely in favour of PWG in Andhra Pradesh.

We reached Vishakapattanam at around 5 in the afternoon and went straight into the Battalion headquarters of 66 Battalion, CRPF at the Indira Priyadarshini Stadium of Vizag. This unit was deployed in Tripura in its previous assignment, till March this year. Most of the officers knew Mr Sharma and Kaushik by name. We received warm hospitality.

Our staff was accommodated for the night in the Battalion headquarters. Accommodation for Mr Sharma, Anup Kumar, Kaushik and me was made at a make-shift Officers' Mess in a posh area, Kailash Giri close to the sea beach. Kailash Giri is located on a hillock on eastern ghats hill range which merges into the sea. There's a park on this hill-top adjacent to the sea. One can enjoy breathtaking view of the sea from here. The name Kailash Giri is because of the presence of the statue of the celestial couple, Shiva-Parvati. We enjoyed a panoramic view of the city, and its beaches.

Mr Sharma said that the city derived its name Vishakapattanam from the Deity 'Visakha', the God of Valour. This region was formerly part of the Kalinga Empire (ancient Orissa) that stretched up to river Godavari. There's reference of this city in the ancient Hindu and Buddhist texts. During the colonial era, the city had its hub in the Waltair railway station. Part of the city still goes by the colonial British name of Waltair. It is also referred to as the 'City of Destiny'.

Local legend states that an Andhra king of 9-11th century while on his way to Benaras rested here. Enchanted with the sheer beauty of the place, he ordered a temple to be built in honour of his family Deity, Visakha. Archaeological sources however reveal that the temple was possibly built between the 11th and 12th centuries by the Cholas. The temple is no longer in existence, as it was washed away about a hundred years ago by a cyclonic storm. Vizag was initially under French control and later came under the British. After independence, it was the biggest district in our country. Subsequently, it was divided into the three districts of Srikakulam, Vijaynagaram and Vishakapattanam.

We witnessed the semi-final match of IPL between Rajasthan Royals and Delhi Daredevils at the officers' mess. It was a one-sided match and Rajasthan Royals won by a whopping 105 runs.

At night, I had a long chat with Harleen. It left me 'Eating Poetry':

> Ink runs from the corners of my mouth.
> There's no happiness like mine.
> I've been eating poetry.

❖❖❖

XXXVII

We resumed our journey towards Nellore from Vizag today, 31st May morning sharp at 6 a.m. We took NH-5 again to cover the distance of about 500 k.m. In the process, we crossed places like Anakapali, Prattipadu, Rajahmundry, Eluru, Vijaywada, Guntur and Ongole. At Rajahmundry, we took our lunch. We reached Nellore by 8 p.m. The weather was extremely hot and we considered a break at Rajahmundry. Mr Sharma contacted the Chief Security Officer, ONGC Tripura, for suitable accommodation. But, confirmation came late. By that time, we had left Rajahmundry.

Despite hot weather outside, we felt comfortable due to the excellent road condition. Kaushik even commented, "A Boeing aeroplane can easily land on this surface, provided there's no overhead electricity line."

Agriculture, horticulture, floriculture and allied nursery keeping are the main sources of livelihood of the people from these areas. A good number of nurseries of fruits and flower plants came into our notice, almost at regular intervals at Eluru, Hanuman Junction, Vijaywada and parts of Guntur. Guntur is a stronghold of left parties as apparent from the posters of CPI. We stopped at Guntur for evening tea. Our boys felt rather comfortable in the atmosphere; after all they had come from a left-ruled state.

Nellore is a stronghold of CPI (M). Lots of posters and party offices came to our notice. Our staff got accommodated in District Police Lines, Nellore, while we were lodged in a private hotel. District police administration made the arrangements.

Today, we listened to stories from the epic Mahabharata again. No sooner had we left Vizag after breakfast, than Anup Kumar suggested to Mr Sharma, 'Sir, you're silent about the Mahabharata these days?"

The latter confessed by saying, "We remained too worried about Aman's case to think of our pastime."

"But we enjoyed every moment of our stay in Orissa", said Kaushik.

"This is another way of enjoying life", he said, "frankly speaking, the influence of the Aryans in southern India was minimal. Pandit Jawaharlal Nehru pointed out in his 'Discovery of India' that the Aryans were limited to northern India, up to the Vindhya mountain ranges. Their progress to the south was stopped by these mountain ranges."

Anup Kumar tried to bring out more stories from him, "How's it possible, Sir? It is said that the epic Mahabharata is present in every breath of the citizens of India!"

He replied with a smile, "Perhaps, I've mentioned about the participation of states in the Kurukshetra battle from southern India, on the very first day."

"I missed that", said Anup Kumar, "as I had not joined your company at that time."

"There's mention of Andhra in the epic Mahabharata", he said. "The kingdom was ruled by a non-Vedic King. It has been termed as Southern Kingdom. Other related kingdoms often mentioned together with Andhra are Pandya, Dravida, Odhra and Kalinga. The state Andhra Pradesh has got its name from this kingdom.

In the epic, the infantry of Satyaki was composed of a tribe called 'Andhras', known for their long hair, sweet language and mighty powers. They lived along the banks of Yamuna river and probably migrated from Andhra kingdom. Andhras and Kalingas supported the Kaurava in the Kurukshetra war. Sahadeva defeated the kings of Pandya, Dravida, Odhra, Chera, Andhra and Kalinga while performing the Raja Suya Yajna."

"Is this migration from one place to another a common phenomenon?" I asked.

"Good question, doctor", he appreciated. "Perhaps, I've spoken about this in my earlier discussion on imperialist characters of the Pandavas. The Andhras were nomads for several centuries. Some tribes migrated and others didn't, and remained in their older settlements. According to Apastambo

Sutra, around 700 BC, some Andhra tribes inhabited the Salva kingdom on the banks of Yamuna river. Apastambo was a sage. His Sutra has been widely practised among Andhra Brahmin families. He wrote these rules in Salva Desam on the banks of Yamuna river. After Apastambo's death, the Andhra tribes crossed the Vindhya mountains, reached the south, and merged with other Andhra tribes. Various Andhra kings considered themselves to be related to Aryans and invited Brahmins from various parts of the Indian sub-continent to immigrate to the land of Andhra by providing incentives such as donation of villages and lands."

"But, sir, why do we term the language of Andhra people as 'Telugu'?" Kaushik queried.

"The etymology of Telegu is not known for certain", said Mr Sharma. "It is thought to have been derived from trilinga, as in 'Trilinga Desa', 'the country of three lingas'. According to a Hindu legend, Shiva as linga descended on three mountains namely, Kaleswara, Srisaila and Bhimaeswara, which marked the boundaries of the Telegu country. Trilinga Desa is the land in between these three Shiva temples namely Kaleshwaram, Srisailam and Draksharaman. Telugu has also been known as 'Tenungu', 'Tenugu' and 'Telungu'.

Telugu is basically a Dravidian language. It's script is derived from Bhattiprolu script, which itself is a variant of Brahmi Script. Telugu vocabulary has been subjected to prolonged influence from Sanskrit and also from Prakriti. It has also been influenced by Urdu.

Interestingly, a British author in the 19th century called Telugu the 'Italian of the East' as all the words in Telugu end with a vowel sound. It is believed that Italian explorer Niccolo Da Conti coined the phrase in the 15th century. Conti visited Vijayanagara Empire during the reign of Vira Vijaya Bukka Raya. Like Turkish, Hungarian and Finnish, Telugu words have vowels in inflexional suffixes harmonized with the vowels of the preceding syllable."

Incidentally, the disciple of Lord Shiva, our great Parasuram was from Konkan region of south India, i.e., coastal

Maharashtra, Karnataka and Kerala. He fought the advancing ocean back, thus saving the lands of Konkan and Malabar.

"I think the influence of the epic in south Indian society will be evident from its literature as well", said Kaushik.

"You're right Kaushik", said Mr Sharma, "in fact, you'll find many regional versions of the Mahabharata in these states. Some are even written in foreign countries like Indonesia, Java, Sumatra and China. These books are very popular in these areas, particularly in Tamil Nadu. Examples of some of these are *Kaka Wins Bharatayuddha* from Java, William Buck's *Mahabharata*, and Elizabeth Seeger's *Five Sons of King Pandu*. The plays of Tamil street theatre, Terukkutu, use themes from the Tamil language versions of Mahabharata, focusing on Draupadi.

Similarly, in early twentieth century, Bhandarkar Research Institute, Pune brought out the biggest compilation of the Mahabharata containing 13,000 pages in 19 volumes. This work is sometimes called the 'Pune' or 'Puna' edition of the epic.

Tamil writer S. Ramkrishna has written a critical analysis on Mahabharata called *Uba Paandavam*. It discusses the story in a non-linear manner from a traveller's point of view.

Similarly, Kanada novelist S.L. Bhyrappa wrote a novel in Kannada titled *Parva*, giving a new interpretation to the story of Mahabharata. He stressed upon the social and ethical practices in these regions and correlated them with the story from the classic."

"Who are the Bengali writers?" I asked.

"There are so many, starting with Kashiram Das, Kaliprasanna Singha, Upendra Kishore Roy Choudhury, Raj Shekhar Basu, Jogindra Nath Sarkar, Gajendra Kumar Mitra, Nrishinga Prasad Bhaduri and many more others", replied Mr Sharma. "Even Samaresh Basu has written at least three beautiful novels, 'Shambha' 'Pritha' and 'Yuddher Sesh Senapati' based on stories from the epic. Tagore has written many poems and his plays 'Chitrangada', 'Bidai Abhishek' and 'Karna Kunti Sambad' are based on the stories from the classic.

Doctor, you'll feel proud that the first complete English translation of the Mahabharata was carried out by a Bengali writer Kisari Mohan Ganguli, published between 1883 and 1896. You'll find his work online. You'll find many condensed versions as well, in English, of the epic written by eminent writers R.K. Narayan, C. Rajagopalachari, Krishna Dharma, Ramesh C. Dutt, Bharat Vaja Sharma and many others."

"Sir, you've not told us anything about your north-east", Anup Kumar pointed out.

"King Bhagadutta of Pragjyotisa, present day Assam, was a central character in Kurukshetra battle", he said. "Oriya, Bengali and Assamese are the three languages that have emerged from one common source: the Magadhan element, called Magadhi Apabhramsa. The vocabulary of Assamese is largely derived from Sanskrit and its structure is also based on Sanskrit grammar. Sarala Das wrote the original Mahabharata from Sanskrit into Oriya in the 15th century. He was the first to break the brahminical domination over the epic. Rama Saraswati, the earliest and foremost Vaisnavite poet in Assam, translated the major portions of the epic in the 16th century. Similarly, Kashiram Das translated the Mahabharata in Bengali in the 16th century."

"Sir, who's the first writer of the Mahabharata in Hindi", said Anup Kumar.

"Mahabharata in Hindi was written a little later, in the 18th century by Gokulnath", said Mr Sharma, as we were entering Nellore city. Without giving us a chance to put further questions, he concluded, "The Malayalam and Marathi versions of the Mahabharata were written by Ramanujam and Mukteswar respectively."

"I hope writer Ramanujam would be the forefather of eminent mathematician Srinivas Ramanujam", said Kaushik, which invited applause.

We had our dinner in our respective rooms through room service. I could see the second innings in the IPL semi-final match between Kings XI Punjab and Chennai Super Kings at

Wankhede Stadium, Mumbai. It was again a one-sided match as Dhoni's team won by 9 wickets.

After the match, I was thinking of my sweet-heart. As if by telepathy, she rang me up just then. Actually, she had also been watching the match. She was passing her time through local sight-seeing with uncle Baldev. Today, they had visited Chilka and had enjoyed a boating session for about two hours. They were fortunate enough to see a couple of dolphins and quite a large number of crazy crabs. Tomorrow they plan to visit places like Nandankanan, Khandagiri, Udaigiri and Konarak temple.

On hearing about the Sun Temple, I couldn't resist my temptation to ask her, "May I expect your company to visit Konark, when we meet in a week's time?"

- Why, is it so special?
- Because you'll be an experienced guide for Konark by the time I meet you again, and the rest can be said in lover's ear alone!
- Ok, I shall keep my promise. Let me gather the experience of a guide first.

I bade her good night, like 'The Highwayman':

Look for me by moonlight;
Watch for me by moonlight;
I'll come to thee by moonlight, though hell
Should bar the way!

❖❖❖

XXXVIII

I spent the first day of June watching TV, and in the process enjoyed good children films Chota-Chetan and Nanha Jaisalmer. Harleen also kept me rejuvenated with occasional chatting over the telephone. She's reciprocating my feelings. I would request her to consider seeking a transfer to CRPF Group Centre, Agartala.

As usual, in our evenings gossips, Anup Kumar made the opening query, "Sir, probably there was no fatherhood of the Pandavas from south India."

We were sitting inside the room of Mr Sharma. He didn't respond to the query immediately, instead he said to me, "Doctor, it would be easy these days to ascertain the fatherhood of the Pandavas through DNA test."

"But one thing is clear that they weren't the descendants of Pandu", Kaushik said.

"Yeah, you can say that, except for the fatherhood of Arjuna", he said.

"Why?" asked Kaushik, "he was the son of Indra."

"I'm influenced by a fresh school of thought given by an expert in this field namely, Indrajit Bandopadhay", said Mr Sharma. "You can read his article on the net. The Pandavas came to Hastinapura with their mother Kunti, after Pandu's death. Pandu had won Kunti in a Swayamvara. Later, Bhishma bought Madri from Shalya and married her to Pandu. He enjoyed the company of his two wives as best as he liked. There was no symptom to show that Pandu was impotent."

After a pause, he asked Kaushik "Is there any offence in this?"

"It'll be a case of bigamy under section 494 IPC, with provision for seven years' punishment. It is a non-cognizable offence and perhaps the police would have very little role to play", replied Kaushik.

"Such cases of bigamy, polygamy, polyandry or adultery you'll find in plenty in the Mahabharata and in most of the cases, it is the Pandavas who flouted the law", he said. "But you've ignored the sale of Madri by Shalya to Bhishma for Pandu. It is a serious offence under section 373 IPC for which Bhishma, Pandu and their associates may be punished with imprisonment upto ten years and with fine."

"But such types of marriage were in existence during the Mahabharata period, and were perhaps termed as 'asura' marriage, as you narrated the other day" said Anup Kumar.

"You're right in one sense, but it'll be an offence as per prevailing laws these days", said Mr Sharma. "Just after a month of his marriage with Madri, Pandu started Digvijaya—'the conquest of world'. On return, he, accompanied by his two wives, Kunti and Madri, went to the forest leaving his excellent palace with its luxurious beds. He loved the woods, and spent time hunting deer.

Probably he didn't go there just to kill deer. Perhaps, he had some stress-related problem, which affected his fertility. He was a religious person at heart. He had a dual identity. He was the legal son of Vichitravirya who was a person of notorious lust. On the other hand, he was sage Vyasa's biological son! His father's lust and his mother's unwilling sex with Vyasa probably caused his illness."

"I think here, there may be a censorship problem", commented Kaushik, which evoked laughter.

But he carried on, "Pandu met with a tragedy. One day Pandu, while roaming about in the woods, shot a deer. He used five sharp and swift arrows. But, the deer was actually a sage, Rishi Kindama. He was enjoying his mate, a deer.

How can a man take the form of a deer? Why would an archer like Pandu need to shoot, 'five arrows' to kill a single or even two deer? Why did not the Rishi die even after being pierced by five arrows?

Rishi was certainly committing an act of bestiality. We find his 'mate' silent. The subsequent behaviour of Pandu is a little strange. He told Rishi Kindama that kings treated the game of slaying animals like slaying enemies. He also brought reference of Rishi Agastya, who performed a major sacrifice by killing deer.

Kindama replied that men didn't shoot arrows at their unprepared foes. What would have happened if he was prepared?

From the use of words like 'foes' 'enemies', etc., one can easily make the conclusion about deliberate killing of Kindama by Pandu. One reason is of course the practice of perverted sex on the part of Kindama. Pandu didn't repent for this killing."

"Is there any offence committed?" asked Anup Kumar.

"Yes, the act of Rishi Kindama, having unnatural sex with a deer, could have attracted a case under section 377 IPC", said Mr Sharma. "He would have been behind bars for ten years and shall also be liable for fine, if it happens today.

Similarly, the act of Pandu could have attracted a case under section 304A IPC for causing death of Kindama through a negligent act. For the killing of deer, he would be punished under section 51 of Wildlife Protection Act, 1972. He would suffer imprisonment for at least two to three years. Killing of the deer may also attract stringent punishment under section 429 IPC. It has a provision of punishment for five years."

"But, if Pandu killed Kindama out of some personal vendetta, it would be a case of murder under section 302 IPC with provision for capital punishment", said Kaushik.

"You're absolutely right", said Mr Sharma. "From the curse given by Kindama, which subsequently caused the death of Pandu, and in an indirect manner the death of Madri, it appears to be a case of homicide. Generally, these curses announced by the sages those days were commensurate with the misdeeds, which provoked the sages to make such announcements."

"This is true", Kaushik supported him.

Mr Sharma went on, "As I've already said, Pandu went to the forest with his wives for finding herbal medicines for treatment of his stress-related problems. When they were there, they came to know about the pregnancy of Gandhari. Pandu wasn't in favour of obtaining offsprings through the niyoga method. The birth of Dhritarashtra and his brother Pandu through the widows of Vichitravirya, namely Ambika and Ambalika through Vyasa, had been smooth as there was no contender for the throne. Bhishma, with his vow, denied the proposal of his step mother Satyavati to produce sons through Ambika and Ambalika.

But, one person was there in the palace, Vidura, the step brother of Dhritarashtra and Pandu, born through a maidservant with the semen of Vyasa. Vidura was always around Dhritarashtra and Pandu. He was the main conspirator and the game maker. Sri Krishna just complemented in the later part of the Mahabharata story.

Vidura propagated that the birth of Duryodhana would bring evil omens for the Hastinapura kingdom. He even suggested that Duryodhana should be killed just after his birth. Gestation period for Duryodhana was unethically mentioned as two years after Gandhari had conceived. It was just to prove that Yudhisthira was elder than Duryodhana. On the other hand, for crowning Parikshit, the son of Abhimanyu through Uttara, period from his mother's womb was calculated.

Thus, Vidura might have, with consent from Satyavati and Bhishma, sent Pandu with his wives to the woods. Then, just after receiving information of Gandhari's conception, he went to the forest in a chariot. After counselling, Pandu agreed to get a child through Vidura. Madri denied the proposal of having sex with Vidura."

Here Kaushik interrupted, "This is polyandry and probably it is still continuing in Haryana belt. Every year, quite a number of girls from Tripura, particularly from south Tripura district get married to boys from Haryana. The ratio of males and females is critically adverse to girls in Haryana. After marriage, these girls gradually get accustomed to polyandry."

"Exactly", said Mr Sharma, "so Kunti chanted the mantra, which once she learnt from Durvasha and invited Dharma. Vidura was the incarnation of Dharma. He came in a chariot to give birth to Yudhisthira through niyoga. Thus, it can be prima facie said that Vidura was the biological father of Yudhisthira."

Here Kaushik said with his sharp sense of humour, "In that case, the first slave king in India was Yudhisthira, not Iltutmish."

Saying this, he paused to ascertain our reaction. But, we remained silent, as we were clueless.

Kaushik said with a smile, "Vidura was born to a maid servant of Ambalika, the wife of Vichitravirya with his biological father as Vyasa. Yudhisthira was born to Kunti, with suspected fatherhood from Vidura."

We all roared with laughter and Mr Sharma said, "You can term the rule of Yudhisthira as a bureaucracy, a government by paid officials, for Vidura was the Prime Minister and a public servant."

It was eight in the evening; and we decided to watch the thrilling final of IPL between Rajasthan Royals and Chennai Super Kings at Dr D.Y. Patil Sports Stadium, Mumbai. Thanks for the all round performance of Yusuf Pathan, Rajasthan Royals lifted the trophy with an apparently mediocre team.

XXXIX

We completed the first day's task without any problem. The number of candidates was less as compared to earlier four venues. Still, about 2,000 candidates from four southern states of Andhra Pradesh, Tamil Nadu, Karnataka and Kerala took tokens. Our staff, namely Havaldar S. Hariharan, Havaldar S. Baradarajan and Rifleman S.K. Madhaban gave excellent service. We're pleased to see that these three boys, basically from Tamil Nadu and Kerala, could communicate with candidates from Andhra Pradesh and Karnataka in their mother tongues. The candidates are physically tough, but some cases of forgery of signatures came to our notice. We marked the group responsible for the same and took extra cautions.

They were from a particular belt of Andhra Pradesh and belonged to Kepmaris.

In the evening, around half past seven we all assembled in Mr Sharma's room to listen to the unfinished story of the previous day. Dinner was also arranged in his room through room service.

He resumed his story, in his inimitable style, "When Kunti chanted her mantra for the birth of Bhima, she invoked 'Vayu'. The forceful God came to her, riding a deer. He didn't have smile on his face, like Dharma. He was very tense to ask Kunti what type of child she was expecting. Unlike Dharma, he had some guilty feeling. This was because Pandu had not been taken into confidence.

Kunti also reacted nervously, with a modest smile. But, she didn't utter any word. Why was Kunti so shy?

We didn't find deer as 'Vahana' of any God. Is it only for indicating the speed? Or, does it have any other significance? Obvious conclusion is that 'Vayu' was somebody residing very close by. He had some association with deer. Who can fulfil the criteria?

The answer is Rishi Kindama who had a connection with deer. In fact, his gotra was Kashyapa.

What are the other associations of a Rishi with deer? Rishi Hrishishringa was the son of a deer. He was from Kashyapa gotra. It was Kashyapa who performed the Yajna of Parikshit at the request of Janamejaya. When the Yajna prematurely ended, Kashyapa revived all serpents. Bhima had Naga connection. Once, Vasuki, after being defeated by Bhima gave away a Naga Kanya to Bhima as wife. Bhima had a son, Bhabhrubahu with the beautiful serpent woman. So there's a possibility that Bhima was fathered by a Naga! Thus, it can't be ruled out that Bhima was fathered by Kindama who was a Kashyapa—naga vamshi."

"It is a possible proposition", said Anup Kumar.

Mr Sharma continued, "Kunti wasn't happy with Bhima. She had even dropped him from her lap. It shows her disgust of the way this child was born! Kunti denied any more association with any other person. Perhaps Pandu too was interested in have his own offspring."

"Now, I can guess the possible motive behind the murder of Kindama", said Kaushik.

"Yes you can tell", he said.

Kaushik replied, "Pandu didn't like the fatherhood of Bhima through Kindama. He took revenge by killing Kindama."

"Excellent guess", he said, "this is also my conjecture. Probably Kindama was a neighbour of Pandu in the woods. He came to know the truth about Pandu's stress-related problems and the fatherhood of Yudhisthira. He approached Kunti, beyond the knowledge of her husband. But Pandu didn't like this perverted person, and killed him."

"The Censor Board may not allow this portion", I suggested.

"This won't affect our story", Mr Sharma said. "Now who's the biological father of Arjuna? Unlike in the case of births of Yudhisthira and Bhima, there's no indication about the manner of arrival of Indra when Kunti invoked Indra.

The age difference between Bhima and Arjuna is one year. After the birth of Bhima, we notice actual seriousness on the part of Pandu to get his own progeny. Probably he was moved by the curse of Rishi Kindama which he took as a boon in disguise, like emperor Dasharatha in the Ramayana.

Dasharatha was childless till he was cursed by a blind Rishi couple following the accidental death of their son Shravan Kumar at the hand of the king. They were fully dependent upon him. The boy went for fetching water for his parents from a spring with an earthen pitcher. Mistaking the sound of filling of the empty container by the boy as drinking of water by animals, the king shot his arrow in that direction causing the accidental death of the boy. His parents suffered massive heart break on receiving this shocking news of the death of their son. They couldn't recover and died. While breathing his last, the sage cursed Dasharatha to suffer similar death, from the shock of reversal of his beloved son. The emperor was blessed with paternity after this curse only.

Pandu resolved that he would please Indra with his asceticism to obtain a progeny through him. As I've said, his problem was psychological. His own birth through his biological father Vyasa all the time haunted him. It had caused a mental barrier in him and left him in a dilemma. He felt that he couldn't produce his own offspring like his father Vichitravirya.

He stood upon one leg from morning to evening and practised other severe austerities with his mind rapt in meditation, for gratifying the Lord of the Celestials. Bhima was in his infancy. But Kunti still undertook rigorous penance. The couple were under treatment of some Vaidya for curing the stress-related problem of Pandu. Kunti had already tasted motherhood. Even if, as a consequence of Kindama's curse, she and her husband died in course of her union with Pandu, it wouldn't cause much harm. Kunti succeeded in her endeavour to get her progeny through Pandu.

The latter termed it to be the grace of Lord Indra whom he had worshiped. Otherwise, there could have been no need for such rigorous penance given Indra's love and lust for woman. It was Indra who raped Tara, the wife of Brihashpati. He would surely have come at the very pronouncement of the first syllable of Kunti's mantra.

Arjuna, indeed, is Indra's son, as Pandu indeed is 'Indra'! Pandu has been compared to Indra many a times. In the Swayamvara, Kunti placed the nuptial garland around Pandu's neck. Pandu was described as 'another Indra' in that royal assemblage of Kuntibhoja. Thus, it is quite possible that Pandu recovered from his stress-related problems to become the biological father of Arjuna.

Bankim Chandra in his *Krishna Charitra* mentioned 'Arjuna' as a synonym of 'Indra'. In the Rig-Veda as well, the name of 'Arjuna' is used as a synonym of Indra."

We patiently listened to the story from Mr Sharma, as he was describing the birth of Arjuna from a different angle.

He said, "Abhimanyu holds the highest status among the Pandavas, though he wasn't the eldest. It indirectly proves that the Pandavas knew at heart about the true carrier of Pandu's blood. In the Adi Parva, Arjuna's son, Abhimanyu was mentioned as the perpetuator of the family. Ghatotkacha was the eldest son among the Pandavas, yet his father Bhima didn't claim that title for him.

Draupadi's five sons have been mentioned many a time, like sons of other Pandava brothers. The focus was always on Arjuna and his sons. He was the true carrier of Pandu's blood.

In the Swayamvara Parva, Karna declared that no other person except Indra or Pandu's son would match him in fighting on the battlefield. Indra wasn't the father of Arjuna in the eyes of Karna.

When Dushasana dragged Draupadi to the Sabha, she cried out not to drag her and not to uncover her, and added that the princes wouldn't pardon him, even if the gods themselves with Indra as their ally took their side. Draupadi did never treat Indra as her father-in-law.

Sri Krishna and Arjuna set the entire Khandavprastha on fire to build their capital, against the desire of Indra. Such action on the part of Arjuna against his father's wish is impossible in the Mahabharata scenario!"

We accepted the reasons cited by Mr Sharma in favour of Arjuna being the son of Pandu himself, contrary to the popular belief that he was the son of Indra. We called it a day.

Anup Kumar is leaving Nellore tomorrow by train. He'll join us at Siliguri on 10th June 2008. Being a BSF officer, he has the advantage of availing Railway warrant. He would like to spend sometime in Kolkata where his wife is staying with his in-laws. We shall be leaving by road on the 4th evening.

XL

Nellore is a very old city. This fact is evident from the pattern of buildings and narrow roads inside the town. It remains busy till midnight as pilgrims for Tirupati Temple, Andhra Pradesh touch this spot for their road journey. We're fortunate to see the Chief Minister of Andhra Pradesh, Shri Y.S. Rajshekhar Reddy, who visited Nellore during our stay on 3rd June.

In the evening, Kaushik and I sat down in the room of Mr Sharma to listen to the story of the remaining Pandavas. After tea, he began with his customary smile, "Till yesterday, we've discussed the fatherhood of the sons of Kunti. Let's now discuss Madri's case.

Arjuna's birth through Pandu elated Madri. She told him that by birth, she was superior to Kunti. But as far as status is concerned, she was inferior to her. She wanted a child through him."

"This is quite evident as Madri didn't want children through niyoga", said Kaushik.

Accepting the views of Kaushik, he said, "But Kunti didn't allow Pandu to have sex with Madri. Instead, she gave Madri the mantra for invoking God to beget progeny. She knew how she had cured her husband Pandu of his stress-related problems. The curse of Kindama definitely played in her mind.

Perhaps, after a prolonged discussion, Madri agreed to conceive through niyoga. With Kunti's mantra, Madri invited twin Ashwini Kumars. They came to her with the speed of light. She gave birth to twins Nakula and Sahadeva. All the Pandavas were born at the interval of one year. Together, it would look like an embodied period of five years. Why is then 'five years' mentioned? This discrepancy has been retained to hint that the Pandavas' birth is a myth."

Here Kaushik intervened, "Once, I read in a newspaper about the birth of twin babies to the wives of twin brothers, who had actually married twin sisters!"

It created laughter. Mr Sharma said, "The epic is silent if there was a twin sister of Madri. The story of the birth of the twins through Ashwini Kumars is untenable, since it doesn't require two men to produce twin babies. Kunti's refusal to disclose the mantra to Madri is also astonishing.

Why should Madri depend upon Kunti, once she's learnt the mantra? Like Kunti she could have chanted it again to beget a son. Ashwins had their ancient home on the Ganges. They could be Gangeya or Matsya like Bhishma's mother or Satyavati's mother. Another school of thought is that they were sons of some Puruvamshi Rishi. They were of black complexion like 'Bhoomi-putra' Rishi, similar to sage Vasishtha."

There was a long pause. We were silent. I was thinking about the depth of his knowledge and passion for the epic. Probably, Kaushik was also thinking the same. We remained practically speechless.

He broke the silence, "Tomorrow we're leaving Nellore. I think I should narrate the story about the death of Pandu and Madri today itself. It comes in the same sequence.

Pandu's sexual problem was infertility, not impotence. Once he had cured it, Kunti kept him under sharp watch to keep him away from Madri. The latter was young and attractive. She feared if Madri got any issue through Pandu, her own status would be at stake. After becoming mother of four children, she also didn't want to conceive again.

It was Arjuna's fourteenth birthday. Spring had set in and they were celebrating Arjuna's birthday with fanfare. Madri took this opportunity to allure a very joyful Pandu to his favourite recess in the forest. Madri was in semi-transparent attire, which tempted him. She wanted physical relationship with Pandu on the very birthday of Arjuna, to have a son like him. Pandu couldn't control himself.

It was a tragedy for both of them. During their union, like Kindama, he died in the arms of Madri. Perhaps of a heart attack! Kunti and the Pandavas were close by. They came running, but it was all over. Kunti blamed Madri at first. But she was mentally matured enough to face such a situation. She became calm. On the other hand, Madri lost all interest in life. She committed suicide.

Now the Rishis assembled. A decision had to be taken. Vyasa entered the scene. His script for the future of the Pandavas was already written.

The Rishis knew the problem. It won't be easy to convince the masses about the birth of the Pandavas. No one would believe that Arjuna alone was Pandu's biological son while the others were born through niyoga. Only the Rishis, Kunti and the Pandavas knew the truth.

Vyasa and the Rishis decided to counter myth with superior myth. This assembly took atleast fifteen days time to arrive upon a decision and consider future course of actions. A strong sympathy wave was created to compel the masses to accept the myth of the birth of the Pandavas. The Brahmins led by Vyasa advocated the myth, to be treated as fact.

The story of the 'God-fathers' of the Pandavas was born.

If we go by the conventional story of the Mahabharata, then one more serious offence will be invited. In the actual Mahabharata, Madri burnt herself on the pyre of her husband to commit sati.

If it happens today, this would have invited a serious case against Bhishma, Dhritarashtra, Vidura and other adult members of the Pandavas and Kauravas families. They would be charged for abetting Madri to commit suicide, an offence under section 306 IPC read with section 34 IPC. This section has a penal provision of imprisonment upto ten years and with suitable fine."

Kaushik said, "Stringent punishment is prescribed in section 4 of Commission of Sati (Prevention) Act, 1987 for abetment to sati. It is clearly stated that notwithstanding the penal provisions in Indian Penal Code, if any person committed sati, or even abetted the commission of such sati, either directly or indirectly, should be punished with death or imprisonment for life and should also be liable for fine. For glorification of sati, there's provision of punishment of 7 years with fine in section 5."

Mr Sharma said, "Thanks for reminding me, Kaushik. In fact this Act was enacted after the commission of sati by an 18 year old girl Roop Kanwar sometime in 1987 at Deora village of Sikar District, Rajasthan. She committed sati on the pyre of her husband Maal Singh."

Kaushik said, "You're right Sir, it was 4th September 1987, which coincided with my marriage day."

"What a coincidence!" I uttered spontaneously.

"It is sad that none of the 45 persons against whom the case was initially established got punished", said Kaushik.

All the Pandavas were minors at the time of this incident. Yudhisthira was 16, followed by Bhima-15, Arjuna-14 and twin Nakula and Sahadeva-13 years. It is horrible to think about the mental state of the Pandavas, especially Nakula and Sahadeva when their mother Madri was ablaze."

"We shall feel proud as Bengalis, for Raja Ram Mohan Roy was one of the pioneers behind eradication of this evil practice—'Sati' in the 19th century", said Kaushik.

Mr Sharma said, "Yeah! But sometimes, I feel surprised why 'Sati' is selective. There are many noble widows in the Mahabharata like Kunti and Satyavati, who abstained from committing sati. Gandhari and Kunti died in a forest fire along with Dhritarashtra."

"Obviously, it depends upon the education and social status of the widow", said Kaushik.

Mr Sharma and I supported the naked truth uttered by Kaushik.

XLI

Today is 6th June 2008, Friday. We left Nellore day before yesterday evening. It is the same track which we followed on 31st May for journey from Vizag to Nellore. The night journey is comfortable for us. We moved non-stop, except for dinner at Guntur and breakfast at Rajahmundry before reaching Vizag the next morning. At Vizag, we made a brief halt, and finally left for Bhubaneshwar around 7.30 p.m. We faced inclement weather at Vizag, but the weather became fair after Srikakulam. Entering Orissa early this morning, again we faced incessant rains. We continued to move cautiously, amidst rain. Finally we reached Bhubaneshwar safely by ten for re-union with Harleen and uncle Baldev.

Before narrating today's happenings, I would like to write something about Nellore. When we started from Nellore, Anup Kumar wasn't with us. Both Kaushik and I weren't impressed with Nellore, and didn't know its importance. So, I asked Mr Sharma why Nellore was chosen as a venue for the recruitment rally.

He said, "Dr Bhaumik, do you know the total area of Nellore district?"

"It may be equal to our West Tripura district", I suggested.

He then looked towards Kaushik. The latter said, "It may be half of our state's area."

"No", he said, "it is bigger than our state's size by at least 3,000 square kilometres."

"I didn't know that", Kaushik confessed.

Mr Sharma asked, "Do you know the background of the name Nellore?"

"No", I responded, this time, "is it interesting?"

"Nellore is famous for high paddy yield", he said, "and so it got its name. 'Nelli' means paddy in Tamil. Nellore was part of composite Madras state until 1st October 1953. The states were reorganized on 1st November 1956, on linguistic basis. This district came under Andhra Pradesh. Nellore played a major role in the formation of Andhra Pradesh. Potti Sriramulu, a Telegu patriot and activist from this area, fasted unto death for the formation of the state. His sacrifice resulted in creation of linguistic based states in the Indian Union."

Both, Kaushik and I were thoroughly amused.

Kaushik said, "Anup Kumar is not travelling with us, so, let me raise his patent question! Is there any Mahabharata connection with Nellore?"

Mr Sharma and I laughed heartily at the question by Kaushik. He said, "Of course, there's some Nellore connection with the Mahabharata. Ancient poet Tikkana Somayajulu was the first to translate the Mahabharata into Telegu. He was from this area. This land also produced Yuga Kavi Guntu Seshendra Sharma. His name was once nominated for Nobel Prize for his contribution to literature. He has been conferred with almost all the awards on literature in our country. He has also written *Adhunik Mahabharatham*.

This land has produced many eminent personalities in various fields. S.P. Balasubramaniyan, one of the India's top singers hails from Nellore. It produced two former Chief Ministers of this state, Dr Bezawada Gopal Reddy and Nedurumali Janardhana Reddy. Puchalapalli Sundaraiah, the great Communist leader who sacrificed his life for the poor practised communism here."

"This may be the reason why there is a stronghold of communists at Nellore", said Kaushik. "I've heard his name from elders in my family."

"He was a very popular Communist leader, and probably he visited our state once or twice", said Mr Sharma. "By the way, do you know Nellore has another name?"

"Another name!" I repeated with astonishment.

He disclosed, "Nellore is also called 'Shrimp capital of India', due to its high production of cultured shrimp. Seventy per cent of prawns are exported to America from this area."

"Sir, how do you gather all this myriad information", Kaushik asked.

He replied with a smile on his face, "Most of you spend your leisure time before the idiot box. I mean to say TV while I prefer to sit with my laptop which has Internet facilities. Besides, I've a penchant for reading issues related to the Mahabharata."

"Sir, this is simply splendid! I appreciate your elephantine memory", this time, I expressed my feelings.

"Doctor, everything depends upon your interests", he said, "despite being a medical officer, I've noticed you keep have an interest in literature."

We were crossing Ichchapuram of Andhra Pradesh to enter into Brahmpur, Orissa in the night. We kept on talking to keep the driver, Joginder awake. It is a four-lane road. We came across very thin traffic after entering Orissa due to the inclement weather. However, we made satisfactory progress.

I had been quiet for sometime. I was in fact thinking about Harleen. It was two in the morning. Everybody was restless, and yearning for tea.

Seeing me silent, Mr Sharma said, "Doctor, there's a good news for you", after saying this, he took a long pause to judge my reaction.

I fell in a deep thought and said, "Good news for me!"

With his customary smile, he replied, "This is really good news for you, for Harleen, for Baldevji and for all of us."

Kaushik and I looked at him eagerly, as he explained, "Dr Pradhan of State FSL, Bhubaneshwar has successfully retrieved the data from Aman's laptop. I had a talk with Dr Pradhan in the evening. He's eager to meet us."

"Fantastic!" both Kaushik and I uttered almost simultaneously.

"Sir, you've really done an injustice by concealing this so far", I said.

"Don't worry", he said, "I've already informed Baldevji. They would behave normally till our arrival. It is quite possible that they're being watched by vested interests.

Baldevji assured me saying, "Wahe guruji ke kripa, mujhe to disha mil gayi. Aap jeise kahenge, waisa hi karenge. Aab Harleen ki khushi hi meri khushi hai."

[By god's grace I've found my path. Now, I'll follow your advice only. Now I want to see Harleen happy.]

"Sir, one request", I said, "Will you please allow me to accompany you to State FSL when you visit Dr Pradhan?"

"Ok, Doctor", said Mr Sharma, "you deserve to lead. You're the first person to scent the mystery surrounding the death of Aman."

"Sir, you're right", Kaushik said, "He's the pathfinder for this mystery."

"Sir, we're ignoring the pain and agony suffered by Harleen for two years", I said, "and the cooperation given by Aman's parents."

"Bravo doctor! Bravo! I was expecting a reply like this from you", he said, "it is spoken like a true lover!"

I felt too embarrassed to react, but I took solace in Browning, till our arrival at Bhubaneshwar:

Escape me?
Never—
Beloved!
While I'm I, and you're you,
So long as the world contains us both,
Me the loving and you the loth,
While the one eludes, must the other pursue.
My life is a fault at last, I fear:
It seems too much like a fate, indeed!
Though I do my best I shall scarce succeed.

❖❖❖

XLII

It is again a hectic day for us at CRPF Group Centre, Bhubaneshwar. Harleen couldn't arrange a vehicle from the Group Centre. Our drivers have been driving continuously for the last two days. So we decided to hire a taxi.

We took a quick breakfast. Then the four of us, Harleen, uncle Baldev, Mr Sharma and I left the CRPF Group Centre at about 11.30 a.m. in an Indica. We went straight to the office of Dr Pradhan. He greeted us and led us to a small conference hall. Another scientist, Mr Basudev Satapati, his junior was also present. After introductions and refreshments, Dr Pradhan gave a printed report to Mr Sharma. He also produced a soft copy in CD.

The latter's face became bright every now and then, as he went through the report. Seeing us inquisitive and eager to know the story, Dr Pradhan broke the silence: "Retrieval of data from the laptop, last used by late Captain Amandeep Sandhu gives me immense pleasure. I've never worked upon a case based on a personal request. But my friendship with Mr Sharma goes back to December, 2002 when we worked together as judges at police duty meet in Bangalore. Since then, we're good friends. When he requested me to take this case, I couldn't refuse. But after achieving the task with assistance from Satapati, I would say that such a case is witnessed only once in a life-time."

Satapati bowed down his head to receive the acclamation, while Dr Pradhan went on, "Fortunately for us, the laptop was in a good condition."

After a pause, he turned towards Harleen, who was sitting between uncle Baldev and me with wet eyes, "Because of this brave lady, we're in this happy mood today. It is a general practice adopted by personnel serving in areas like armed forces, police, and high security fields to use different passwords for different e-mail servers. They also frequently change the passwords. Similarly, they adopt other precautionary measures like keeping important files stored outside the computer device. Dr Bedi gave us a Yahoo ID and password of Captain Amandeep based on his place of birth.

We checked all the files in the laptop. But these had been hacked and destroyed. We checked if any e-mail was sent from this laptop by Amandeep prior to his death. To our utter dismay, we couldn't find any evidence of any e-mail being sent by him. For three days, we were totally hopeless. By a sheer fortune, Mr Satapati noticed a draft when we opened the mail box in yahoo.id provided by Dr Bedi. The print out of this is with Mr Sharma presently."

Mr Sharma by this time had finished his reading. He requested Dr Pradhan to allow him to narrate the findings in a gist which Dr Pradhan accepted gleefully. Mr Sharma began, "Captain Aman put a heading for his draft, 'Dear I Always Remember You.' It is in fact the diary of Captain Amandeep Sandhu, for the period of his stay at Bharatpur for 'Operation Bikram'. Captain Nilesh Rahane was his bosom friend and his batch-mate from basic training days. He was occupying the room next to him. But Captain Rahane betrayed him, the details of which I would narrate soon.

As the troops were assembling in Rajasthan from various corners for 'Operation Bikram', there was another activity at Bharatpur Officers' Mess behind the curtain. Captain Rahane hails from the Dantewada district of Chhattisgarh. On the night of Sunday, 18th April 2006, Aman heard Rahane having a telephonic talk with someone regarding smuggling of ammunitions. The latter was bargaining on rates of 'seeds'. They were using the term 'harvesting', a number of times. Aman became very suspicious, and soon he identified two other tentacles in the form of Major Mahipal Singh in charge of Ammunition Depot Bharatpur and Lt. Colonel Suresh Paul of Captain Rahane's unit. He realized that the word 'harvesting' meant the quantity of ammunitions which could be siphoned out in course of the armed exercise 'Operation Bikram'. Similarly, 'seeds' meant 'ammunitions'. Aman didn't know the persons to whom these ammunitions would be sold.

Aman committed the biggest blunder by disclosing this information to Brigadier S.H. Yadav who was his first Commandant. He told Yadav about the developments on 21st April 2006 over the telephone. The latter advised him not to relate this over the telephone, or send the same though e-mail. Instead, he should give his email-id and password to Mr Yadav, and advised him to post his observations as a draft. This would enable Mr Yadav to read the information gathered by Aman. At the same time, there wouldn't be any record available regarding any e-mail sent by Aman. Mr Yadav also cautioned him not to share this information with any other person. In the event of any leakage of this information, the perpetrators would become careful and it would become difficult to catch them. In fact, they may harm Aman in some way."

Mr Sharma looked towards Dr Pradhan and Mr Satapati; they expressed satisfaction over the narration, so he continued, "It is needless to say Brigadier Yadav was also hand-in-glove with the racket. He shared the information received from Aman with his accomplices, especially Captain Rahane. Rahane behaved normally with Aman, and in fact he became friendlier. Captain Rahane used to lead a fast life and maintained relations with many girls.

The last explosion in the ammunition depot took place on 28th April 2006. These explosions were carried out to destroy the evidence of supply of ammunitions to undesirable elements, who had been engaged in waging a war against our states. In this case, it was the Maoists, as confirmed by my source.

After these explosions in the Black Panther Rifles' Ammunitions depots, a high level inquiry committee was constituted. All the troops were asked not to leave Rajasthan till the inquiry was over. On 29th April 2006 in the morning, Captain Rahane came to the room of Aman with photographs of some girls saying that his wife was coming, and she would stay for two days with him at Bharatpur. Aman didn't know that Captain Rahane was married, and so he was taken by surprise. Rahane replied that they were actually living together and the recovery of photographs of these girls by his wife (or would-be-wife) Sandhya would jeopardize the prospect of their marriage. Rahane promised that he would take back the photographs as soon as Sandhya left the mess. Aman couldn't turn down the request of Captain Rahane. So he kept those photographs in his room.

Sandhya came in the afternoon of 29th April 2006. She was a beautiful lady and probably a high-society girl. She behaved like the wife of Captain Rahane, and went to the mess for dinner on Saturday night with Rahane. Aman also attended the dinner. She was introduced to Aman in the afternoon itself by Rahane. Aman was sitting alone, enjoying the music. At one point of time, Sandhya joined him with a glass of wine in her hand while Rahane was enjoying his drinks in the bar. At her request, he took a glass of a soft drink. Major Mahipal was taking pictures at the party. He also took photographs of Aman and Sandhya, sitting together at the table. Some couples were dancing on the floor. Sandhya requested Aman to join her for a dance. Aman looked towards Rahane and the latter asked him to go ahead with Sandhya. So he danced with Sandhya. This was also caught on camera. Sandhya attended dinner the next evening as well, and behaved in a more friendly manner with Aman."

Mr Sharma stopped here.

This time uncle Baldev responded, "Jab main wahan gaya Aman ki dead body lane ke liye, tab wohi tasvir mujhe dikhayi gayi. Kuch tasvirein shayad Aman ke saman ke sath bhi bhej di thi, jinhe dekhne se laga ki Aman saach mooch divana ho gaya tha. Ye sab batein Brigadier Yadav sab ke samne hui, aur main viswas kar baitha. Mera sara gussa Harleen beti ke upar ja kar para.

> Maine keh baitha, Baisakhi ke dauran agar Harleen sagai ke liye razi ho jati, shayed yeh din dekhna nahin parta. Mere munh se woh lafz Yadav sab ne chhin liye, aur Harleen ke upar mera gussa aur barha diya. Mein soch bhi nahi saka, iske peechhe itna gehera raz hein.
>
> Wahe guru ke kripa, mera bhram ab tut gaya. Babuji, aap log vidwan hein. Jitna paisa lagein main dene ke liye taiyar hun, lekin mein chahta hun aise ghinoni harkat

karne walon ko kadi se kadi saza mile, taa ki mere Aman ki atma ko shanti mile.

Aur ek bat hein. Mere karan Harleen beti do sal tak itna kasht uthayi. Mein Harleen ko khush dekhna chahta hun. Aap logon ke ane se phir se bacchi ke man mein raunak aa gayi. Mein ummid karta hun yeh raunak aagey bhi barkarar rahegi."

[When I went for taking Aman's dead body, they showed me these photographs. Some photographs were probably with the belongings of Aman. Seeing these, it appeared to me that Aman had gone astray. This I had discussed in front of Brigadier Yadav and I became angry with Harleen.

I said that if during Baishakhi, Harleen had agreed for the sagai, this couldn't have happened. Yadav Saab took these words from me and incited me against Harleen. I couldn't imagine that there was such a deep-rooted conspiracy behind the event.

By God's grace, I've realized my fault. Sir, you're wise men. I'm ready to pay whatever money is required but, I want to see that the killers of my son Aman face stringent punishment, so that his soul may rest in peace.

Another thing, on account of me, my daughter Harleen had suffered a lot. I want to see her happy. I've noticed that she's regained zeal to a great extent in your company. I hope that this will continue in future as well.]

Uncle Baldev couldn't hold his tears. Mr Sharma consoled him by embracing him and showing solidarity towards his vow to fight against the murderers of his son, Aman. Harleen also started weeping which made me embarrassed, as I tried my best to console her.

We left the office of Dr Pradhan a little after 1 p.m. and went to the office of advocate Abhishek Pattanaik to apprise him about the latest developments.

Mr Sharma told Pattanaik about our movement plans, as we were leaving for our next venue Siliguri via Barrakpore tomorrow. Pattanaik spoke to his friend, Shri Pawan Kumar Sharma, Ld. Senior Advocate, Rajasthan High Court, Jaipur Bench over the telephone and narrated the case. Ld. Senior counsel Mr Sharma agreed to take up the case of Captain Amandeep. It was decided that Mr Pattanaik would prepare the draft for filing a Writ in Rajasthan High Court for registration of a murder case on the basis of freshly-found evidence relating to the death of Captain Amandeep Sandhu at Bharatpur, Officers' Mess of Black Panther Rifles on 2nd May 2008. Further, it would be prayed for endorsement of the investigation to Central Bureau of Investigation (CBI). If any further clue transpires from the documents likely to be received under RTI, it'll be tagged with the case through supplementary prayer.

Uncle Baldev and Mr Sharma would meet Pattanaik at his residence in Bhubaneshwar in the evening. Since Mr Sharma was the main architect of the ongoing investigation, he should see the draft before departure for Siliguri. We provided photocopies of all the documents to Mr Pattanaik. Uncle Baldev declared that he would pay Pattanaik handsomely. But Pattanaik replied that he would take only nominal fees. He felt it to be his moral responsibility to fight against the enemies of our country. The Maoists have become a serious threat to India's internal security and they're swallowing tax payers' money too.

We returned to our campus quarters at three in the afternoon. Kaushik was waiting for us for lunch. So we went straight into the dining hall without changing clothes. He was eager to listen about the latest developments.

Mr Sharma said, "It is all well, on all fronts. You better spend some time with Dr Bhaumik after lunch in his room. He'll tell you the entire story. By the way, our boys shouldn't miss the opportunity to visit Konark Sun temple. Baldevji and I would be busy in finalizing the Writ Petition to be filed before Jaipur Bench of Rajasthan High Court, at advocate Pattanaik's residence.

It is summer season, so it'll be pleasant till eight in the evening. What I suggest, you take the mini-bus with our boys and leave for Konark by half past four."

Uncle Baldev also supported the plan.

Kaushik said, "It'll be very much strenuous for Dr Bhaumik to accompany us, for he needs rest."

"In that case, you come to my room after lunch", Mr Sharma said, "I'll tell you the story behind Aman's death. Let Dr Bhaumik take some rest. Our appointment with the advocate is at 7 in the evening."

"You're so caring", I thanked Mr Sharma.

"My dear Dr Bhaumik", Mr Sharma responded, "you should remain fit and keep others also fit, both mentally and physically."

This rendered me speechless. We hurriedly finished the lunch and went inside our rooms.

❖❖❖

XLIII

We reached Konark around six in the evening. The daylight was beginning to fade. We took a professional guide to save time. He led us to the 13th century Sun Temple and went on with his description, stopping at places allowing us to take photographs: "Konark is a small town in the state of Orissa, 65 kilometres from Bhubaneshwar. Built with black granite by king Narasimhadeva between 1236 to 1264, it is also called the Black Pagoda. The temple is a World Heritage site. It takes the form of chariot of Arka, the sun god, and is heavily decorated with stone carving. The entire complex was designed in the form of a huge chariot drawn by seven spirited horses on twelve pairs of exquisitely decorated wheels. The entrance is guarded by two lions, which are crushing a war elephant. Each elephant again, lies on the top of a human body. The temple symbolizes the majestic strides of Sun God. At the entrance of the temple, there's a Nat Mandir. This is where the temple dancers used to perform dances in homage to Sun God. All around the temple, there are various floral and geometric patterns. There are also human, divine and semi-divine figures in sensuous poses. These contain couples in various amorous poses, and are derived from the Kamasutra".

Our boys were hesitating to put questions to the guide in the presence of Harleen. So, I told Kaushik, "I'm going with Harleen, as she has seen the temple only five days back. You call us after you've finished."

Our staff grinned at my proposal, while Kaushik said, "Ok, Dr Bhaumik."

Away from our comrades, we sat side by side on the steps of the main temple facing towards Nat Mandir, with some ruined structures, half repaired by the Archaeological Survey of India towards our back. Harleen was wearing a magenta coloured salwar-kameez with a dupatta round her neck. She was at her very best and the developments which took place today made her feel relieved. "Face is the mirror of our mind", presently I could read her mind from her face under the moon.

I told her, "It was after visiting this temple that once poet Rabindranath Tagore wrote: 'here the language of the stone surpasses the language of men'. I think you've forgotten to become a guide for me during this visit to Konark."

I kept my hand on her hand which she didn't mind. We passed few moments silently and then she broke the silence, "I may not have the quality of a guide. That's why I didn't promise that day. But since you've mentioned about Tagore's comment on the sculpture, I'm telling you a story of a sculptor written by our Punjabi writer, Rajendra Singh Bedi.

> The sculptor was a young girl Kirti in her early twenties. Her father Narayan was a great sculptor. But at his sudden death, Kirti fell in serious financial crisis with her ailing mother. She had seen her father at his work, and had inherited the art as well. So she took up the work of

sculpting on wood. She preferred to prepare human figures and devas.

Maganlal, a bachelor in his early forties was a shopkeeper where her father used to sell his products. His antique shop was located in a mixed populated area, close to the shop of a travel agent Siraj. The latter made frequent trips to Khajuraho and other places with foreign tourists. Kirti usually visits Magan's shop in the evening to sell her products. On her way to the shop, she was often teased by Siraj, which she couldn't evade.

Magan is a cheater. He pays nominal amounts of five to ten rupees per piece, on the pretext of mediocre quality of the products. He knows that the products are even better than those of her father. He sells these sculptures by imparting to them an antique look, keeping these under earth and pouring acids. Magan earns a lot by this treachery. He always insists that Kirti should make 'nude sculptures' which would fetch her more money.

She makes a clear confession before Magan that the main problem in preparing 'nude' sculptures is non-availability of models. Finally, one day, Kirti told Magan that she would bring a 'nude' next week. Magan promised to give her rupees one hundred for the same. As per her promise, Kirti came to his shop after one week with a 'nude sculpture', a lady changing her wet clothes. Magan was pleased with the quality of the work. However, Kirti had to bargain hard to earn rupees one hundred from Magan. She had fever. Besides, her mother was admitted to the hospital.

Pleased with the work of Kirti which would definitely fetch ten times the amount he had spent, Magan asked her to try to prepare 'amorous sculptures' for which he would pay handsomely. He was even ready to give her advance to ensure her visit to Khajuraho for seeing the models. Kirti left Magan's shop silently without taking any advance, frustrated by the slyness of Magan.

After Kirti left his shop, Magan took the 'nude sculpture' for dipping it into acid for defacement and to give it an antique look. Just at that moment, he noticed that the face of the sculpture was similar to Kirti. Magan realized that in the absence of a model, Kirti probably stood in front of a mirror with wet clothes to bring perfection to her work, and in the process she caught a cold.

Next week, Kirti brought an amorous sculpture and fetched rupees one thousand. Kirti was desperate this time in bargaining as she was now alone. She had lost her mother in the interim period. She also confirmed that she went to Khajuraho with Siraj. To his great astonishment, Magan discovered that in the 'amorous sculpture', the male figure was none other than Siraj, and Kirti was of course the female."

"It's an amazing story", I said. The clock was showing half past seven. Our comrades were engaged in shopping in the stalls in front of the temple. We stood up, hand in hand, walked down the steps silently to have a look for the last time at the big chariot wheel. Suddenly, I couldn't resist myself, and kissed her taking her in firmly in my arms. She didn't resist as long as I held her, only some drops of water from her eyes and her breathing gave me indications about her warmth. We were silent during our return. The anxiety of future separation evoked Laurence Hope:

For this is Wisdom; to love, to live
To take what fate or the gods may give,
To ask no question, to make no prayer,
To kiss the lips and caress the hair,
Speed passion's ebb as you greet its flow
To have, – to hold – and – in time, – let go!

XLIV

We reached Barrakpore Police Training College, West Bengal by road on the evening of 7th June, after covering a distance of about 650 k.m. in a day. Initially, we moved along NH-5 up to Baleswar via Cuttak and Bhadrak from Bhubaneshwar. From Baleswar, we followed NH-60 and touched localities like Jaleswar, Datan, Belda and Kharagpur. At Kharagpur, we stopped for lunch at around 2 p.m. After lunch, from Kharagpur we took NH-6 to cross places like Debra, Panskura, Kolaghat, Bagnan, Dankuni, Dunlop, Sodepur and Barrakpore. Major portion of the route passed through the rural areas of Bengal.

I did not notice any characteristic change in its nature from what we generally read in literature of the three Banerjees', Tarashankar, Bhibhuti Bhusan and Manik; except that the highways are developed in patches, and vehicles are moving 24 × 7. Most of these areas are flood-affected, as evident from the traces of straws attached to trees even at great heights.

Last night, we returned to the campus at Bhubaneshwar at around 10 p.m. Uncle Baldev and Mr Sharma came from the residence of Mr Pattanaik after another half an hour. Before that, I gave Harleen the gift which I had purchased in Ranchi. She accepted it smilingly. Mr Sharma was satisfied with the draft prepared by Advocate Pattanaik. Harleen and uncle Baldev would leave for Delhi tomorrow afternoon by Bhubaneshwar-Delhi flight, and then avail the connecting Indian Airlines flight for Jaipur from Delhi the same evening. They would be accompanied by Shri Himesh Nanda, a Junior of Mr Pattanaik. Writ Petition would be filed on 9 June 2008, Monday at Rajasthan High Court, Jaipur Bench by Shri Pawan Kumar Sharma, Senior Advocate, Rajasthan High Court. Mr Sharma didn't want to comment further on the case.

Uncle Baldev and Harleen waved hands with wet eyes at the time of our departure from CRPF Group Centre, Bhubaneshwar in the morning. Uncle made me further emotional with his words. Embracing me he said, "*Puttar*, *mein janta hoon tumse batein kar ke, Harleen beti ko bahut sukun milta hai. Tumhare upar jo uska vishwas hai, use barkarar rakhna. Agey kya hoga yeh to vakht hi batayega. Agar Wahe Guru ki kripa hui, to tum dono ki dosti, rishte mein bhi badal sakti hai. Tumhare aur Harleen mein mujhe koi kami nazar nahi ayi.*"

[My son, I know that my daughter Harleen feels happy speaking to you. You should live upto her faith in you. What'll happen in the future, time only can say. By God's grace, your friendship may be converted to a relationship. I've not noticed any shortcomings between you and Harleen.]

I touched uncle Baldev's feet, and thanked him for those kind words. Harleen also touched the feet of Mr Sharma and uncle Baldev, to which Kaushik remained a silent spectator.

Till lunch we were in sad mood, Mr Sharma and I were practically dozing in the seats. Only Kaushik, Narayan and Joginder were speaking at times. Lunch at Kharagpur in a roadside restaurant stimulated us greatly. We tasted a Bengali recipe after more than a month. Our boys were jubilant with the quality of food. Kaushik had taken his basic training at Barrakpore Training Institute where we would stay tonight.

Mr Sharma said, "It is this location from where the Sepoy Mutiny had started in 1857. Mangal Pandey was a Sepoy in the 5th company of the 34th Bengal Native Infantry, which had its headquarters at this location.

Kaushik said, "I've seen the film *Mangal Pandey*, the Rising 2 to 3 times. It is an excellent movie; Amir Khan plays the role of Mangal Pandey."

"Lots of criticism of this movie has come to my notice, in newspapers", said Mr Sharma. "Is there any distortion of facts in the film?"

"I don't think so", said Kaushik. "Story of the film somewhat goes like this: In 1857, India was ruled by the British East India Company. Mangal Pandey was a Sepoy, a soldier of Indian origin, in the army of the East India Company. Pandey, while fighting in the Anglo-Afghan Wars, saves the life of his British commanding officer William

Gordon resulting in a strong friendship between them, transcending both ranks and race.

Gordon rescues a young widow, Jwala, played by Ameesha Patel, from committing sati. Afterwards, he falls in love with her. Meanwhile, Heera, portrayed by Rani Mukherjee has been sold into prostitution to work for Lal Bibi. Lal Bibi is a typical Mashi in red light area, played by Kiran Kher. There's a spark of attraction between Heera and Pandey, and a liaison follows.

Gordon and Pandey's friendship is challenged following the introduction of a new rifle, the enfield rifle musket. In reality, as in the film rumours began to spread among the Sepoys that the paper cartridges that held the powder and ball for the rifle were greased with either pig fat or beef tallow. Since the process of loading the cartridge required the soldier to bite the cartridge open to pour in the loose powder, the soldiers believed that the process would require them to consume pork or beef, an act abhorrent to Muslim and Hindu soldiers, respectively, for religious reasons.

In the film, Gordon investigates the matter and assures Pandey that the cartridges are free from pollution. Keeping his trust in Gordon, Mangal bites the cartridge. But he soon discovers that the cartridges are actually greased with animal fat. The rumour of this imposed pollution is the spark that ignites the resentment in the country. Mutiny breaks out, led by Pandey. At one point, Pandey and Gordon become involved in direct hand-to-hand combat, as the latter tries to dissuade the Sepoy from what he believes to be a futile exercise that'll only lead to death. Pandey is captured and executed, despite the protests from Gordon, who reasons that Pandey will be revered as a martyr, and his legacy will cause more uprisings. This turns out to be correct, as the film closes, with scenes of nation-wide revolt against the British rule.

The film ends with a montage, drawings of the historical rebellion and the narrator describes the progress of the Indian Independence movement over the next century. The montage ends with documentary footage of Mohandas Karamchand Gandhi leading the Indian National Congress during peaceful protests against British rule in 1940s, eventually forcing the end to colonialism in the sub-continent".

"Excellent!" said Mr Sharma. "Kaushik, you've given such a vivid description of the film. It is really splendid. It shows how you've loved the film."

"So, Kaushik is the man of the match today", I said.

"Certainly, you can say, man of the moment", said Mr Sharma, as we entered into Barrakpore Police Training Complex located on the banks of the river Ganges. Kaushik led us to the Officers' Mess. But, except for the Ganges, nothing else enthralled us. The Officers' Mess, the accommodation, internal roads and the periphery of the complex—all were highly congested. Some armed battalion's headquarters were also housed in the campus. We couldn't see much as it was drizzling. However, we spent quite sometime sitting on the cemented bathing ghat of the Ganges, despite the inclement weather. The illuminated town on the other side of the river looked quite charming with occasional passing of steamers and boats in the river.

Looking at the Ganges, I couldn't be as brave as Mr Sharma to put her in the dock over the charge of infanticide of her seven new-born sons, the elder brothers of Debavrata, our Bhishma. I tried to judge her age but the sound of waves was breaking my concentration. So, I remembered Abram Joseph Ryan;

> Some reckon their age by years,
> Some measure their life by art;
> But some tell their days by the flow of their tears.
> And their lines by the moans of their hearts.

❖❖❖

XLV

Today is 9th June 2008, Monday. Yesterday, we reached Siliguri at night at about 11.30 p.m. Our progress was smooth from Barrakpore along NH-34 till we reached Shivbari, 10 k.m. short of Siliguri, at around half-past nine. Hundreds of supporters of Gorkha Jan Mukti Morcha (GJMM) were on the streets protesting against Bengali people from Siliguri and adjoining areas. We noticed lots of brick throwing, and even damaging of tourist vehicles.

We heard that tension was prevailing in Siliguri as GJMM had given a boycott call over the last few days, in support of their demand for Gorkhaland. They weren't allowing tourists' vehicles to ply towards Darjeeling and the hills. We cautiously crossed the spot and managed to find a restaurant near Sevok tri-junction for our dinner. Finally, we reached our place of stay at BSF Group Centre, Salgadu, Siliguri. As the name suggests, the campus has come up amidst shal forest with a sizeable Gorkha population all around. We were apprehensive that the ongoing agitation might affect our recruitment rally.

Our journey in the morning however didn't begin on so sullen note. The weather was sunny in the afternoon after a short drizzle in the morning. Harleen conveyed their safe arrival at Jaipur, the previous evening. Uncle Baldev had informed us about the admission of the Writ Petition in Rajasthan High Court when we were crossing Kaliachawk market, Malda, in the afternoon. The case would come up for hearing on 14th June 2008, Friday.

Their counsel Mr Pawan Kumar Sharma was satisfied with the Writ Petition and the documents annexed with it. He made it optional before uncle Baldev if they would like to stay at Jaipur, for he was confident that the Rajasthan High Court, Jaipur Bench would pass a verdict in favour of petitioner Baldev Sandhu. The court took the time for calling the records urgently from the lower court at Bharatpur. Uncle Baldev decided to board a night super bus with Harleen on Monday evening itself, leaving Shri Himesh Nanda, the junior of Mr

Pattanaik to assist senior advocate Mr Sharma. Mr Nanda was associated with the preparation of the Writ Petition from the very beginning.

Our journey was very pleasant despite the poor condition of NH-34, compared to highways in states like Andhra Pradesh, Punjab and Delhi. We took breakfast at Krishnanagar and purchased a good number of CDs of Bengali songs, mostly Rabindra Sangeet. We enjoyed the songs very much.

Our convoy moved through NH-34 from Barrakpore, touching places like Barasat, Krishnanagar, Palashi, Baherampur, Morgram, Ingrajbazar, Pandua, Raiganj, Karandighi, Dalkhole, Bagdogra and Siliguri. The joke of the day was our discovery of synonym of National Highway No. 34 with the 34th Bengal Native Infantry, parent unit of Mangal Pandey. The other similarity was of course the weight of the enfield bullet, 34 grams of pure lead.

Fortunately for us, on 9th June the markets and the shops were open. Our boys wanted to visit the malls in Siliguri and Bagdogra for purchasing imported items. There was a call for a strike in Darjeeling District from 10th June onwards.

Siliguri is a unique town as 15 out of 47 wards of Siliguri Municipal Corporation fall in neighbouring Jalpaiguri district. Our recruitment venue is in the Jalpaiguri portion of Siliguri Municipal Corporation, but even in this part of the city, we noticed the activists of GJMM moving openly with swords and other lethal weapons outside BSF Campus in drunken condition.

We spent the afternoon of 9 June gossiping in the house of Dr R.K. Panja, Professor of Political Science, NBU, at Kadamtali, Siliguri. He had been a teacher of Mr Sharma. The conversation between the teacher and the disciple was quite absorbing for Kaushik and me. We could gather vital knowledge about the ongoing conflict in Darjeeling. The following are the excerpts:

> As with other low intensity conflicts in India, such as Jharkhand and Uttarakhand, the Gorkhas seek independence from the state, but not the country. Within

many Indian states, one ethnic group dominates a number of linguistic, ethnic and religious minorities. This holds true here also for majority is Bengali from West Bengal.

Separatist leaders have exploited complaints from the Gorkhas about neglect and domination by the Bengalis to mobilize the Nepali speaking minority of the Darjeeling hills, emphasizing their concern for Gorkha identity. Yet, that very idea is controversial, and there's a lack of agreement among the locals on what 'Gorkha' means.

The Gorkha, an ethnic group originally from Nepal, migrated to India during and after British rule. Many were recruited in the colonial army. In today's Darjeeling however, the term Gorkha is applicable to all Nepali speaking people. It is a political, rather than a multi-ethnic group consisting of indigenous tribes of the area, and Nepali immigrants with Indian citizenship.

The Bengalis own most places of business in the hills. The Nepali speaking locals, however, perform menial jobs, and resent the success of Bengalis, whom they consider to be outsiders in the hills. Moreover, they blame the government of West Bengal for their underdevelopment. But the Gorkhas are quite united.

While the six-month old GJMM party and its leader Bimal Gurung want nothing less than an independent Gorkhaland within India, the former radical, Subhash Ghishing had dropped that idea in favour of a more viable solution of greater autonomy. Ghishing and his Gorkha National Liberation Front (GNLF) led a violent two year conflict in the 1980s for a separate state. In 1988, he accepted a political settlement, signing a tripartite agreement with the governments in Kolkata and New Delhi that gave a great deal of autonomy to the newly founded Darjeeling Gorkha Hill Council (DGHC), the governing body of the district of Darjeeling. Ghishing has been the Chairman of the DGHC since its inception.

In 2005, the same parties signed another memorandum of settlement to include Darjeeling in the sixth schedule of the Indian Constitution, which addresses administration of tribal areas. According to the agreement, the DGHC would be granted more powers. For the GJMM and its leader Bimal Gurung, the sixth schedule solution is a betrayal of Gorkhaland.

While many are blaming the West Bengal government for neglecting the hills, others claim that it is the fault of the local administration and the ruling GNLF itself. They accuse the DGHC for siphoning funds and claim that some GNLF functionary including Ghishing, have amassed personal fortunes with funds allocated for development. These accusations have sparked anti-GNLF sentiments in Darjeeling and surrounding villages.

Yet, many locals fear that neither autonomy nor independence will change their fate. They refer to the state of Jharkhand where tribal population was successful in gaining independence from the state of Bihar in 2000, as an example.

Today, Jharkhand is still facing serious problems from Maoists, which we've witnessed recently. Pace of development is still a utopian proposition, despite rich mineral resources of the state.

Professor Panja concluded the topic with these words: "This agitation will continue as long as volatile situation prevails in adjoining Nepal, the country of Nepali speaking people. The reason, however, I'll not explain."

XLVI

Today is the second day of our rally at Siliguri. Anup Kumar joined us day before yesterday in the night. On his arrival, we began to receive special care. After all, he's a BSF officer, and we're staying in BSF campus. Local police and BSF assisted us in the smooth conduct of the recruitment rally, despite a tense situation in Darjeeling district, and in particular, Siliguri town.

We could manage time for our evening chatting. As usual, Anup Kumar asked a question about the epic, "Is there any reference to the north-east in the Mahabharata?"

Sometimes I had noticed, after raising a question, Anup Kumar didn't pay the required attention to the answer, which was not the case with Kaushik. As for me, my profession is different from that of my other comrades, and probably I had much interest in Mr Sharma's narratives.

Mr Sharma was expecting this question, and so he replied quickly, "Apart from participation of King of Pragjyotishpur, present day Assam namely Bhagadutta in Kurukshetra war, Manipur is famous for the Chittrangada-Arjun affair. Tagore has written a beautiful drama 'Chitrangada' on this based on this event. Bhima married Ulupi, believed to be the princess of Nagaland. Similarly, another school of thought is that Hidimba was from present day Dimapur."

"One thing is clear that the Pandavas did visit the north-eastern states", said Kaushik.

"How are you so sure?" asked Mr Sharma.

"Because all these ladies like Chitrangada, Hidimba and Ulupi retained their sons with them, and they didn't move with their husbands", replied Kaushik. "This practice is still in existence in these states."

"You're right, Kaushik!" said Mr Sharma, "and it is one of the reasons for which there's a sense of dislike among the tribes from these places towards the people from the mainland.

Perhaps, I've said this earlier as well. In all these marriages, the Pandavas met initial resistance.

There's yet another interesting opinion about the north-east. Arunachal Pradesh was covered by the waters of the great Tethys Sea in the cretaceous period. The formation of the Himalayas brought the present Arunachal on the map of the Indian sub-continent. After the onslaught upon Kshatriyas by Parasuram, and during post-Mahabharata period, a large number of defeated Kshatriyas migrated to south-east Asia through this area. This is the reason for the spread of Hindu culture in the eastern world.

As regards Tripura, the ancestors of Tripura kings namely Trilochana participated in the Rajsuya of Yudhisthira. They took the side of the Kauravas in the Kurukshetra battle. Tripura is regarded as Kirat land. You'll also find a story of pious large egret and corrupt Brahmin Gautam, in the epic. It is related to this land."

The name of Yudhisthira prompted Kaushik to put another question, "Sir, you've told us about the births of the Pandavas, it'll be unfair on your part if you don't tell us about the births of the Kauravas."

"In that case I should start with Vidura", said Mr Sharma, "I've already mentioned how Lord Dharma was cursed by sage Mandavya and was incarnated as Vidura. He was born to the maid servant of Ambalika, the wife of Vichitravirya. So he was the step brother of Pandu and Dhritarashtra. He was the Prime Minister of Hastinapura with Dhritarashtra as the king after Pandu had retired to the forest. Moreover, he was the father of Yudhisthira as I had narrated earlier.

When Kunti conceived in the woods, Gandhari had two years' pregnancy. Vyasa gave her a boon of becoming the mother of one hundred sons, a reward of her service and devotion to the sage. When she heard about the birth of a son to Kunti, she became restless for she had not become a mother, even after two years of conception. Without the knowledge of Dhritarashtra, she had undergone an abortion. A mass of flesh came out of her womb.

When Vyasa got the information, he immediately rushed there and examined the mass of flesh. He said that it was possible that progeny could be retrieved from this mass of flesh. He asked Gandhari to keep one hundred pitchers ready and arranged the pouring of water on the mass of flesh constantly. Obviously, the water contained some medicine or chemicals. The mass of flesh got divided into several parts. Each of these parts was kept in an earthen pitcher. Still one part was left out. Gandhari wished for a daughter. Vyasa arranged the same in another earthen pot. After another two years' period, first Duryodhana was born in an earthen pitcher; which might be a case of a test-tube baby or cloning. The other ninety-nine brothers of Duryodhana and his sister Dushala were born in the same manner within a span of another one month. The gynaecology was at its best during the period of Mahabharata."

After a pause, he said, "The birth of Dronacharya also took pace in a somewhat similar manner. His father was the great sage Bharadwaj. One morning, he was taking a bath in the Ganges. Apsara Ghreetachi also came there for a bath. All of a sudden, the wind blew away the clothes of Ghreetachi. Bharadwaj couldn't resist his temptation seeing the naked youthful beauty of Ghreetachi and his semen oozed out almost spontaneously. With the sperm donated by Bharadwaj, and probably with the union of female cells from Ghreetachi, the embryo of Drona was formed outside his mother's womb in an earthen pitcher."

"Is there any offence committed here?" asked Anup Kumar.

"Certainly not!" said Mr Sharma, "but there's a ban on producing human clones. Further, it is evident that Vidura deliberately spread rumours of the birth of Sun-like son of Kunti, when Gandhari was pregnant. It is quite possible that Vidura was aware of the birth of Karna, Kunti's first child before she got married to Pandu. But it was never declared publicly either by Kunti or Vidura or any body. The information about Kunti becoming a mother was conveyed by Vidura, to cause Gandhari to try for premature child-birth. She ended up with termination of her pregnancy. But, because of the excellent work done by sage Vyasa, Gandhari's children could see the light of this universe. When Duryodhana was born, Vidura and his associate Brahmins made propaganda of evil omens in the form of cawing of crows and eerie sounds from animals like donkeys, jackals and vultures amidst a cyclonic storm."

"What may be the reason behind this?" asked Kaushik.

He explained, "If you think of it logically, you'll find there was no evil sign. It was the month of Bengali Chaitra, corresponding to April-May and such stormy weather was quite natural. Vidura raised the issue of crowning prince Yudhisthira as the king-in-the-making. This was gladly accepted by Dhritarashtra, and he wanted to know before his court if Duryodhana would get a chance to become the king, once Yudhisthira's rule was over. Vidura reacted to it sharply by saying that his newly-born son Duryodhana should be killed for the welfare of the country. It indicates the hatred of Vidura, the Prime Minister of Hastinapura towards an infant. He was his nephew, even then he thought of his death!"

It was ten in the night. Mr Sharma said, "Since, we're here for one more day, I shall narrate some more stories relating to Duryodhana tomorrow."

So, we called it a day.

XLVII

Today is our penultimate day of stay at Siliguri. We assembled in the lobby for our evening chatting for the final time. It is raining outside, but we're happy that despite inclement weather, we could complete our rally. Mr Sharma, Kaushik and I, we three are leaving by train tomorrow afternoon from New Jalpaiguri to Kolkata. Our men will also leave tomorrow for Tripura under the leadership of Ajit Debbarma by road, after dropping us at the railway station. Anup Kumar has booked his train ticket for day after tomorrow.

Today we've not put any questions to Mr Sharma. He picked up on his own from where he had left yesterday, "Bhima was born the same day as Duryodhana was born. So, at the time of this discussion in the royal court, the other Pandavas were yet to be born. In that sense, Vidura was advocating for Yudhisthira, perhaps his progeny.

Duryodhana was very much worried. His father being blind, the kingdom was ruled by Pandu. After his death, Yudhisthira, the heir-apparent, would in course of time become the king. Duryodhana thought that as his blind father was quite helpless, he must prevent Yudhishthira's accession to the throne, and contrived a way of killing Bhima.

The reason for his hatred towards Bhima was that the latter excelled among all the royal princes in physical prowess. He used to bully Duryodhana and the other Kauravas by dragging them by their hair and beating them. A great swimmer, he would dive into pools, with one or more of them clasped helplessly in his arms, and remain under water till they were almost drowned. Whenever they climbed up on a tree, he would stand on the ground and kick at the tree and shake them down like ripe fruits. The Kaurava brothers used to sustain bruises as a result of such practical jokes of Bhima.

Duryodhana made arrangements to carry out his resolve since he thought that powers of the Pandavas would decline with the death of Bhima. He and his brothers planned to throw Bhima into the Ganges, imprison Arjuna and Yudhisthira and then seize the kingdom and rule it. Duryodhana went with his brothers and the Pandavas for a swim in the Ganges. After the swim, exhausted, they slept in their tents. Bhima had exerted himself more than the others and his food had been poisoned. He felt drowsy and lay down on the bank of river. Duryodhana bound him with wild creepers and threw him into the river. The evil Duryodhana had already caused sharp spikes to be planted on the spot. This was done purposely, so that

Bhima might be impaled on the spikes and lose his life. Fortunately, there was no spike in the place where Bhima fell. Poisonous water-snakes bit his body. The poisonous food he had taken was counteracted by the snake poison and no harm was caused to Bhima. The river washed him to a bank.

Duryodhana thought that Bhima must have died as he had been thrown in river infested with poisonous snakes and fanged with spikes. So, he returned to the city with the rest of the party in great joy.

When Yudhisthira enquired about the whereabouts of Bhima, Duryodhana informed him that he had preceded them to the city. Yudhisthira believed Duryodhana and as soon as he returned home, he asked his mother whether Bhima had returned home. His anxious question brought forth the reply that Bhima hadn't yet returned, which made Yudhisthira suspect some foul pay against his brother, and he went again with his brothers to the forest and searched every where, but Bhima couldn't be found. They went back in great sorrow.

Some time later, Bhima awoke and trudged wearily back home. Kunti and Yudhisthira welcomed him with great joy. On account of the poison that had entered his system, Bhima became stronger than before.

Kunti sent for Vidura and told him the secret: "Duryodhana is wicked and cruel. He seeks to kill Bhima since he wants to rule the kingdom, I'm worried."

Vidura replied: "What you say is true, but keep your thoughts to yourself, for if the wicked Duryodhana is accused or blamed, his anger and hatred will only increase. Your sons are blessed with long life. You needn't fear on that account."

Yudhisthira also warned Bhima and said: "Be silent over the matter. Hereafter, we've to be careful and help one another and protect ourselves."

Duryodhana was surprised to see Bhima alive. His jealousy and hatred increased. He heaved a deep sigh and pined away in sorrow.

Sharma took a long pause, and began, "This is a story of Mahabharata. Probably this is the only story where

Duryodhana was alleged to be directly involved in an offence against the Pandavas.

But interestingly, the writer of Mahabharata is again harsh against the Kauravas. The offence committed by Duryodhana and his associates would attract section 307/120(B) IPC for attempted murder of Bhima through poisoning and other schemes, in furtherance of a criminal conspiracy. The sections have maximum penal provision of imprisonment for life. But they're likely to get relief for they were juvenile at the time of commission of the offence. Further, it would have been difficult to prove the case due to contradicting evidence. It is really doubtful if any person can survive after being thrown into a river, with hands and legs tied and poisoned. The Pandavas and the Kauravas had gone together to the banks of the Ganges, still other Pandavas didn't notice anything. The possibility of use of sedative doses upon other Pandavas can't be ruled out.

It is peculiar that a virtuous person like Vidura didn't have the courage to bring this incident to the notice of Bhishma and others. By concealing this sin, Vidura and Kunti have become sinners and probably spoiled the life of Duryodhana and other Kauravas. Any man of prudence will have doubts if this incident was a false allegation on behalf of Vidura and Kunti. It may also be noted that the Kaurava brothers were severely tortured by Bhima. Acts of Bhima would have also invited cases under section 323 IPC for voluntarily causing hurt or even under section 325 IPC for voluntarily causing grievous hurt.

The maximum punishment under this section is seven years' imprisonment and shall also be liable for fine. Advocates on the side of the Kauravas would have demanded addition of section 307 IPC stating the acts of Bhima like clasping the Kaurava brothers in his arms, and putting them under water till they were almost drowned or causing their fall from trees, constituted the offence of attempted murder. Advocates on the side of the Pandavas would claim Bhima to be a juvenile to shift the trial to a juvenile court.

But one thing is sure that the Pandavas and the Kauravas would find it difficult to stay outside the prisons."

❖❖❖

XLVIII

I'm composing this Diary sitting at Agartala. Today is June 14, 2008, Saturday. This morning Mr Sharma and I've returned from Kolkata by an Indigo flight after journeying by Teesta-Torsa Express overnight from New Jalpaiguri. Kaushik has also travelled with us from New Jalpaiguri junction upto Kolkata. But he stayed back at Kolkata to spend a few days with his relatives. Anup Kumar is probably in the train now.

As I was writing, I received a call from Harleen. She was beaming with joy to announce the judgment of Rajasthan High Court, Jaipur Bench. In the court, the learned public prosecutor on behalf of the Rajasthan government didn't put any objection to the prayer for re-investigation of the entire affaire related to death of Captain Amandeep Sandhu, at Bharatpur Officers' Mess of Black Panther Rifles on 2nd May 2006 through CBI, after registering a formal murder case. Accordingly, the court passed the judgment allowing the Writ Petition filed by uncle Baldev.

I could make out the exultation of Harleen, as she repeated, "Main bahut khush hoon, aaj...I'm very pleased today."

I recited, "Main bhi bahut khush hoon...me too."

"Kyun... why?"

"Ab tumhari khushi mein hi meri bhi khushi hai...now your pleasure is my pleasure."

"Aur kuchh...anything more?"

"Tum Agartala Group Centre mein badli karalo...you get transferred to Agartala Group Centre."

"Yeh kyun...why this suggestion?"

"Kyun ki, 'U' kabhi 'bhi' 'Q' se alag nehin hota hai...I love you as Q loves U'."

She didn't ask any further questions, only her hilarity reverberated in my ears. I looked towards the sea of light outside and cried to myself with joy!

Light, my light, the world-filling light,
the eye-kissing light, heart-sweetening light!
Ah, the light dances, my darling, at the centre of my life;
the light strikes, my darling, the chords of my love;
the sky opens, the wind runs wild, laughter passes over the earth.

The butterflies spread their sails on the sea of light.
Lilies and jasmines surge up on the crest of the waves of light.

The light is shattered into gold on every cloud, my darling,
and it scatters gems in profusion.

Mirth spreads from leaf to leaf, my darling,
and gladness without measure.
The heaven's river has drowned its banks
and the flood of joy is abroad.

Bibliography

Ashok Mitra, *Bharater Chitrakala*, Anand Publishers Pvt. Ltd., Kolkata.

Dr. B.R. Kishore, *Mahabharata*, New Delhi.

Bankim Chandra Chatterjee, *Bankim Rachanabali*, Sahitya Sansad, Kolkata.

Birendra Mitra, *Kurukshetre Devshivir*, Nath Publishing, Kolkata.

C. Rajagopalachari, *Mahabharata*, Bharatiya Vidya Bhavan, Bombay.

Dr. C.S. Shah, *Introduction to Mahabharata* (Internet edition).

The Commission of Sati (Prevention) Act, 1987 (No. 3 of 1988).

Durga Madhab (John) Mitra, *The Letort Papers—Understanding Indian Insurgencies: Implications for Counterinsurgency Operations in the Third World*, U.S. Army War College.

http://www.diehardindian.com/demograph/moredemo/aryan.htm

http://www.vishalaarwal.voiceofdharma.com/articles/indhistory/whatisamt/parte.htm

Dhiresh Bhattacharya, *Mahabharater Ekshoti Durlov Muhurtha*, Anand Publishers Pvt. Ltd., Kolkata.

Ekaler Hindi Galpaguchcha, National Book Trust of India, New Delhi.

Gajendra Kumar Mitra, *Panchajanya*, Mitra & Ghosh Publishers Pvt. Ltd., Calcutta.

Hindi Galpaguchcha, National Book Trust of India, New Delhi.

Indrajit Bandyopadhayay *Mahabharata—The Mystery of the Pandava 'God-Fathers'—Part-1* (Internet edition)

JatLand.com, *The Mahabharata Tribes.*

Dr. Jayantanuja Bandyopadhyaya, *Mahakavya-O-Maulabad*, Allied Publishers Pvt. Ltd., Kolkata.

Kamal Kumar, *Code of Criminal Procedure, 1973*, Kamal Law House, Kolkata.

Klaus K. Klostermalier, *A Coincise Encyclopedia of Hinduism*, Oneworld Oxford Publications, England.

Mayadhar Mansinha, *A History of Oriya Literature*, Sahitya Academi, New Delhi.

Mahabharata, Bengali translation of the Indian epic Mahabharata in Prose by Late Kaliprasanna Sinha, Vols. I and II, Tuli-Kalam, Calcutta.

Maitreyi Devi, *Na Hanyate*, Prima Publications, Kolkata.

Mani Bhaumik, *Code Name God: The Spiritual Odyssey of a Man of Science*, Bengali translation by Ranjan Bandyopadhyaya, Anand Publishers Pvt. Ltd., Kolkata.

Mark Tully, *India's Unending Journey*, Rider, Ebury Publishing.

Malayalam Galpaguchcha, National Book Trust of India, New Delhi.

Narendra K. Sinha, *The Story of Rama—A Mythological Novel*, Fusion Books.

Nrishinga Prasad Bhaduri, *Krishna Kunti Ebong Kauntey*, Anand Publishers Pvt. Ltd., Kolkata.

Nrishinga Prasad Bhaduri, *Mahabharater Chay Prabeen*, Anand Publishers Pvt. Ltd., Kolkata.

The Oxford History of India, Oxford University Press.

Premchander Galpaguchcha, National Book Trust of India, New Delhi.

Ratanlal & Dhirajlal, *The Indian Penal Code*, Wadhwa and Company Pvt. Ltd.

Rabindranath Tagore, *Geetanjali*, Biswabharathi Granthan Bibhag, Calcutta.

Suprakash Roy, *Santal Bidroha*, Radical Impression, Kolkata.

Subodh Chakraborty, *Tourist Guide*, Kamini Prakashanaloy, Calcutta.

Mone Rekho, An Autobiography, by Suchitra Mitra, Aajkal Publishers Pvt. Ltd., Kolkata.

Samaresh Basu, *Kalkut Rachana Samagra*, Maushumi Prakashani, Calcutta.

Telugu Galpaguchcha, National Book Trust of India, New Delhi.

Urdu Galpa Sankalan, National Book Trust of India, New Delhi.

Wikipedia, the free encyclopedia.

Upendra Kishore Roychoudhury, *Cheleder Mahabharata*, Saksharata Prakashan, Pachimbanga Niraksharata Durikaran Samity.